Using Geodata & Geolocation in the Social Sciences

SAGE was founded in 1965 by Sara Miller McCune to support the dissemination of usable knowledge by publishing innovative and high-quality research and teaching content. Today, we publish over 900 journals, including those of more than 400 learned societies, more than 800 new books per year, and a growing range of library products including archives, data, case studies, reports, and video. SAGE remains majority-owned by our founder, and after Sara's lifetime will become owned by a charitable trust that secures our continued independence.

Los Angeles | London | New Delhi | Singapore | Washington DC | Melbourne

Using Geodata &

Geolocation in the

Social Sciences

Mapping Our Connected World

David Abernathy

Los Angeles | London | New Delhi
Singapore | Washington DC | Melbourne

Los Angeles | London | New Delhi
Singapore | Washington DC | Melbourne

SAGE Publications Ltd
1 Oliver's Yard
55 City Road
London EC1Y 1SP

SAGE Publications Inc.
2455 Teller Road
Thousand Oaks, California 91320

SAGE Publications India Pvt Ltd
B 1/I 1 Mohan Cooperative Industrial Area
Mathura Road
New Delhi 110 044

SAGE Publications Asia-Pacific Pte Ltd
3 Church Street
#10-04 Samsung Hub
Singapore 049483

Editor: Robert Rojek
Assistant editor: Matthew Oldfield
Production editor: Katherine Haw
Copyeditor: Richard Leigh
Proofreader: Andy Baxter
Indexer: Martin Hargreaves
Marketing manager: Sally Ransom
Cover design: Francis Kenney
Typeset by: C&M Digitals (P) Ltd, Chennai, India
Printed and bound in Great Britain by Bell and
Bain Ltd, Glasgow

Library of Congress Control Number: 2016941198

British Library Cataloguing in Publication data

A catalogue record for this book is available from
the British Library

ISBN 978-1-4739-0817-8
ISBN 978-1-4739-0818-5 (pbk)

At SAGE we take sustainability seriously. Most of our products are printed in the UK using FSC papers and boards.
When we print overseas we ensure sustainable papers are used as measured by the PREPS grading system.
We undertake an annual audit to monitor our sustainability.

For Heather, Colin and Campbell

Contents

List of Figures

About the Author

David Abernathy is Professor of Global Studies and Geographic Information Systems at Warren Wilson College in North Carolina, USA. He holds a PhD in Geography from the University of Washington in Seattle. His teaching and research interests are currently focused on the combined use of open source geospatial software and low-cost computing hardware to develop accessible tools for collecting and analyzing spatial data. He has also been interested in the unique geography of Panama for more than two decades, studying the political ecology of disease eradication in the Canal Zone and mapping biodiversity conservation in the Panamanian rainforest.

Companion Website

The companion website for *Using Geodata and Geolocation in the Social Sciences* can be found at https://study.sagepub.com/abernathy

Visit the site for:

- Links to all of the websites and free software packages discussed in the book
- Downloadable versions of all datasets presented in the book

1

Introduction

The Power of Where

 **Overview**

This chapter looks at:

- Maps, mobilities, and spaces of flows
- The connected age: location awareness and the "internet of things"
- Harnessing the geoweb
- The structure of the book

There are around 2 billion smartphones in the world, so chances are you own one of them. If so, think about the ways you might use your device during a vacation. As you plan your trip, you explore places and get driving directions using digital maps and imagery. On the road, you search out places to eat and refuel, paying attention to traffic information ahead in case you need to find an alternative route. Upon arrival, you consult a subway map to see where to go and when the next train will arrive. You take pictures and video of interesting sites and post them on Twitter and Facebook. Perhaps you decide to use the coupon that popped up on your smartphone screen when you walked by a particular shop. As you prepare to return home, you receive a notification that your flight has been slightly delayed and has changed gates. You check an airport map to find a restaurant close to the new gate, then use the extra time to look back at the map from yesterday's hike to see exactly how many miles you walked. Once you have finally landed back at home, you wearily check your smartphone to see where it was you parked your car.

What is so remarkable about the above scenario is that it does not seem all that remarkable; you probably have done most of these things without giving them much thought.

We have come to expect information to appear when and where we need it, and to be able to communicate with anyone at anytime, no matter where they are – something that Leisa Reichelt (2007) calls "ambient intimacy." The normal barriers of space and time have seemingly been so reduced as to practically vanish. We can be on a video call, texting with a group of friends, and posting comments on social media sites (sometimes simultaneously!) without knowing or caring where all of those people happen to be.

But sometimes caring where those people are – or will be – is precisely the point. While the role that smartphones and social media played in social movements like the Arab Spring and Occupy is still under debate, these tools unquestionably ushered in a new way to coordinate the movement of individuals in geographic space. By having access to decentralized, immediate communication networks such as Twitter, networked groups can quickly mobilize in place and just as quickly dissipate. "Flash mob" protests can seemingly emerge out of nowhere, dissolve, and reappear elsewhere as networked protesters use ambient intimacy to keep track of each other as well as any potential threats.

Both the politically charged action of coordinating a protest across geographic space and the seemingly mundane task of mapping directions across town require the use of technological tools that have only recently emerged. Once confined to the relatively fixed position of desktop computers and mainframes, the internet has diffused to laptop computers, smartphones, and many other devices that are extremely mobile. Cellular networks, WiFi, Bluetooth® and other wireless forms of communication have allowed us to carry the internet with us almost everywhere we go. Global positioning systems tell us where we are on the face of the Earth with startling accuracy. We always have a location, and we always have access to the network. We live in a *geoweb*.

Broadly defined, the geoweb is a network of individual nodes whose geographic position can be identified and communicated on the internet. For something to be considered as part of the geoweb, it must be both geolocated and connected. *Geolocation* refers to the identification of the real-world location of some phenomenon, such as a smartphone, a car, or a tweet, using some sort of standard coding system. The most common coding system for geolocation is the coordinate system of latitude and longitude, but there are also many other systems used in geolocation (street addresses, ZIP codes, etc.). *Connectivity* simply means that geolocated phenomena must be connected to the internet in some way in order to be considered as part of the geoweb. Marking your location on the face of the Earth using a global positioning system (GPS) would not make you part of the geoweb, for example, unless that location was made accessible to other parts of the network (to determine your proximity to a certain subset of your friends, perhaps).

The geoweb also includes any data collected from a geolocated and connected node, from the speed of your car to your check-in on the Foursquare app to photosynthetically active radiation levels in a rainforest. Our definition of the geoweb can be expanded, then, to include what we can refer to as "geodata" – data that have some spatial or locational component. As such, the geoweb refers to *a distributed digital network of geolocated nodes that capture, produce, and communicate data that include an explicitly spatial component.*

The smartphone is an important and increasingly ubiquitous example of a geoweb node, but it is by no means the only one. Much of our physical world is rapidly being connected to the geoweb, from the scale of the individual (clothing, cars, homes) to the city (lighting systems in parking decks, motion sensors in roads and bridges) to entire ecosystems (rainforests, oceans). As such, we are gathering more and more data that can be analyzed and visualized geographically. The geoweb can help us better understand social activity in specific places – we might, for example, be interested in examining a set of Twitter and Facebook posts from a specific part of a city, or perhaps we would like to measure the fluctuation in air quality across an environmental sensor network. By generating data that are both geolocated and connected, we can begin to ask questions and seek answers that might otherwise be impossible.

This book is about the emerging geoweb and its implications for how we might go about asking such questions and seeking answers about the world around us. How can we take advantage of an increasingly geolocated and connected world to better under-stand human society and the environment? What tools can we use to collect and visualize geolocated data? How do we deal with issues of privacy, data accuracy, and fears of a "surveillance society" as the geoweb continues to grow and expand? In short, how will an emerging world in which everything is individually geolocated and globally net-worked change the way we interact with ourselves and our environment?

MAPS, MOBILITIES, AND SPACES OF FLOWS

Humans have long sought to understand and visualize space and place in order to both make sense of the world and navigate through it. From early cave paintings to the cart-ography of the ancient Greeks to the National Geographic world maps on elementary school walls, maps have served as tools for describing the Earth. "Geography" first emerged with Eratosthenes, who calculated the size and shape of the Earth and developed a grid system for mapping places, and was formalized as an academic discipline in the eighteenth century. Today's cartographers and geographers tend to use computers as they continue advancing our understanding of space and place.

The concepts of space and place are too important and powerful to be relegated to a single academic discipline, however. The power of "where" can be found across the arts and sciences, from disease diffusion models in epidemiology to the development of historical gazetteers in the digital humanities. Understanding and visualizing the "where" of almost any phenomena – the location, the proximity to other phenomena, the spatial distribution, the movement – can often help us better understand the "why." As such, one can find a bewildering array of maps that have been created to help make sense of human society. From city zoning to political redistricting, from ethnicity to sexuality, and from wealth to health, space is a construct that humans use to organize, define, and differentiate themselves.

The emergence and widespread adoption of the internet, beginning in the 1990s, gave rise to a new way to conceptualize and visualize space. Made up of a rapidly expanding collection of interconnected computers, "cyberspace" emerged as a vast digital network that reconfigured society in myriad ways, including the ways in which space and place are constructed and interpreted. Suddenly nodes and networks were as important to our understanding of geography as the concepts of territories and borders, if not more so. The world shrank, in essence, as our global digital network enabled real-time communication without regard to physical distance. We became a network society.

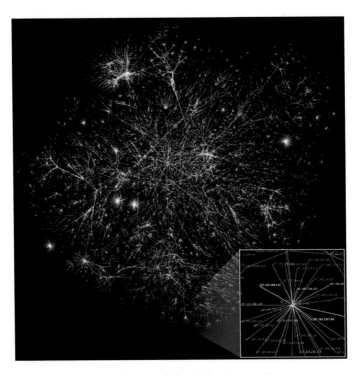

FIGURE 1.1   Mapping cyberspace (Source: Wikimedia Commons)

The sociologist Manuel Castells (2000) uses the term "space of flows" to describe the emergent social relations in a network society. More important than the space of places, he argues, is the movement (of information, capital, people, ideas) between places. While networks have been around for quite some time, Castells argues that during the 1970s we saw the emergence of new information technologies that have transformed society in unique ways. We now live and work within an integrated global network that ties together financial markets, media, employment, communication, and almost every other aspect of human life. Our digital networks reduce the "friction of distance," in essence,

4

allowing us to move more information across greater distances than ever before in human history. Our daily lives now take place in the midst of what Rainie and Wellman (2012) call a "new social operating system."

As the social sciences came to terms with the internet and the network society in the 1990s, there was a growing realization that people, things, and ideas were more mobile than ever before. A "spatial turn" in the social sciences, and later the humanities, emerged as movement and mobility were recognized as being vital to the understanding of society. Rather than putting an "end to geography," as some proclaimed global communication networks would accomplish, the emerging network society actually made geography more important, since it enabled movement and mobility like never before. Research across the breadth of academic disciplines sought to understand the spaces of flows as they accelerated across multiple networks.

THE CONNECTED AGE: LOCATION AWARENESS AND THE "INTERNET OF THINGS"

On May 1, 2000, President Bill Clinton accepted a recommendation from the Department of Defense to end "selective availability," an intentional degradation of location information provided by GPS satellites that was originally implemented for national security reasons. Overnight, GPS receivers improved locational accuracy from approximately 100 meters to less than 20 meters. Civilian use of GPS soon exploded, as GPS chips were included in everything from mobile phones to car navigation systems to farm equipment. The amount of geolocated data being generated increased dramatically.

At around the same time, the internet was limping through the first dot-com market collapse but nevertheless was maturing as a revolutionary tool for communication and information distribution. Mobile phones were on their way to becoming the most rapidly adopted consumer technology in history, as emerging 3G data speeds allowed users to access the growing internet with their mobile devices. Computer processing chips and sensors of all types were becoming more powerful even as they were shrinking and dropping in cost.

By around 2002 or so, these three network technologies (global positioning systems, cellular communication, and the internet) were integrated enough to give us the foundations of the geoweb. For the first time in history, we had the ability to identify an exact location on the face of the Earth, link that location to the internet (often using mobile devices and cellular communication) and begin examining its relationship with other surrounding phenomena. And as technology continued to advance, we began to see more and more geolocated and connected nodes being added to the geoweb.

In the years since the geoweb first emerged, there has been tremendous growth in the amount of location-based data being generated. From digital maps and imagery used in geographic information systems (GIS) to digital photographs that have been "geotagged" to animals tagged with radio frequency identification (RFID) chips, geodata have rapidly proliferated. The geoweb continues to evolve as the internet spreads ever further into the physical world and as the amount of data generated increases markedly. The geoweb, then, is an important part of two larger trends in our present-day digital society: the era of "big data" and the emerging "internet of things" (IoT).

The internet of things refers to the expansion of the internet beyond computers and mobile phones to other aspects of the physical world. Today, objects such as cash registers, lighting systems, bridges, and thermostats are connected to the internet, and they are generating data, responding to changes in their environments, and often accessible to users on the network. Nodes on the IoT are not necessarily part of the geoweb, since there may be applications that do not require geolocation, but quite often geolocation is an integral component. An estimated 26 billion things (not including computers and phones) will be connected to the internet by 2020 (Gartner, 2013), and many of these will be incorporated into the geoweb as they utilize geolocation data in important ways.

The proliferation of these devices, coupled with an ever-increasing capacity for data storage, has resulted in a dramatic increase in the amount of data being captured and stored each year. "Big data" has emerged in recent years as the broad term for our realization that we are increasingly awash in data and that we need to find ways to effectively harness them in order to improve our decision-making capabilities. Geodata are not inherently big data, but often we see large-scale sensor networks or complex GIS datasets that are so large as to challenge our existing tools for analysis, storage, and visualization. Also, as the IoT continues to expand, it seems likely that organizing data spatially will be increasingly important.

HARNESSING THE GEOWEB

As mentioned above, there was a "spatial turn" that led to disciplines beyond geography explicitly examining the role of space and place as factors influencing social phenomena. Efforts to spatially integrate the social sciences and humanities have led to interdisciplinary courses, research centers, and projects that attempt to more fully engage space and place as fundamental to our understanding of human society. GIS has been applied to all sorts of research questions beyond its original home in the natural sciences, from asking why certain voting patterns appear to questioning why and how certain cultural practices spread from one place to another. We have come to understand the power of "where" when attempting to better understand the "why" and "how."

Space and place are even more relevant to social science research in an era of an increasingly interconnected geoweb. We now have the ability to collect and study more geolocated data than ever before, at spatial and temporal scales that we might have thought impossible just a few years ago. As such, we need to develop a robust toolkit to help us make sense of the bewildering volumes of data that are generated every day. How might we collect and visualize geodata in a way that could help us answer our research questions? How do we go about understanding the roles of place and space in an unprecedented era of human connectivity?

This book is designed to help you incorporate geodata into your research. Whether you are a first-year student in the social sciences or a seasoned researcher wanting to expand your analytical skill set, this book will provide you with the necessary background and introduce you to many of the tools being used to collect and visualize geodata today. From sensor networks to social media, from the promise of a connected society to the perils of surveillance and lost privacy, the implications of a world increasingly enveloped in a geoweb are profound. This book will help you begin to make sense of it.

THE STRUCTURE OF THE BOOK

The book consists of two main sections. Part One places the geoweb in a broad context, outlining a brief history of geodata and examining both the potential benefits and costs of a world where more and more phenomena are geolocated and connected. It concludes by examining the different types of geodata that you will explore in Part Two of the book. Part Two is the "hands-on" portion of the text, introducing several tools and strategies for identifying, collecting, and visualizing location-based data.

Throughout the book, specific software tools are introduced so that you can explore some of the possible ways to collect and visualize geodata. An emphasis is placed on the use of free and/or open source tools, both to minimize the expense involved in working with geodata and to demonstrate the importance of open source software tools and data when working with the geoweb. Closed, proprietary datasets and software tools make the collection and visualization of geodata much more difficult and expensive. The tools introduced in this text are in no way comprehensive, but rather are meant to serve as relatively easy-to-use examples of the types of software tools available. Links to download these tools are available on the companion website https://study.sagepub.co/abernathy.

What this book does not do

While this book is designed to introduce you to several of the tools for collecting and visualizing geodata, it is not a book on data analytics. Some basic models for data exploration and analysis will be included in the book, but readers seeking more in-depth statistical tools or modeling techniques will be directed to other works that more fully address these topics. Likewise, while cloud computing and tools like Hadoop will be mentioned in the text, this is not a book on big data computation. The goal of the book is to provide you with a solid foundation for understanding the geoweb, as well as collecting and visualizing geodata, as you advance your own research questions in the social sciences and humanities. It is intended to be a broad introduction, so further readings and analysis tools will be included where appropriate.

This section concludes with an outline of the contents of each chapter.

Part One: The geoweb in context
Chapter 2: A brief history of the geoweb

While the concept of a geoweb is a relatively new phenomenon, location-based data have a long, rich history. This chapter provides a brief overview of the history – and geography – of geospatial data, our efforts to collect and analyze them, and how recent technological advances have enabled the geoweb's emergence.

Chapter 3: "Big geodata": managing spatial data in a connected age

Building on Chapter 2, this chapter discusses the broader context within which the geoweb is emerging: the era of "big data" and the "internet of things." Charting the tremendous increase in data production since the 1970s – particularly since the dawn of the internet in the early 1990s – this chapter illustrates how the geoweb is an example of "big data" that has several unique aspects.

Chapter 4: Citizen cartographers: neogeography, VGI and the democratization of data production

This chapter examines the dramatic transformation in data production, analysis, and visualization that has occurred over the last dozen or so years. Once limited to the GIS specialist or professional cartographer, spatial data have been democratized and are easily created by and available to almost anyone with access to a set of increasingly inexpensive tools. Global positioning systems are now widely available in handheld devices, and many software programs and mobile applications have been developed to enable the quick and easy production and dissemination of location-based data. This chapter discusses the many important ramifications of the democratization and decentralization of geospatial data creation.

Chapter 5: Challenges of the geoweb: data accuracy, privacy, and surveillance

While Chapter 4 largely celebrates the emergence of the geoweb, this chapter highlights some of the challenges and concerns that have arisen as location-based data have become near-ubiquitous. Privacy issues, long a top concern among many who find more and more of our daily human transactions taking place online, become magnified when the internet becomes increasingly "location aware." Recent revelations as to the extent to which the National Security Agency conducted internet surveillance have only served to heighten these fears. Certainly issues of privacy and surveillance must come into play as location-based data are increasingly used for research. Another concern for the researcher is the accuracy of data on the geoweb, particularly if much of the data is created by the "neogeographer" rather than the "expert." The chapter closes by arguing that by paying close attention to these challenges, the geoweb can be effectively incorporated into our research. Ultimately the geoweb allows us to ask more new research questions – and hopefully get more new answers – than we could without this vast new trove of location-based data.

Chapter 6: Introduction to geodata: types of geodata; how do we identify and gather location-based data?

This chapter introduces the reader to the various types of geodata that can be collected for research in the social sciences and humanities. The chapter first distinguishes between types of space (absolute, relative, topological) and how important it is that the researcher understand which type of space is most useful for the research question being asked. Next, the chapter discusses the temporal spectrum of geodata – from extremely specific to indeterminate – and what this might mean for the researcher in terms of data collection, analysis, and visualization. The chapter then outlines the tools for capturing and visualizing geodata that will be introduced in Part Two of the book.

Part Two: Capturing and visualizing geodata

Chapter 7: Capturing absolute location with the Global Positioning System

The ability to precisely locate some phenomenon on the face of the Earth – whether it be a car, a mobile phone, a Facebook post, or a disease outbreak – lies at the very heart of the geoweb. As such, the first chapter focusing on a specific form of capturing geodata will cover the ways in which global positioning systems are used to identify absolute space in terms of latitude and longitude. The chapter will briefly cover how a GPS works, how its adoption worldwide has enabled the geoweb, and how GPS data can be incorporated into social science research.

Chapter 8: Geocoding, geotagging, and geoparsing

As discussed in the previous chapter, latitude and longitude coordinates enable the researcher to identify a precise location on the Earth's surface. Yet we tend to spatially organize places using very different coding systems, such as street addresses and ZIP codes. Geocoding refers to the process of converting such geographic data to latitude and longitude coordinates. This chapter will address the systems used to geocode spatial data and will provide examples of geocoding software and geocoding datasets. The chapter also examines geotagging (adding coordinate information to digital data, such as a photograph) and geoparsing (extracting geodata from unstructured data, such as a news article or book).

Chapter 9: Social media geodata: capturing location-based Twitter data

The proliferation of data produced with social media tools such as Twitter has drawn the interest of many social science researchers. This chapter examines some of the ways in which the volunteered information posted on Twitter can be studied spatially. From simple web-based queries to more complicated analyses using the R programming language, this chapter provides several examples of ways to extract geodata from Twitter.

Chapter 10: Mapping the emerging internet of things

This chapter explores the explosion of geodata being generated across the internet of things. After first providing some examples of the IoT and sensor networks, the chapter then introduces approaches to the collection of geodata being generated by the IoT. The final section of the chapter turns to the creation of geodata using the Arduino microcontroller. Exercises are included that demonstrate how to create a sensor node and connect it to the internet.

Chapter 11: Visualizing data in geographic information systems with QGIS

Geographic information systems have been used to store, analyze, and display spatial data for the past few decades. But only in the last few years have the software tools for spatial analysis been accessible to the non-expert. This chapter explore the rise of GIS for the "neogeographer" and provides a gentle introduction to GIS for the non-technician using the free and open source toolkit called QGIS. The basics of visualizing vector and raster data will be covered in a series of exercises.

Chapter 12: Working with geodata in GRASS

This chapter introduces another powerful set of geospatial tools known as the Geographic Resources Analysis Support System (GRASS). Like QGIS, GRASS is free and open source, and it includes many useful modules for analyzing geospatial data. Several exercises are included to get you up and running with GRASS, including examples of how to examine 3D and temporal data. The final exercises of the chapter demonstrate how GRASS and QGIS can be used as an integrated system by adding a software plugin in QGIS.

Chapter 13: Working with geodata in R

This chapter returns to the R programming language to examine how it can be used as a GIS. The chapter explores the RStudio development environment for R, as well as several R packages that provide tools for geocoding and mapping. Later exercises include using R for visualizing Twitter data, accessing R within GRASS, and creating an interactive web mapping application using the library of tools called Shiny.

Chapter 14: Web mapping

While desktop GIS tools such as QGIS and GRASS remain popular, recently there has been a proliferation of tools for collecting and visualizing geospatial data directly in a web browser. This chapter contains exercises for working with geodata across several of the most popular and useful online mapping tools, including Google Maps, OpenLayers, CartoDB, and Leaflet.

Chapter 15: Epilogue: Weaving the Geoweb

This chapter concludes the book by stepping back and discussing the broader implications of a rapidly evolving geoweb, including an examination of the technological, social, and political issues that must be addressed as the geoweb matures. The chapter also summarizes the benefits to incorporating location-based data into social science research.

 **Chapter summary**

This chapter introduced and defined the geoweb as a distributed digital network of geolocated nodes that capture, produce, and communicate data that include an explicitly spatial component. The geoweb emerged from a set of technological advances in communication networks (GPS, cellular communication, the internet) as well as advances in our ability to collect, store, analyze, and visualize geolocated data. The social sciences and humanities have begun to more explicitly integrate spatial analysis into questions about human society, incorporating geographic information system and other tools in research. The goal of this book is to help you understand the implications of the geoweb, know how geodata can be captured and stored, and learn several techniques for visualizing geodata.

The geoweb represents nothing less than a revolution in how we understand ourselves and the world around us. As more people, devices, and things become "location aware," we can see patterns, map relationships, and connect places as we have never done before. As we do, we will necessarily grapple with challenges of all kinds, from the ethical issues surrounding privacy and personal data to the larger societal questions about living in a digital age of global connectivity. We will also hopefully make new discoveries and learn ways to improve lives as we continue to advance the geoweb. The power of "where" has been with us for much of human history, but never has it been as vividly important as it is today.

PART ONE

The Geoweb in Context

2

A Brief History of the Geoweb

Overview

This chapter looks at:

- The origins of *geography* and *geodata*
- Geodata goes digital
- The emergence of geographic information systems
- Launching the Global Positioning System
- Birth of the "location-aware" mobile device
- Mashing up mapping
- Developing a "planetary nervous system": sensors, data, and the internet of things

THE ORIGINS OF *GEOGRAPHY* AND *GEODATA*

The term *geodata* refers specifically to computerized geographical data. The geoweb is made up of many types of geodata, from digital elevation models to aerial imagery to the current location of your smart phone. Without computerized geographical data, the geoweb would not exist. Yet efforts to understand the world around us by collecting and mapping information clearly have a long history, and advancements in geographic thought that took place hundreds of years ago were also necessary prerequisites for the emergence of the geoweb. This chapter examines some of the important highlights in geographic thought and technology upon which the geoweb is built. From the earliest attempts to make mathematical sense of the Earth to the emergence of geographic information systems, there were many scientific advancements necessary to pave the way for a globally interconnected geoweb.

Geography means, literally, "earth writing" and typically refers to efforts to describe the Earth visually through maps. Humans seem to have always had a desire to learn about and depict the world around them, judging by the basic maps found on cave walls and tombs from Greece to China that date back to thousands of years BC. Some of this early cartography used symbols, such as points and curved lines, to form literal representations of the world, while other maps focused more on mythological representation based on religious beliefs. While many of the earliest maps were clearly created freehand, there is evidence that some early cartographers incorporated geometry and surveying techniques into their work.

Important mathematical contributions to cartography were made by Eratosthenes, the astronomer who first used the word "geography," around 250 BC. He calculated the circumference of the Earth with some accuracy by comparing the angular difference between the sun's rays at two different cities in Egypt. This marked the beginning of the science of geodesy – the systematic effort to measure and understand Earth's geometric shape. Eratosthenes also used a grid system of imaginary lines – meridians and parallels – to develop a coordinate system for referencing places on a map, which was an important precursor to our existing system of latitude and longitude.

A few hundred years later, Ptolemy published the eight-volume atlas *Geographia*, which included several improvements in mathematical representations of the Earth. His work included a map projection that provided a more accurate representation of a spherical Earth on a flat surface, as well as a coordinate system that took the Equator as the primary line of latitude (Figure 2.1). Ptolemy is also credited with cartographic conventions still used today, such as orienting north at the top of a map and using a legend.

FIGURE 2.1   Ptolemy's world map (Source: Wikimedia Commons)

While Ptolemy's parallel lines of latitude were very close to those used today, the error in his lines of longitude was significant, as he had to rely on estimates from merchant travelers to chart them. Accurately calculating longitude at sea remained a difficult problem to solve well into the eighteenth century, when clockmaker John Harrison invented the marine chronometer that enabled accurate timekeeping at sea. Up until that point, ship navigators could only guess at their east–west location, meaning that valuable time and often lives were lost.

With the problem of calculating longitude solved, there was now an accurate system for pinpointing geographic location on the Earth by simply providing a pair of coordinates that described one's distance from the Equator (where the latitude was set at zero) and from a baseline meridian (where longitude was set at zero). Unlike the Equator, however, there was no natural geographic feature that determined which line of longitude should serve as the meridian of origin. Different countries selected meridians that served their own purposes for navigation and time; there was, for example, a Washington meridian in the United States, a Paris meridian in France and an Antwerp meridian in Belgium. Even so, there was often no standard time in a given country, which became increasingly problematic as rail transportation expanded. In the United States, time was set by individual rail companies rather than the government, leading to chaotic timetables and a growing plea for the standardization of time.

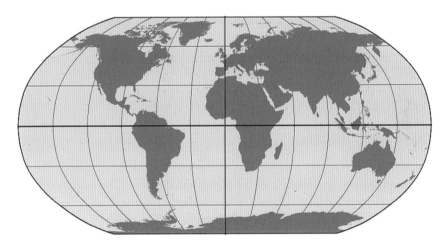

FIGURE 2.2   Prime Meridian crossing through Greenwich, England (Source: Wikimedia Commons)

In 1884, the International Meridian Conference was held in Washington, DC, in order to determine a meridian that could be used to coordinate time and travel around the world. Delegates at the conference chose the meridian crossing through Greenwich, England, as the line of origin for longitude (Figure 2.2), though France did not recognize this decision and continued using the Paris meridian for three more decades. For the first time in history, there was a (largely) agreed-upon graticule of latitude and longitude that provided a common geographic coordinate system throughout the world. It was now possible to pinpoint any place on Earth simply by sharing a pair of numbers.

The same year that the world was becoming more united through geography and time, the continent of Africa was being divided. At the Berlin Conference of 1884, several European powers agreed to carve out colonial territories across Africa, placing much of the continent under colonial rule at the turn of the century. Colonial expansion fueled an increasing interest in mapping and geography as the European powers sought to describe and categorize their newfound territories. In the Western Hemisphere (a social construction made possible by the general agreement on the Greenwich Prime Meridian), the United States saw an increasing interest in geography as well, with the National Geographic Society forming in 1888 and formal academic departments emerging in universities by the turn of the century.

The two world wars in the twentieth century served as unfortunate catalysts for the production of geographic science and geodata. Whereas maps had often been extremely inaccurate in prior conflicts, by the First World War Britain's Ordnance Survey was producing millions of maps, and aerial imagery was being used to give military leaders a bird's-eye view of the battlefield. The Second World War saw a continued dramatic increase in the production of geographic data, as tactical maps and war plans, aerial imagery, topographic maps, architectural drawings and more were created by almost every conceivable branch of the US government. In addition, maps became widespread in the communication (and miscommunication, through cartographic propaganda) of the war's developments to civilians around the world. Newspapers and magazines across the globe published a wide variety of maps in an effort to explain what was happening throughout the conflict.

GEODATA GOES DIGITAL

The Second World War also helped usher in the era of modern computing that would bring cartography and geography into the digital age. *Colossus*, the first programmable digital computer, was developed by the British during the war to assist in breaking codes of the Enigma machines used by the Axis powers. In the United States, the ENIAC computer was designed primarily to calculate tables for the aiming of artillery. By the war's end the value of digital computing was clear, and steady advances in technology (the transistor, the integrated circuit, data storage units) fostered an increase in the commercial use of computers. The instructions fed into these computers also became more complex, and gradually the concept of "software" took hold as operating systems and programming languages increased the flexibility of computer hardware.

The year 1957 brought two technological "firsts" that were crucial prerequisites for the geoweb. The first digital photograph was created when Russell Kirsch and his team at the US Bureau of Standards developed the drum scanner for converting conventional photographs into scanned images. By creating an input device that could transform a physical photo into something that could be read and stored by a computer, Kirsch helped set the stage for the conversion of geodata from analog to digital. While the pixel resolution of the first digital image (a photo of Kirsch's three-month-old son; Figure 2.3) was rather paltry by today's standards, the invention of scanning technology was extremely important in advancing digital mapping.

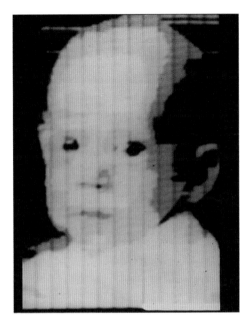

FIGURE 2.3   An image of Russell Kirsch's son created with the first digital scanner (Source: Wikimedia Commons)

In October of that same year, the Soviet Union launched *Sputnik*, the first satellite sent into space. In addition to being the forefather of the satellites that would eventually be used for today's global positioning systems, Sputnik put pressure on the United States to promote its own research and development of satellites and other defense technologies. The Advanced Research Projects Agency (ARPA) was established just a few months after *Sputnik* was launched – the agency that would construct the precursor to today's global internet.

ARPA established a computer communication link between the University of California, Los Angeles and the Stanford Research Institute in October 1969, just months after the first moon landing. Known as ARPANET (see Figure 2.4), the network began to expand to include additional universities and research facilities as the US Department of Defense, NASA, and other governmental agencies began conducting internet research. It would take several additional technological advances, such as the standardization of a protocol for connecting independent networks (TCP/IP), the release of the internet for commerce, hypertext, and the web browser (first created by Sir Tim Berners-Lee) before the internet would begin to grow dramatically. Once these pieces were in place, however, the internet did indeed begin to expand at a rapid clip: by 1994 there were an estimated 25 million people on the internet, according to Internet Live Stats (www.internetlivestats. com/internet-users/#trend, accessed January 2016); 20 years later that number was closer to 3 billion.

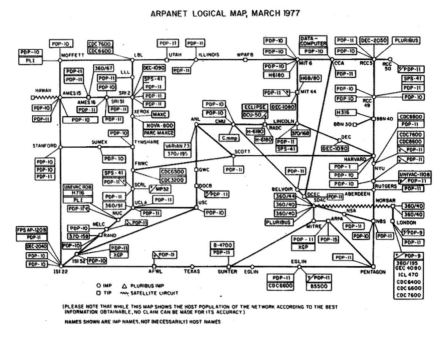

FIGURE 2.4   ARPANET logical map, 1977 (Source: Wikimedia Commons)

THE EMERGENCE OF GEOGRAPHIC INFORMATION SYSTEMS

The same year that man first stepped foot on the moon and ARPA first created the network connection that would evolve into the internet, Jack Dangermond and his wife, Laura, founded the Environmental Systems Research Institute (ESRI). The main goal of ESRI was to organize and map spatial information in order to assist land planners in making informed land use decisions. Eventually the company would produce a software product with the combined capabilities of displaying Earth information and connecting that information to a management database. Known as ARC/INFO, the software was the first commercial geographic information system (GIS). ESRI remains an industry leader today, with its ArcGIS software being used widely in government and commercial industries around the world.

The first use of the term "geographic information system" slightly pre-dates the formation of ESRI, however. In the early 1960s, the Canadian government was becoming increasingly interested in inventorying and monitoring its natural resources. The Canada Land Inventory (CLI) was created to collect, map, and analyze land use data, and Dr Roger Tomlinson produced a feasibility study to determine whether computers might prove valuable in the mapping and analysis of land inventory data. Credited with coining the term "geographic information system," Tomlinson helped develop the Canadian Geographic Information System to handle the large amounts of data that were being generated by the CLI. Tomlinson's GIS was important in that it went well beyond digital cartography, enabling users to query out subsets of spatial data, overlay multiple data layers, and conduct geoprocessing analyses such as calculating area and buffering geographic features.

GIS caught on quickly across many agencies of the US government, from the national efforts of the US Geological Society to state-level highway inventories. It spread globally as well, as individuals and organizations around the world quickly realized that GIS could be applied to spatial problems of all kinds, from tracking the spread of disease to mapping socioeconomic variations in city neighborhoods. As computers shifted from large mainframes to desktops and as processing power, data storage, and graphics continued to become both better and cheaper, GIS was widely adopted as a key analytical tool for understanding spatial phenomena.

This widespread diffusion of GIS led to a rapid increase in the amount of geodata being produced. Early users scanned paper maps with the descendants of Kirsch's technology or digitized points, lines, and polygons using a graphics tablet and digitizing pen. As the internet began to mature, websites emerged that served as repositories of geodata that could be downloaded and loaded into a GIS. Soon there were digital versions of municipal streets, hydrography, land use, and other physical features, along with an increasing volume of sociospatial data such as population density, race, income, and much more. Cartography was revolutionized, as maps could quickly and easily be redrawn to accommodate changes instead of having to be painstakingly reproduced by hand.

Of course, this proliferation of data and digital maps would be worthless if there were not ways to accurately model the geographic location of real-world phenomena on a two-dimensional computer screen. For GIS to be of use, it needed to be able to capture the absolute location of whatever was being mapped (typically using the coordinate system of latitude and longitude) and preserve spatial relationships between those locations when transforming the globe into a flat surface (using map projections).

There are many types of map projections, but what they all have in common is that they have some method for mathematically transforming the locational coordinates of a three-dimensional spherical surface to a two-dimensional plane. It is not possible to perfectly preserve all aspects of a sphere on a flat surface, meaning that any map projection must distort one or more of a globe's features: shape, area, distance, or direction.

As such, different map projections have been developed to preserve different properties for different purposes. While the problem of map projection was not new as GIS emerged, the development of accurate projection algorithms was an important aspect of GIS software development.

As we saw earlier, the idea of determining geographic location by using a grid of latitude and longitude has a long history. Yet a unified global geographic coordinate system did not emerge until the 1960s, as many countries had national surveys based on different models of the Earth's shape. In other words, while a system of latitude and longitude provides precise location on a perfect sphere, it does not when that sphere becomes distorted. Since the Earth is an ellipsoid, not a sphere, these distortions must also be taken into account when devising a geographic coordinate system. As technology for measuring the shape of the Earth improved, from surveying tools to Doppler radar to optical data from satellites, global geodetic systems began to emerge. The most recent of these geodetic systems, the World Geodetic System 1984 (WGS 84), is now the one used by another technological advance that helped lead to the emergence of the geoweb: the Global Positioning System (GPS).

LAUNCHING THE GLOBAL POSITIONING SYSTEM

Fifteen or so years after the launch of *Sputnik*, an era of space exploration was in full swing. Several countries had launched satellites, the United States had put a man on the moon, and spacecraft had sent back imagery from as far away as Jupiter. It was around this time that the US Department of Defense began discussing the idea of developing a global navigation system using satellites to improve upon the terrestrial navigation systems that existed at the time. Many military prototype satellites were launched beginning in 1978, and in 1983 President Ronald Reagan declared that the developing global navigation system would be made available for civilian use. The first modern GPS satellite was launched in 1989, and the system was declared to be fully functional in April 1995, with 24 satellites in operation.

The Global Positioning System is comprised of three main components: the space segment, the control segment, and the user segment (see Figure 2.5). The space segment is made up of the satellites that are evenly spaced in orbit around the Earth, so that there are at least six satellites in view at any given time on any point on the surface of the planet. The control segment, which is maintained along with the space segment by the US Air Force, consists of a main control station, additional monitoring stations, and several ground antennas. The user segment is made up of GPS receiver units (such as dedicated GPS units or mobile phones). Combined, this system provides a way for any user to quickly identify coordinates of latitude and longitude with exceptional accuracy.

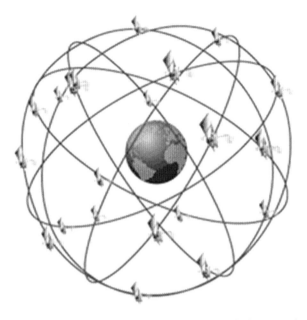

FIGURE 2.5   Configuration of GPS satellites (Source: Wikimedia Commons)

GPS accuracy was intentionally reduced at first, however. While the system was made available for civilian use, military concerns led the US government to intentionally degrade the location accuracy to around 100 meters, a process referred to as "selective availability." By 1996 the decision had been made to eliminate selective availability by the year 2000, and President Clinton and the Department of Defense ended it on May 1 of that year. Literally overnight, the accuracy of the GPS satellite signal improved tremendously, reducing the amount of location error from 100 meters to 20 meters or less. Suddenly a whole range of new applications were made possible. The GPS revolution was poised to erupt.

Commercial GPS receivers had been available before the end of selective availability, but they were expensive and not widely adopted. After Clinton's directive, however, there was a growing demand for GPS receivers and the market grew quickly. GPS navigation could soon be found in millions of cars and boats as well as in dedicated handheld units. The improved accuracy made GPS useful for roadway navigation, outdoor activities such as hiking and camping, and as a tool for supplementing data in geographic information systems. Sales of personal navigation devices increased dramatically for many years following the elimination of selective availability, only slowing as a newer device emerged as the navigation tool of choice for someone wanting access to the GPS: the mobile smartphone.

BIRTH OF THE "LOCATION-AWARE" MOBILE DEVICE

By the mid-2000s, there were millions of mobile phones with embedded GPS receivers, but often access was restricted to emergency use (as in the e911 system in the United States) or by the carrier (which might require additional fees and software for tapping into location information). But the growing popularity of the "smartphone" – a mobile phone with enough computing power to give the user access to email and the internet, and software flexible enough to allow the user to download many different types of applications – brought an increasing demand for access to location-based services. Smartphones quickly overtook stand-alone GPS devices and personal navigation systems as users began accessing location and directions directly from their mobile device.

The mobile phone did more than just give users a convenient way to access location information, however. Traditional GPS receivers were exactly that – they received signals from the GPS satellites and used that information to plot the device's latitude and longitude. Mobile phones, on the other hand, were two-way devices. In other words, a mobile phone could not only retrieve location information, but also *transmit* it. A mobile phone was not merely a passive device that displayed one's geographic position, but rather an active node on a growing network of devices that could both send and receive spatial data. The GPS communication system, the network of cellular phone communication, and the internet were becoming interwoven into an integrated network that contained an unprecedented amount of geospatial information.

This integration of the one-way GPS signal transmission into a two-way mobile communication system was nothing less than a geospatial revolution, bringing rapid changes in location technology that brought fantastic new capabilities as well as a host of new fears about privacy and surveillance. We began mapping directions, searching for places nearby, and "checking in" on social media sites at the same time we began worrying about how this information might be used by those collecting it. Our GPS location was not just our own anymore, but was tied up in a growing web of location data that made that location at once more powerful and more of a concern.

Developers of mobile phone software quickly incorporated GPS capabilities into all sorts of software applications. A phone's geographic location could be accessed by a search engine, for example, so that a search for "Italian restaurants" would bring up only those restaurants nearby, offering driving or walking directions to each. An athlete could use a "coaching" app that tracks distance and speed and offers words of encouragement during a workout. Photographs from a phone's camera could be geotagged and plotted on a digital map and shared with others. And during a social event, or protest, or natural disaster, networks of connected and geolocated mobile phones could be used to meet up with friends, organize marches, or locate missing loved ones.

For any of these software applications to be of use requires the end user to voluntarily share his or her geographic location. Volunteered geographic information (VGI) has dramatically changed cartography and map-making (Goodchild, 2007). Until recently, only trained cartographers or GIS technicians had the know-how and capabilities to create maps, but now we see vast amounts of geospatial data being created by amateurs who willingly share their latitude and longitude with others. As we will see in Chapters 4 and 5, this "neogeography," coupled with the "always on" location-aware capabilities of mobile devices, creates new possibilities and raises new concerns over privacy and surveillance at the same time. Mobile devices can map, and they can be mapped – allowing us to alter our relationship with geography in ways we are only beginning to understand.

MASHING UP MAPPING

The proliferation of VGI across a rapidly growing network of mobile devices capable of connecting to the internet has contributed to the evolution of what we mean by a GIS. People tended to think of a GIS as primarily a software application that runs on a desktop computer, but increasingly geographic information migrated to the internet. Digital mapping applications and virtual globes emerged as internet-savvy individuals increasingly looked to the web for access to geospatial information. And as is so often the case with the internet, the tools for accessing and visualizing geospatial data tended to be free, rather than the thousands of dollars typically charged for commercial GIS software. Maps and map-making were suddenly accessible to anyone who had access to the internet.

While most of the first internet maps were simply static pages that replicated paper maps, later online maps were interactive and could be manipulated and even edited by a user. The rise of a more collaborative and interactive World Wide Web – commonly referred to as "Web 2.0" – allowed for more and more of the functionality of a traditional GIS to be replicated on the internet, and made it easier than ever for a non-professional to create digital maps. Internet users with very little or no programming experience could produce digital cartography and share it with others by combining existing mapping applications (e.g., Google Maps) with other data. Known as "mashups," these new maps displayed all sorts of new datasets that were not included in traditional cartography. From maps of urban potholes and public restrooms to global carbon calculators and space satellite trackers, thousands of different map mashups appeared online.

An important component of many internet software applications that helped spawn mashups is the application programming interface (API). An API provides a set of tools that allows different software services to talk to one another. A Twitter or Facebook post, for example, might include a Google Map showing the location of the person sharing the post. Or a website might pull together data from Google Maps, the Federal Aviation Administration and automatic dependent surveillance broadcasts to create a map of real-time air traffic patterns. By letting different software services talk to each other and share each other's data, APIs facilitate the creation of new digital tools and datasets that would not be possible if those software services walled off access. You will have an opportunity to look more closely at some of the more popular APIs later in this book.

DEVELOPING A "PLANETARY NERVOUS SYSTEM": SENSORS, DATA, AND THE INTERNET OF THINGS

By the late 2000s, software applications and internet services sharing data across mobile phone networks and around the web had become commonplace in many parts of the world. Even poorer regions have seen wireless networks mushrooming up, providing connectedness to places that have never had access to land-based communication networks. There were an estimated 5 billion mobile phones by 2010, and a study by the United Nations in 2013 showed that more people had access to mobile phones in the world than had access to toilets. Mobile phones have taken over from personal computers as the primary tool for accessing the internet. And each year, the percentage of new phones containing GPS receivers increases. We are rapidly becoming a mobile, mappable society.

The GPS receiver chip inside a mobile smartphone is but one of the many sensors found inside the handheld unit. Today's phones also contain cameras, light sensors, accelerometers, and gyroscopes. Some phones include sensors for temperature and humidity as well as 3D image capture. Soon, phones could include sensors for everything from monitoring personal health to capturing air quality data. And since a mobile smartphone is actually an entire computer that is connected to the internet, all of the sensor data collected by the device can be stored, shared, aggregated, and visualized. The large and growing collection of internet-connected mobile devices is nothing short of the world's largest wireless sensor network.

Many of the sensors embedded in our mobile devices are also finding their way into several other aspects of our physical world. It is not just phones that are now "smart"; the internet is now extending into objects as diverse as household appliances, automobiles, farm equipment, and clothing. Sensors can track everything from home sprinkler systems to bridge vibrations to shopping behavior in a mall. This growing integration between the physical world and cyberspace, and the increasing amount of data it is generating, is often referred to as the "internet of things." Any data generated by the IoT that have a spatial component – where location matters – can be considered to be part of the geoweb.

As connected sensors continue to permeate our world, the volume of data generated will continue to expand rapidly. Already we are said to live in an era of "big data," where we are able to generate in mere days an amount of data that would have taken years or even decades not long ago. In his book on big data, the photographer Rick Smolan says that we are witnessing the emergence of a "planetary nervous system" as we generate more and more data that are increasingly interconnected (Smolan and Erwitt, 2012). We now have far more data on our social and environmental worlds than ever before, and we are only beginning to understand how to make sense of them.

One key way of making sense of a world awash with data is through geography. Location, movement, proximity, distance, clustering, diffusion, and other spatial aspects

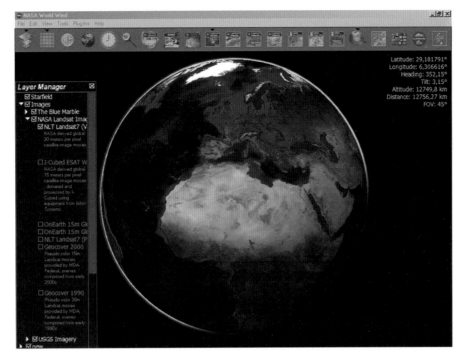

FIGURE 2.6   Screenshot of NASA's World Wind digital globe (Source: Wikimedia Commons)

of data can help us understand and visualize the world of big data around us. This is the promise of the geoweb: that the collection and visualization of large volumes of spatial data, being generated by everything from mobile phones to smart cities, can help us better understand our social and natural environments.

Tools and platforms for data visualization have evolved rapidly in response to the explosion of data coming from the IoT. For data containing spatial information, a whole host of web applications and GIS tools are available for mapping and geographic visualization. Digital globes such as Google Earth provide powerful tools for combining multiple layers of geographic information like aerial imagery, street networks, terrain, and near-real time weather (see Figure 2.6). These web-based maps and globes are increasingly available on mobile phones, and these handhelds are also incorporating new tools for "augmented reality" that give us digital layers of information overlaid on top of the physical world captured by the phone's camera. For example, you might have an app on your phone that lets you "see" what restaurants are inside a building, or you might play a game like Google's Ingress that gives you an imaginary world of gameplay that is set atop the real world around you. The emerging geoweb will increasingly bring the physical and digital worlds together, seamlessly integrating networked sensor data into the space around us.

Chapter summary

This chapter has touched on just a few of the many technological advances that have led to the emergence of a globally interconnected network of location-aware devices, geolocated sensors and spatial data: the geoweb. From the earliest maps to today's precise global positioning systems, humans have long sought to understand the world around them by organizing data spatially. The integration of various communication networks, from the GPS network to cellular networks to the increasingly ubiquitous internet, has led to a level of global connectivity never before seen. As this global network continues to add nodes and collect ever more data, the spatial organization and visualization of these data will only increase in importance. A world of "big data" being created by the "internet of things" requires a fundamentally new sort of cartography.

Further reading

Easton, R.D. and Frazier, E.F. (2013) *GPS Declassified: From Smart Bombs to Smartphones.* Lincoln: University of Nebraska Press.

3

"Big Geodata"

Managing Spatial Data in a Connected Age

 **Overview**

This chapter looks at the "Four Vs" of big geodata:

- Volume
- Velocity
- Variety
- Veracity

On December 17, 2011, Mohamed Bouazizi set himself on fire outside a provincial police headquarters in Tunisia after his vegetable cart was confiscated. Bouazizi's self-immolation is widely viewed as the tipping point that led to increasing social protests and civil unrest in Tunisia, eventually leading to the toppling of that country's long-standing president, Zine El Abidine Ben Ali (Beaumont, 2011; Worth, 2011). Throughout the growing protest movements in Tunisia, as well as in other protest movements such as Occupy Wall Street in the USA and the Arab Spring protests across the Arab world, social media outlets such as Facebook and Twitter grabbed attention as playing an important role as tools for resistance.

In Tunisia, flows of information across social networks supplemented the traditional forms of media communication, leading to a tremendous amount of data being produced throughout the months of protest. Internet use spiked across the country as bloggers, journalists, and activists used the decentralized social media networks to raise awareness, organize specific protests, and communicate to the outside world. Twitter hashtags and retweets, along with Facebook posts and other internet communication, allowed for a rapid dissemination of information as events unfolded.

While the role social media played in actually helping to *cause* protests like the uprising in Tunisia has been a topic of debate (Gladwell, 2010; Shirky, 2011), what is clear is that these new communication networks have allowed for a considerable increase in the amount of data being produced around such events. The production and dissemination of information is no longer only the domain of large broadcast networks; it is now possible for almost anyone who consumes information to also be a producer. Anyone with access to a laptop computer or a mobile phone can create or record words, images, sounds, and video recordings that can instantly be uploaded and distributed across the internet. So much information is being produced and shared, in fact, that our traditional tools for making sense of it have often become overwhelmed. The more data we produce, the more we need new tools and techniques for collecting, storing, analyzing, and visualizing them.

This is, in essence, the idea behind the term "big data." While we are still grappling with exactly what we mean by big data, one of the most common definitions can be summed up as the "three Vs," a framework first proposed by analyst Doug Laney (2001). The first is *volume* – the sheer amount of data we now produce each day is so great that we find ourselves struggling to capture it all. The second is *velocity* – not only are we producing more data than ever but we are doing so faster than ever. Twitter users alone, for example, generate approximately 6000 tweets every second of every day. The third 'V' is for *variety*. Data generated on Twitter, which are generated rapidly and at high volume, are but one type of data flowing across the web. Factor in other social media sites, emails, millions of web pages, YouTube videos, sensor networks of all sorts, satellite imaging, and the myriad other sorts of data being generated daily, and you have a cacophony of data that we can hardly comprehend. The amount of data generated in an "internet minute" is truly mind-boggling.

This chapter positions the geoweb as a framework for making sense of data in this new era of information abundance. As our tools for collecting and managing data have evolved, we have learned how to acquire, store, and visualize vast amounts of data. Yet we are only now beginning to understand how we might ask new questions of these data as we seek to better understand ourselves and the world around us. And as we are generating more data from more sources than ever before, verifying the accuracy of the data produced is also a considerable challenge. Using the "three Vs" as a guide – and adding a fourth, *veracity*, as a means for considering data accuracy – this chapter examines the rapid growth of digital data over the past several years and charts the transition of location-based data from geographical information to "big geodata." But first, we should consider the nature and evolution of data in society.

GOT DATA?

Consider an earth scientist measuring seismic activity, a sociologist conducting interviews, or a historian poring over archival records in a library. Each of these individuals is engaged in the activity of research through the collection of data. Data make up the most elemental and abstract form of observations, measurements, or recordings that we then combine and relate in different ways in an effort to derive meaning from the world around us. We might arrange data in a list, a graph, a map, a relational database, a photograph, or some other organizational framework. We store data we have collected on paper, in audio and video recordings, and on computer hard drives so that we can preserve, share, compare, append, and otherwise make use of them in the production of human knowledge.

While today we say we live in the "information age," it is more accurate to say that we are living through the most recent information revolution in a long history of technological transformations. The graphical representation of the spoken word, or writing, is considered to be one of the early revolutions in information technology and provided the basis for a more permanent means for storing data. The invention of the moveable type printing press led to another information revolution, as the mass production of books and journals led to an unprecedented circulation of information and ideas. The telegraph and telephone facilitated long-distance communication throughout the nineteenth century. In the earlier decades of the twentieth century, radio (and later television) broadcasts were used to communicate information, while film and magnetic tape were being employed in the storage of data.

Today's information age began in the 1970s, as advances in computer processing power and data storage led to widespread adoption of the personal computer. Data could now be created and transmitted as electrical signals and stored on the magnetic tape inside portable floppy disks. Thus began the transformation of a world made up primarily of analog data to one where digital data would begin to dominate, setting the stage for an impending "information explosion." The 1980s and 1990s brought us the cellular and computer networks that formed the backbone of today's internet, providing the platform for human creativity and collaboration that led to another transformative leap in the circulation of ideas. The volume of data began to grow exponentially.

VOLUME

On May 23, 2012, the search giant Google paid tribute to Bob Moog, the father of the modern music synthesizer, by posting a "Google doodle" of a playable synthesizer. Google doodles, which are stylistic changes to the Google logo to represent holidays, special events, and birthdays like that of Bob Moog, are often interactive. In the case of the synthesizer doodle, visitors to the Google homepage could manipulate the controls of the synthesizer and record a 30-second snippet of music. During the single day that the Google doodle was online, more than 300 million visitors created *more than 50 years'* worth of music. That's more than 440,000 hours of music created in a 24-hour period.

Storing half a century's worth of music made with a Google doodle might seem rather pointless, but it does illustrate how quickly large volumes of data can be generated. To take a more scientifically relevant example, we can look at the field of astronomy, where we have rapidly increased the amount of data being generated by telescopes. The Hubble telescope, launched in 1990, collects approximately 120 gigabytes of data – the equivalent of more than 1000 meters of books on a shelf – each week. The Galaxy Evolution Explorer telescope gathered over 20 terabytes, or more than 20,000 gigabytes, over its ten-year lifespan. Yet these both pale in comparison to the amount of data that is expected to pour in from the Square Kilometer Array (SKA) telescope that is scheduled to begin operation around 2020. Made up of hundreds of thousands of radio telescopes, the SKA will collect more than a million terabytes per day, which is more data than is currently generated by the entire World Wide Web.

The volume of data generated on the internet each day is now so large that we find it hard to describe. In 2012, Intel tried to articulate the data deluge by breaking down our activity into an "internet minute," where we produce more than 2 million Google searches, 6 million Facebook views, and 30 hours of YouTube video. While impressive, those numbers already seem almost archaic as both the number of internet users and the amount of data storage continue to grow each year. It is estimated, in fact, that as much as 90 percent of the data generated in the world has been created in just the last few years. This data generation shows no sign of abating, as the number of networked devices continues to proliferate across the globe and the cost of producing and disseminating information is practically nothing.

Our data-rich society causes some to lament that we face constant "information overload." Indeed, we live in a world of overflowing email inboxes, spam, 24-hour news, and a multitude of social media sites that provide a never-ending stream of content. Yet information overload has actually been with us for a long time. After Gutenberg and the printing press, more books than an individual could read in a lifetime were cheaply available. The sociologist George Simmel was writing about the information overload of urban life back in the early 1900s. Instead of thinking of our current era as simply one of information overload, however, Clay Shirky (2008) urges us to consider it as one of filter failure. We need, in other words, new and better tools for making sense of the data that we are generating at an unprecedented rate.

VELOCITY

Part of the reason why our past tools for filtering data are failing is that data are now being generated faster than ever. We used to rely on the morning newspaper and the evening news for our daily updates about the world around us. Now as soon as a news event happens it is immediately communicated online via news websites, Twitter, Facebook and myriad other digital tools. We can go to the web to check real-time traffic information, follow a hashtag on Twitter to see what others are reporting about a live event, and consult an app to see if it will be raining in the next 10 minutes. Stock trades now happen in milliseconds over high-speed fiber optic cables, and webcams, sensors, and mobile phones communicate live imagery and data almost instantly from around the world.

One of the reasons why we are seeing a rapid increase in both the velocity and volume of data being generated is that we have the capability of storing extremely large quantities of data in computer memory. Not too long ago, computer storage was expensive, meaning that we had to decide which data were worth keeping and which were not. As computer memory technologies advanced and the cost per megabyte of storage plummeted, we greatly increased our data storage capacity. The gigabyte of storage that might have cost you around $1000 in the mid-1990s, just as the internet was gaining momentum, now costs only pennies. We also now have access to large amounts of computer storage in the "cloud," which means we do not even have to own the physical memory ourselves – we can store our data online. Data storage has become cheap and plentiful enough that we typically do not have to worry about running out.

Of course, storing our rapidly growing volumes of data is only one of the problems. Another is having the capability to process data quickly enough to be able to make decisions or put the data to work in a meaningful way. Collecting information on traffic flow and congestion is not useful if it takes an hour or two to get that information mapped and distributed to an app on a mobile phone. Much of the data we collect is extremely time-sensitive and will not be of much use to us in the future – we need ways to make sense of large datasets in real-time.

Computer processing power has kept pace with computer storage in terms of growing more powerful even as it becomes cheaper. Almost everyone is familiar with Moore's law, which predicts that the number of transistors on a computer microprocessor will double approximately every 2 years, giving us ever greater computing power in a smaller and smaller amount of space. The fact that advancements in microprocessing power have been near-exponential for years means that there is truth in the common observation that there is far more computing power in the typical smartphone than there was in the Apollo 11 mission that took men to the moon.

Even with Moore's law, the velocity and volume of data we produce now are so great that single computers, even supercomputers, cannot process them quickly enough. Big data computing requires clusters of computers that are networked and programmed to work together. These clusters can grow quite large – Google, for example, has well over 1 million computer servers clustered in data centers around the world. Google has also developed software systems to break up large volumes of data for analysis and prioritize tasks, which is important for an organization that receives more than 40,000 search queries per second.

Our advances in computer storage and processing have made it possible for us to capture massive volumes of data and analyze those data almost instantly. As such, we are collecting more data, and different types of data, than we ever have before. From sensors embedded in a city's infrastructure to wearable devices monitoring our health, we are gathering a variety of datasets that were not feasible just a few short years ago. This presents the third challenge for managing data in a connected age: the sheer variety of data we are now dealing with.

VARIETY

As the internet of things continues to connect more and more of the physical world to the networked digital world, the volumes of data we generate are increasingly diverse. There are constant streams of data flowing at all scales, from the very local, such as wearable (or perhaps swallowable) health technology that provides data on an individual human body's condition, to the universal, as in the extremely large datasets being produced by today's telescopes. We capture imagery with everything from the camera on a mobile phone to a closed-circuit security camera in a city building to the many satellites orbiting Earth. We monitor a large variety of data, both environmental (temperature, precipitation, wind currents, earthquakes, etc.) and social (traffic patterns, migration, political campaign donations, commodity chains, and where our friends are). We post updates to social networks, report our location to various apps on our mobile devices, send brief missives via messaging applications such as Twitter and SMS, and perform map searches to see what coffee shops might be nearby. We have had access to some of these data for quite some time, while others are new thanks to the emerging tools of the geoweb. But one difference is that the recent technological advances outlined above make it possible for us to now capture these streams of data. All of them.

Capturing these messy and disparate streams of data, however, can be difficult, and it can be more difficult still to find ways to analyze and visualize them. We may find ourselves wanting to compare data from two or three very different datasets – say, a collection of tweets, a series of photographs, and environmental sensor data from the same place – only to find that they are organized in very different ways. There is no common language for the internet of things (though there are several efforts to create one), which makes "translation" one of the challenges of big data.

In the past, data analysis could be done by downloading a dataset, inserting it into a relational database such as MySQL, and running commands on a local computer. With big data all three of these activities are at best extremely time-consuming and at worst impossible. Transferring enormous datasets over networks can stress bandwidth capabilities and hard drive storage capacity. Processing data on a local computer can overwhelm the memory and CPU of that machine, resulting in a crash. And relational databases assume an orderly set of structured data, which, as we have just seen, is often not the case in today's world of jumbled data streams.

Local analysis on a relational database can still be a useful approach to data analysis, and we will look at powerful tools such as QGIS that provide a suite of applications for data analysis later in this book. The point here, though, is that the sheer variety of data that we now collect and store takes all sorts of different digital forms, and we are beginning to develop new tools and approaches to deal with the messiness that is big data. "Cleaning up" data is still a common and time-consuming chore, but we are also in the process of constructing new digital tools that are more comfortable handling ambiguous and unstructured data from myriad sources.

Given the three Vs of big data, it often makes more sense for us to take our analysis to the data rather than attempting to bring the data to us. Increasingly, big data necessarily reside in the "cloud," where we can apply new tools like Hadoop on datasets that are scattered across hundreds of networked computers. Tools providing alternatives to traditional relational databases are emerging rapidly, using different structural forms for organizing and analyzing data. Mapping and visual analysis tools are also evolving, providing ways to interface with multiple datasets and create useful visualizations.

THE FOUR VS OF BIG GEODATA

Geodata are certainly no exception when it comes to the tremendous increase in data capture over the past couple of decades. Indeed, much of what we call big data includes some sort of geolocational information, meaning that we can now create more maps, track more things, and visualize more spatial data than ever before. Harnessing the power of "where" is often an explicit goal of big data analysis, and as such we are collecting spatial information at an unprecedented pace. Below is a brief description of how geodata are evolving in an era of big data.

Volume

Just as advances in our telescope technology have led to enormous leaps in the amount of data we are able to capture on outer space, our tools for terrestrial imaging have led to an abundance of data as well. From the first fuzzy images of Earth taken by a satellite more than 50 years ago to today's high-resolution photographs collected by commercial satellites like *GeoEye* and *DigitalGlobe*, we have been curious observers of our planet home. Remote sensing, a term used to describe this ability to capture data about Earth from above, has improved to the point that we now have vast datasets being generated constantly. We can now collect data across the electromagnetic spectrum, allowing us to get high-quality imagery, thermal data, and other radiometric information as it is captured by sensors on board some of the many satellites orbiting the Earth.

The data collected by the US *Landsat* satellites provides one example of the quantity of Earth observation data being amassed. The first *Landsat* was launched in 1972, and captured fewer than 1700 photographs in its short lifespan. By contrast, *Landsat 5* was launched 12 years later and captured more than 2.5 million images of the Earth's surface. *Landsat* data were stored at various ground stations around the world until 2010, when the Landsat Global Archive Consolidation effort began acquiring and organizing all *Landsat* data and making them freely available online. *Landsat 8*, launched in February 2013, has begun capturing even more observation data across nine spectral bands, from land imaging to thermal infrared to cirrus cloud detection. Each day, *Landsat 8* captures approximately 400 1-gigabyte images that are processed and made available by the US Geological Survey (USGS). By capturing these data and ensuring that they are consistent with the imagery collected over the past several decades, the USGS oversees a collection of geodata that is vitally important for all sorts of scientific endeavors, from disaster relief to urban planning to the study of climate change.

Yet the *Landsat* data collection effort is but one component of the USGS Land Remote Sensing Program, which in turn is but one effort to systematically collect geodata. There are hosts of other geospatial datasets being collected every day, from the location of every aircraft currently in flight to the tracking of components in a company's supply chain. Thanks to the emerging technologies of the geoweb, more and more of our world is mappable and trackable. And unlike *Landsat 8*, which only captures an image of the same place on Earth every 16 days, much of the geodata we map and track requires constant updating and near-real-time communication.

Velocity

One of the most beneficial uses of the large volumes of data collected by the *Landsat* program is the analysis of land cover change over time. Scientists have used multiple satellite images of the same place to examine everything from deforestation in the Amazon to urban sprawl in the United States. By comparing a series of multiple images over time of the same place on Earth, we can understand and study change that happens slowly over the years – change that we might not otherwise be able to visualize as easily.

Yet much of the geodata we collect in today's era of big data is not focused on slow rates of change, but rather is gathered and analyzed for spatial decision-making that takes place in real time. The mapping tools in your mobile phone are not normally used to show what things looked like in the past; instead, they show you where you are *right now* in relation to where you want to be. If the software that calculates your driving directions is even a minute too slow, the information it generates will be practically useless. We expect our devices to be able to absorb location data, analyze them, and then turn them into spatial information of use to us right at that moment. In short, we expect our devices to be both aware of, and able to immediately respond to, our current surroundings.

The fact that we have come to expect this high level of spatial information processing from small and portable electronic devices in many ways demonstrates the advances in computing hardware and software outlined above and in the previous chapter. By shrinking down our microprocessors, sensors, and GPS chips to a size that fits in a handheld device, and by seamlessly networking that device to the internet where we can access the power of cloud computing, we have extended the internet into the physical world. As we have done so, it has become increasingly important for us to interconnect the spatial locations and activities of our physical world with data and information captured and stored in our digital world. We have begun to so intertwine these two worlds – physical space and cyberspace – that we often move among them without noticing. This is, in essence, the geoweb, and it requires the capability to capture and process data at spatiotemporal scales that are larger and faster than we have ever before been able to meet.

While Google's self-driving automobiles, which must collect and analyze approximately 1 gigabyte of data every second, might seem the epitome of the tremendous velocity of geodata, there are many other examples all around us. Turning again to our mobile phones, there are a multitude of spatial datasets we can access in real time. We can see a radar image of current weather conditions, find out the exact location of airplanes in mid-flight, or observe recent crime activity in a nearby city. We can view geolocated tweets based on hashtagged keywords, or we can map the location of friends who are sharing their position over a social network. We can collect data with our mobile device, upload them to the internet, and then view them on a digital map along with those of any number of other contributors to the "crowdsourced" mapping application. Just as the amount of data processed in an "internet minute" can be difficult for us to comprehend, so too is the velocity and volume of geospatial data moving throughout the geoweb at any given moment.

Variety

As mentioned above, we are not only generating lots of data at rapid speeds but also many new and different types of data. Geodata are no different. Much of the data we now generate has some sort of spatial component, and as such has become part of the evolving geoweb. Sometimes the spatial component of data is quite clear – a set of geographic coordinates, for example, that are structured in Geographic Markup Language on the web. But often geodata are not so structured, such as when places are simply mentioned in social media posts or blog posts. Making sense of these types of geodata and structuring them in such a way that they can be incorporated into the geoweb in a useful way is a key challenge as we continue to generate more and more spatial data.

A common, web-based street map provides a good example of how we have seen the volume, velocity, and variety of geodata grow over the past few years. Not too long ago, a street map in a GIS was not much more than a digital representation of a physical street map. It had symbology and colors representing the size and type of road, perhaps labels for street and city names, and perhaps a few other visual elements. We began to add additional attributes to the streets, such as speed limits and number of lanes. Then came geospatial topology, which allowed us to set rules that governed the relationships between elements of our digital map, giving us the ability to locate street addresses or generate driving directions. We put all of this up on the internet, and soon we had early web mapping sites like MapQuest. This was an impressive digital feat in and of itself, but it was only the beginning.

Today's online street map still shows locations and provides directions, but it also might include the current state of traffic flow, including reports and images posted from others as they come across accidents, road construction, or other possible driving delays. You might also see points (or even 3D polygons) representing nearby restaurants, and with one click you can access photos, menus, and user reviews. Another click gives you access to recent aerial imagery of the region, or perhaps the underlying terrain if you are walking or cycling instead of driving. You might even choose to "fly in" to a specific street and view photographs of that exact location. The digital map serves as an organizational tool for managing a variety of datasets being generated by different entities at very different spatiotemporal scales.

Because so many now rely on maps such as this on a daily basis, and because erroneous or incomplete geodata on the map can be frustrating or even deadly, the accuracy of geodata in today's digital mapping applications is extremely important. You have probably heard stories of car accidents caused by faulty GPS data, or of people getting lost on back roads as they blindly trust the driving directions provided by their mobile device. Our digital maps are improving daily, yet the amount of data required to maintain these maps and make adjustments in the face of constant change means that our digital maps are in constant flux. We no longer live in a world of static maps – our cartography today is a constant swirl of geodata being generated from many different sources. Given that several of these sources are not geospatial professionals, but simply mobile device users such as yourself, there is one final 'V' that we must examine in our exploration of geodata as big data: *veracity*.

Veracity

We saw in Chapter 2 that geography and map-making have a long history. For most of that history, cartography was left to the professionals. Kings and colonizers relied on the skills of commissioned geographers to delineate the contours of contested lands. Geographic societies sprang up as clubs for the wealthy and elite. The arrival of digital map-making and analysis through geographic information systems democratized cartography somewhat, but the expensive hardware and software required, along with the technical knowledge necessary to operate them, meant that the production of geospatial information remained confined to a small group. Today, however, anyone with a mobile device can generate geodata and share it with others. The production of geodata is no longer solely in the hands of the experts.

Sometimes referred to as "neogeography," this new world of user-generated geodata and volunteered geographic information has transformed the way we produce and consume maps. We do not typically pore over a thick atlas or stand above a well-crafted globe; instead, we place ourselves inside the map and let the spatial information order itself around us. We voluntarily share our location, check in at certain establishments, upload pictures and videos that are georeferenced, and plot our latest hike on a topographic map. We can collect data that are submitted to a geographic database for use by others, like the National Phenology Network in the United States. We can generate new geographic data by adding features to a digital map like OpenStreetMap. Or we can tag our social media posts with our location, creating data that might be used in a social science research project of which we are not aware.

We are, in essence, part of the map itself instead of a detached observer from above, and our maps increasingly reflect our individual selves instead of a common abstraction.

The newest versions of Google Maps, for example, are tailored for the specific user – features may or may not show up on the map, depending on your past digital behavior. If you have reviewed a restaurant, checked in somewhere on a social media app, plotted driving directions, or generated some other type of geodata, that information can be used to construct a custom map for you. Your cartographic present is increasingly shaped by the geographic information you have generated yourself in the past.

That an increasing amount of the geodata we consume is produced by non-experts – ourselves as well as anonymous others – can be cause for both celebration and alarm. A map that is customized for us based on our tastes and preferences might seem prescient and useful, or it might lead us to wonder what sorts of interesting things are being left off our map. A database full of spatial information that has been crowdsourced by unknown volunteers might enable new scientific insights, but the quality and accuracy of the data may come under question. The geoweb is increasingly made up of geographic data that are not made by professional cartographers working with painstaking exactitude, but are being generated by us. In the next chapter, we will take a look at this transformation in the production of geodata from information which is limited but expertly produced to our current geoweb full of almost limitless spatial information, but of varying quality, that can be produced and shared by everyone.

Chapter summary

This chapter sought to situate the data of the geoweb in the larger emerging world of "big data." Using the explanatory framework of the "three Vs," we have seen how we now produce almost unimaginable quantities of data, at faster rates, and with more tools, and with no signs of slowing down in the coming years. The challenge of big data, and for the geoweb when it comes to big geodata, is to be able to harness the tools that allow us to capture all of these data and do something with them. That we can now collect geodata at spatiotemporal scales that were previously impossible, and combine those datasets with those provided by others to better leverage our own data, means that the geoweb allows us to think in new ways about how we go about doing research. What does it mean when we can collect *all* of the data, instead of just having to take small samples? How do we assess accuracy when geodata can be so diverse in terms of both the tools and the individuals creating them? As the geoweb becomes more democratized, pervasive, and ubiquitous, how can we apply it to better understand our world without undermining privacy?

The next two chapters of Part One examine these issues in greater detail. Chapter 4 further explores the concept of "citizen cartographers," delving deeper into what it means for the geoweb when an increasing amount of geodata is being generated by the everyday user of technology instead of the geographic experts. How might this decentralization of data creation make possible exciting new approaches to the collection and visualization of geodata? Chapter 5 then turns to questions and concerns about a world where geolocation is "always on" and more aspects of our lives are mappable. The geoweb may well give us a new way of looking at the world, but what if it also gives us new tools for surveillance and new means for invading privacy?

(Continued)

As we have seen, the geoweb has emerged as a product of our most recent information age. The widespread adoption of the internet gave us an unprecedented tool for the sharing of information, and a whole host of other technological advancements gave us the power to collect, store, analyze, and visualize that information. We began to include some sort of spatial information in the increasing volumes of data we generated, and we put the power to create spatial data in the hands of the everyday citizen. We can all map, and increasingly we can also be mapped. The next two chapters explore the ways in which we make meaning of this, and also take precautions, as the geoweb continues to grow in its presence and importance in our daily lives.

Further reading

Rainie, L. and Wellman, B. (2012) *Networked: The New Social Operating System*. Cambridge, MA: MIT Press.

Mayer-Schönberger, V. and Cukier, K. (2013) *Big Data: A Revolution that Will Transform How We Live, Work, and Think*. London: John Murray.

4

Citizen Cartographers

Neogeography, VGI and the Democratization of Data Production

 **Overview**

This chapter looks at:

- The wisdom of crowds
- Crowdsourcing and the geoweb
- Neogeography and VGI
- Social media and VGI
- Sousveillance, smart mobs, and counter-mapping

If you type "Encyclopedia Britannica" into an online search engine, chances are that the first website listed will be the online home for that famous compendium of knowledge that has been published since 1768. Chances are also good that the second listing in your online search will be an article in Wikipedia, an online encyclopedia that has been published since 2001. Going a step further, typing "history of Encyclopedia Britannica" into a search engine will almost assuredly return a Wikipedia article first. In fact, typing "history of" followed by most any subject will likely take you to the same source of information time after time: Wikipedia.

The concept of organizing human knowledge into a categorized collection of essays has a long history. For much of that history, the approach taken to constructing an encyclopedia has been to identify some number of experts who contribute comprehensive essays on topics in their various fields. By limiting content to only that produced by experts, and by subjecting that content to extensive peer review, an encyclopedia could be trusted to provide a highly accurate survey of human knowledge. Wikipedia changed all of that, and changed it quickly. Turning the traditional model of knowledge curation on its head, the founders of Wikipedia argued that there should not be a central organizing body in charge of the systematic compilation of information; instead, why not leverage technology to allow anyone to contribute to the construction of a digital encyclopedia? The idea took off – by 2002 Wikipedia had over 1000 entries, according to an entry on the site itself (Wikipedia, 2015), and by 2014 it had more than 32 million and was one of the most visited websites in the world.

While Wikipedia has received significant criticism for this new crowdsourced model of the encyclopedia and is often considered to be less authoritative than encyclopedias that limit authorship to experts, Wikipedia today is one of the world's largest and most widely used reference works in human history and was shown to be nearly as accurate as *Encyclopedia Britannica* as early as 2005 (Giles, 2005). In contrast to traditional print encyclopedias, which are expensive, bulky, and quickly out of date, Wikipedia is free, available to anyone with an internet connection, and continuously updated. Rather than rely on a small group of experts to compile the entire written collection of human knowledge, the Wikipedia model argues that letting anyone contribute and edit, even "amateurs" who may know far less than the experts, ultimately strengthens the compilation and results in a much richer and more complete collection of information. The ultimate form of peer review, according to this model, is one where everyone can be a peer.

This same transformation – from a limited set of information created by a limited set of individuals to a near-limitless collection of information created by a vast number of contributors – has taken place in the production of geospatial data. Whereas throughout history we have seen cartography and geography limited to the well-trained experts, over the past several years the ability to create and visualize geospatial information has been greatly democratized. We still have professional atlases and globes, to be sure, but the majority of geodata being produced today does not come at the hand of the professional cartographer, but instead from everyday users of digital technology. We no longer passively consume the geodata created by experts – we are now active contributors to the production of geodata and can add our own spatial knowledge to that produced by expert and amateur alike.

OpenStreetMap is one example that applies the Wikipedia model to the production of digital maps. Instead of being produced by a handful of cartographic experts, the online map is the product of well over a million individuals who voluntarily contribute geographic information and make cartographic edits. Like Wikipedia, OpenStreetMap is free and is continuously being updated and refined by volunteers around the world. It has been adopted as the mapping platform for several organizations needing to supply geospatial information, including humanitarian groups dedicated to emergency response and disaster recovery. Following the 2010 earthquake in Haiti, for example, Crisis Commons worked with OpenStreetMap data to create the most comprehensive digital map of roads, hospitals, and other infrastructure vital to the post-earthquake recovery efforts. OpenStreetMap was also used by Ushahidi (a Swahili word for "testimony"), an organization that constructed a "crisis map" of eyewitness reports and other volunteered information to help organize rescue and recovery in the earthquake's aftermath.

The shift in the production of geodata from a handful of experts to almost anyone carrying a digital device has profound implications. Indeed, the geoweb would not exist if this transformation had not occurred. This chapter examines the rise of the *citizen cartographer* and explores some of the ways that the democratization of geodata production is changing how we both create and perceive the world around us. In a world where every consumer of geodata can also be a producer, we are beginning to uncover new geographies that no handful of experts could possibly hope to construct. The geoweb, in short, is largely being produced from below.

THE WISDOM OF CROWDS

In his book *The Wisdom of Crowds*, writer James Surowiecki (2004) recounts the story of a British scientist who attended a livestock exhibition in order to test a theory. The scientist, working under the assumption that only a few people in a population have the appropriate skills and know-how to run a society, decided to perform a statistical test on all of the entries in a livestock weight-guessing contest held at the exhibition. Since most of the guessers were not experts – some, but not many, were butchers or farmers – the scientist assumed that the average of all of the guesses of an ox's weight would be far inferior to the predicted weight chosen by those with skill and experience. Instead, he discovered that the average of the total collection of guesses came within 1 pound of the actual weight of the animal. The collective mind of the crowd ended up being much smarter than that of any one individual.

When we take Surowiecki's example and amplify it with the internet, we can find all sorts of cases where a digitally connected "crowd" is able to do some pretty impressive things. The Linux operating system, for example, was started by Linus Torvalds, who early on released his code to the web, where anyone with interest and some technical expertise could use, modify, and distribute the code. The operating system quickly grew in both complexity and popularity as users around the world, often with no knowledge of the others involved, contributed code and fixed existing bugs. Unlike Microsoft's Windows, an operating system developed by programmers all employed by an individual corporation, Linux was being developed voluntarily, for free, by people connected by nothing more than a love of computing and an interest in seeing Linux succeed. And succeed it did – Linux is now a leading software platform for computer servers and can be found on most of the world's fastest supercomputers. Google's popular Android OS, found on more than 1 billion portable devices, is based on the Linux kernel. It might seem incredible, but an operating system developed by an uncoordinated "crowd" of users scattered around the globe has produced software that rivals, and often bests, operating systems that have been painstakingly developed within the closed walls and hierarchical structure of a corporation.

Another example of leveraging the crowd to address a seemingly intractable problem can be found at the intersection of biochemistry and video games (Khatib et al., 2011). Scientists had been struggling for more than a decade to solve the folding structure of a particular simian retroviral protein used in animal models of HIV. Researchers at the University of Washington decided to create a video game, called Foldit, to see if gamers might be able to contribute to the research. Astonishingly, hundreds of thousands of gamers took to the game quickly, and the protein folding structure was solved in a mere 3 weeks. Just as in the case of the ox weight-guessing contest, the collective wisdom of an uncoordinated crowd trumped that of a handful of experts with lifetimes of experience.

CROWDSOURCING AND THE GEOWEB

The Foldit example above is an example of a particular category of crowdsourcing, often referred to as "citizen science." From the morphological classification of galaxies to the monitoring of aquatic resources, a growing number of scientific research projects rely on the voluntary participation of thousands of non-scientists with nothing more in common than an internet connection. The amount of data generated by these volunteers far exceeds what researchers would be able to collect if they had to rely on a staff of paid experts.

In many cases, such projects depend on capturing the geographic location for the data being collected by the crowd. In these instances, scientists turn to the geoweb in order to acquire geospatial data of relevance to the research at hand. By collecting the time and place at which data are collected by individual participants, researchers are able to construct geospatial models that can assist in solving problems or uncovering patterns that would otherwise be extremely difficult or impossible to do.

The GLOBE (Global Learning and Observations to Benefit the Environment) Program is one such example of where geodata are an essential component of the project. GLOBE relies on teachers and students at schools around the world to collect research-quality environmental measures that are then included in a global database. Since its beginning on Earth Day in 1995, more than 10 million students have contributed more than 100 million environmental observations in over 110 countries. Each measurement taken is georeferenced, meaning that scientists and students alike can map the data and make predictive geospatial models based on long-term data observed over a large geographic area. Clearly, data collection at this scale requires the contribution of the crowd.

Researchers increasingly rely on the enabling technologies of the geoweb to gather geospatial data from those participating in citizen science. Given that GPS technology is embedded in a large and growing number of mobile devices, researchers can easily acquire the geographic coordinates that mark the specific location in which data are gathered. From the Audubon Society's Christmas Bird Count to the National Ecological Observatory Network's Project BudBurst that monitors seasonal plant changes, new datasets are being generated at spatiotemporal scales that would not be possible without the combination of citizen scientists and the geoweb. In essence, such crowdsourced projects succeed by allowing citizens to serve as nodes in a vast network of voluntarily submitted geodata.

NEOGEOGRAPHY AND VGI

The above examples of geodata being captured, created, and shared by non-experts are all part of the substantive shift from a world where geographic information tended to be relatively scarce, technically cumbersome, and expensive to produce to a world where the geoweb provides access to geographic information that is abundant, often simple to produce, and practically free. Just as the internet, and later the interactive tools commonly referred to as "Web 2.0," made it much easier and cheaper to produce, distribute, and share content, the geoweb has engendered a new era of spatial data production and sharing that is revolutionizing the traditional field of GIS. New digital tools have emerged that make it much easier to capture or create spatial data, and increasingly we seem willing to share those data openly with the public in hopes that we will gain something in exchange for our sudden lack of privacy.

The terms "neogeography" and "volunteered geographic information" have been coined to describe this significant transformation. Neogeography, or "new geography," helps us define the distinction between the traditional tools and approaches of the geographic information systems expert and the new tools and techniques of the citizen cartographer. Volunteered geographic information (VGI) refers more broadly to the phenomenon of our growing ability and willingness to share spatial information online in ways that can be used by ourselves and others. There are certainly concerns that arise when we begin discussing these terms, from privacy issues to data accuracy problems to the marginalization of those without the necessary tools. These will be addressed in the following chapter. For now, we can examine further some of the more positive implications of the emerging geoweb.

In many ways, we can trace the beginnings of neogeography and VGI to the mid-1990s, just as the internet was beginning to pave the way for change. There was a growing concern that GIS as a field was problematic in several ways, from its roots in military planning to the concern that it serves to perpetuate existing social inequalities. John Pickles's *Ground Truth*, published in 1995, argued that the social implications of GIS, not just the technical ones, needed to be studied as geographic information increasingly pervaded many aspects of our lives (Pickles, 1995). The following year, the term "public participation geographic information systems" (PPGIS) was born out of two meetings of the National Center for Geographic Information and Analysis. The idea behind PPGIS was to identify tools and strategies for empowering marginalized populations and make GIS more inclusive and accessible to the non-experts. While the results of these efforts have been mixed, the emergence of PPGIS and a more critical examination of the role of GIS in society helped open the door for a nascent neogeography.

Around a decade after *Ground Truth* and PPGIS, the internet had matured to the point that users around the world were not just reading static web pages, but were producing, collaborating, interacting, and sharing across emerging social media sites, video sharing sites such as YouTube, and any number of blogs, wikis, and other web applications. Commonly referred to as Web 2.0, this messy new world of user-generated digital information became so pervasive, and was so clearly indicative of a dramatic social shift, that in 2006 *Time* magazine's person of the year was "You." Clear signs of "disruption" were appearing as industries as diverse as news, music, advertising, publishing, and yes, GIS, felt the impacts of a dramatic drop in the cost of producing and sharing information.

While many of the more technical analytical tools of GIS largely remained on the desktop computer, neogeography began to explode when new tools for creating and visualizing geodata emerged on the internet. Google Maps and its API were announced in 2005, and since then the application has steadily added tools that allow users to create their own maps by "mashing up" Google Maps and other sets of spatial data. That same year, Google also announced Google Earth, a 3D viewer that gave users a tool for visualizing a massive amount of aerial imagery, terrain data, and other geographic information around the world. Almost overnight, map-making and 3D visualization were brought out of specialized computer labs and into the homes of millions.

By the time Apple CEO Steve Jobs announced a new product called the iPhone in January 2007, the blending of the GPS network with cellular networks meant that geographic information was quickly going mobile. GPS chips were increasingly being embedded in mobile devices, and new software applications allowed users to capture, display, and share (voluntarily or not) geodata from almost anywhere. The Web 2.0 tools that brought GIS to the internet also began to distribute it across millions of mobile devices. Recognizing the utility of a device that was always on and locationally aware, mobile device users began plotting driving directions, querying spatial databases, geotagging photos, and "checking in" at various locations so that friends nearby could keep tabs on their whereabouts. Our spatial location was becoming increasingly social, and citizens were becoming sensor nodes in a rapidly expanding network of volunteered geographic information (Goodchild, 2007).

SOCIAL MEDIA AND VGI

On March 26, 2006, Jack Dorsey typed the words "just setting up my twttr" into a new software tool that was being designed for small-group short messaging service (SMS) communication. The following year, at the South by Southwest Festival in Texas, the social networking and microblogging platform known as Twitter caught on among attendees as the number of posts, or tweets, rose to more than 50,000 per day. Seven years later, while

Germany was engaged in a surprisingly lopsided rout of Brazil in the semi-final of the World Cup, the #BRAvGER hashtag was tweeted more than 500,000 times in one *minute*. Worldwide, millions of Twitter users post around a half billion tweets every day.

Twitter is a prominent example of a social media platform where content is entirely user-generated and voluntarily shared among social networks. Tweets are limited to 140 characters, but can include links to photos and websites. Users can choose to send a tweet directly to a single individual, like an email, but most posts are sent by individuals to everyone who follows them in their Twitter network. And by using a hashtag, users can post to a much broader audience, since anyone knowing the hashtag can see what others post. This makes Twitter a somewhat unique social media platform, since users can choose what type of communication method they desire for each tweet: one-on-one, within a closed social network of followers, or broadcast to everyone via hashtags. Twitter, like the internet itself, allows users to not only voluntarily share information, but also choose how – and among whom – that information will be shared.

In 2009, Twitter co-founder Biz Stone announced that a new API was being developed for the platform that included geolocation support. Twitter users could now opt to include latitude and longitude in tweets and search for tweets by geographic location. By allowing users to include location metadata in individual tweets, Twitter effectively promoted user posts from volunteered information to volunteered geographic information. Suddenly, a new trove of user-generated data was not just social – it was now also spatial. Twitter had become part of the geoweb.

Twitter is only one example of a popular social media platform that incorporates location into user-generated content. Other popular platforms include Facebook, Google+, LinkedIn, Foursquare, and Instagram. Some are explicitly focused on location, like the place-based check-ins and link to OpenStreetMap in Foursquare, while others allow users the option of including location data if desired, like Instagram. Google+ includes a rich set of tools for controlling location data; a user can, for example, decide to share his or her exact location using latitude and longitude to a certain subset of individuals on the network, while only sharing city location (or no location at all) to other users. Likewise, users on Google+ can use their location to search for people, places, and recent posts that are currently nearby. Facebook lets users opt in to a "Nearby Friends" geolocation feature that provides alerts when other members of one's Facebook network are nearby. Combined, these and other social media platforms are generating an immense amount of geodata and make up an increasingly important component of the geoweb.

It is no surprise that social scientists and other researchers have picked up on the wealth of new data being generated by this entirely new medium. There are some questions and concerns about using social media data for research and analysis (see Chapter 5), but the potential value of such a preponderance of volunteered social data means that many tools and studies have been developed to help make sense of it all. The concepts and theories of social network analysis pre-date the emergence of online social media sites, but now there are vast new datasets and sophisticated tools for visualization and analysis of social networks. Instead of conducting expensive and time-consuming interviews and focus groups, researchers can turn to social media as a means for extracting data on a host of important topics. Instead of prompting participant responses with specific interview questions or soliciting particular behaviors, researchers can instead observe human behavior and interaction on a large scale.

While arguably still in its infancy, social network analysis on large datasets from social media platforms has already begun to reveal interesting and important new insights into human behavior. Research has been conducted on Facebook networks, for example, to see how one's network serves as a collection of peers that can influence everything from mood to risky behavior. Sociologists at Cornell University studying around 500 million tweets were able to discern fluctuations in the collective "mood" of the Twitter users over time (Golder and Macy, 2011). The National Football League in the United States developed a tool for monitoring fan engagement during games by analyzing Twitter data. Public health researchers have examined social media data to better understand various ailments, symptoms, and medications used. By capturing large quantities of volunteered social data and looking for trends and correlations, researchers have opened up exciting new areas of research on the human condition.

Adding a spatial component to the analysis of social media opens up even more possibilities, giving researchers an opportunity to situate social behavior geographically. In the Cornell study mentioned above, the researchers not only measured the collective mood of a Twitter population, but also analyzed the fluctuations in mood over time and place. They developed a global "mood map" that showed the variation in mood, as determined from specific sets of keywords taken from tweets, across countries, time zones, and other geographical regions. Similarly, other types of "sentiment analysis" have been conducted with georeferenced social media data, from the study of regional variation in the opinions on political parties and candidates to the simple mapping of tweets referencing "happy new year" as each time zone reached midnight on December 31. Location is quite often an important factor in determining human activity and behavior; as such, our increasing ability to monitor and map our everyday lives as played out on social media gives us a new window on society. And because the data we collect are now more easily accessible by more people than ever before, we have opened up opportunities to create maps and study spatial relationships that might perhaps be of more interest and relevance to the marginalized and disfranchised than the work of the cartographic experts.

SOUSVEILLANCE, SMART MOBS, AND COUNTER-MAPPING

Many of the technological advancements in the production of geodata, from the computer to aerial photography to the satellites that make up the Global Positioning System, were developed for military purposes. Maps and geographic information systems have been used to monitor activity over large territories, improve navigation and targeting for weapon systems, and designate geographical areas that are deemed desirable from a tactical standpoint. Surveillance of human activity can be found everywhere, from militarized borders to highway speed limits, from the high-resolution imagery of military satellites to the closed-circuit television imagery collected by banks and many other urban inhabitants with an interest in controlling territory. Collecting and organizing information spatially can be a powerful means of control.

The use of geographic information technology to monitor territorial activity – the cartographic "gaze" – is a clear example of the concept of "governmentality" made popular by the French philosopher Michel Foucault (1979). Using Jeremy Bentham's panopticon (a prison structured in such a way as to allow one observer to monitor all of the inmates) as a metaphor, Foucault describes how surveillance can maintain societal order and discipline. Cartography and the constant collection of spatial information by militaries and governments can be seen as a means to perpetuate power by controlling populations and reinforcing the territorial imperatives that legitimize the state. In a phrase attributed to the late geographer Bernard Neitschmann, who recognized the relationship between knowledge and power and advocated for indigenous communities to map their own territories, it is either "map or be mapped" (Bryan, 2009).

One promise of the emerging geoweb is that the recent technological advances in the capture and dissemination of geographical information might turn the concept of cartography as surveillance on its head. If everyone has the tools to collect data – whether it be text, photographs, video, sound, air quality, or other measurable phenomena – and immediately share such data with others over a decentralized network, then perhaps society can monitor as easily as it can be monitored. This idea of sousveillance, the theory that systematic observation can be conducted "from below" just as it has historically been conducted from above, is a relatively recent concept that has grown as the digital technologies of the geoweb have begun to diffuse widely throughout society. States and militaries continue to closely monitor human activity over space, to be sure, but only in recent years has technology provided the means for the systematic monitoring of human activity directly from the populace.

Geographical sousveillance has been referred to as "counter-mapping" (Peluso, 1995). As cartography and spatial information have been increasingly understood as important tools for consolidating and maintaining power, efforts to resist or contest top-down authority by constructing an alternative cartography have grown in recent years. From the participatory mapping of indigenous peoples attempting to regain control over natural resources to the volunteer community cartographers trying to strengthen local food systems in urban centers, examples of decentralized geographical sousveillance are increasingly abundant. As the geoweb continues to expand and evolve, the ability to collect, disseminate, and map data from below will be made ever easier.

Take, for example, the software application called Waze. This community-based traffic and navigation tool shows a real-time map of user-generated content on everything from heavy traffic to police traps and allows users to quickly submit their own data from the road. While sharing information on the location of the cheapest gas prices might not quite be the same as working with indigenous peoples to protect their land, it does demonstrate the concept of geographical sousveillance: information that was once either unknown, withheld, or provided only from a top-down centralized organization is now collected, shared, and visualized in real time on a freely accessible digital map. Information that was previously "silenced" by being omitted from official maps can now be accessed by anyone with an interest in using it. Similar applications post all sorts of other layers of data on digital maps, from the location of public restrooms to street art to food banks. Such collections and recombinations of geodata – called "mashups" – clearly demonstrate the power shift in cartography from expert to neogeographer.

Another way in which the geoweb facilitates the decentralization and redistribution of power is by transforming the relationship between communication networks and geographic space. Before the internet, the tools for one-way broadcast and two-way communication were largely separate. We could disseminate information to large numbers of people via radio, television, and the printed page, and we could communicate via telephone to another person, but there was no one tool that allowed us to do both. As such, organizing any sort of social activity was slow and difficult, and typically required the gathering of a group of individuals in physical space. As a result, any sort of public protest was typically foretold well before the event actually took place, and authorities could be prepared to control or suppress the assembly.

Once cellular networks and the internet were linked, however, we saw a new form of communication emerge that allowed individuals to coordinate information among groups and across specific networks. Suddenly groups could organize and coordinate in networked space without having to gather in physical space until they chose to do so. The creation of this new means of digital communication, which gave users the ability to "narrowcast" to a specific, defined group of individuals, arguably disrupted the panopticon of government surveillance by removing spatial proximity as a prerequisite for social organization.

One trivial, but often amusing, result of this new communication network is the sudden eruption of groups into song and dance in public space, a phenomenon dubbed "flash mob." Seemingly spontaneous and at random, but actually coordinated ahead of time by individuals using digital communication tools, dozens or hundreds of people might break out in applause in a hotel lobby, sing a showtune on the subway, or begin performing the zombie dance from Michael Jackson's *Thriller* in Grand Central Station in New York. Those individuals left out of the communication network are taken by surprise as the strangers around them, typically all absorbed in their own activities of daily life, begin coordinating their actions and cooperating in synchronized routine – all without having ever come together to practice beforehand.

While one can find many examples of flash mobs that have been created with no other purpose in mind beyond harmless fun, there are also those who have used the power of this new form of communication to organize groups for social causes and protest movements. The Harlem Shake, a dance parody in which the scene transforms from one lone dancer to a large crowd dancing, went viral on the internet in 2013, with thousands of groups uploading their own version of the dance online. While the vast majority of these videos were created for sheer amusement, in some cases the performance had underlying social and political tones. Youth activists in Egypt, for example, performed the Harlem Shake outside the Muslim Brotherhood's headquarters in Cairo as a means of protest against the Islamist rulers. In Tunisia, conservative Salafists tried but failed to stop the filming of the Harlem Shake at a language school in Tunis. While some participants in these forms of protest have been arrested, the quick formation and dissolution of a large group – coupled with the ability to upload or stream the video immediately over the internet – makes such social movements difficult to suppress.

Building on this idea of the flash mob, where a group forms in a single location for a short period of time to perform a coordinated act, groups have performed more sophisticated activities that take place over a broader geographical space. During the Arab Spring uprisings in the Middle East and the Occupy Wall Street movement in the United States, groups communicated over decentralized digital networks to coordinate protest activities in different parts of a city or across several cities in a country. Location-based digital tools such as Foursquare and Meetup were employed, along with other tools like Twitter hashtags and Facebook groups that facilitated decentralized communication, to help groups quickly organize and come together in physical space and just as easily dissolve. By eliminating the need for spatial proximity or centralized communication before coming together in protest, social movements become much more difficult to predict and prevent, as well as much tougher to stop. Dispersing a group in physical space is one thing, but disconnecting it in digital space is exponentially harder.

What we are witnessing in these examples, from a harmless flash mob to a prolonged social protest, is the recognition that digital tools provide us with an ability to extend and transform our notions of geographic space in important new ways. Our immediate physical surroundings are one form of geography; our digital, networked "surroundings" are another. By connecting the two and moving information across a complex and decentralized collection of communication tools, we now have an ability to form what Harold Rheingold (2003) calls "smart mobs." Human organization and collaboration are taking on new sociospatial forms as we mix together geolocation and computer-mediated communication with ever more powerful digital tools.

 Chapter summary

This chapter has centered on one key premise: that the ability to produce, acquire, disseminate, and aggregate geospatial information has undergone a transformational shift away from expensive and exclusive to near ubiquitous and practically free. By combining our tools for geolocation with our tools for communication and visualization on the internet, we have begun to weave a geoweb that is increasingly widespread in its

(Continued)

adoption by everyday individuals. As we have begun to understand the power and utility of a growing network of geolocated phenomena, we seem increasingly willing to volunteer our spatial location in return for the additional information we can then access. And by coordinating our location with that of others, we are beginning to see how "mashing up" physical space with the topology of digital social networks can create entirely new geographies of social interaction.

By democratizing the production of geodata, we have seen a tremendous growth in the amount and types of spatial data being produced every day. Just as Wikipedia is expanding in scope and size at a rate that would be impossible for a board of editorial experts to accomplish, so too are the volume, velocity, and variety of geodata being produced by the neogeographers of today whose main cartographic tools are a web browser and a mobile phone. We have only just begun to realize the power and potential of the collected cartography we create when we voluntarily share data from our location over the geoweb. In fact, many would argue that our relatively newfound ability to combine information on physical location with our digital communication tools is nothing short of revolutionary, as it puts unprecedented power in the hands of many and provides us with a whole new way of producing knowledge.

At the same time, however, there are others who do not view the emergence of the geoweb with such optimism, arguing instead that our increasingly location-aware networks are in fact reducing our civil liberties while they strip us of privacy and overflow with inaccurate information. They argue against the technological utopian belief that the production of geodata has been democratized, pointing out the ways in which geospatial information is created and used by governments and corporations alike for surveillance purposes. Other critics simply question the reliability of geodata produced by those without the skills and scientific know-how of the geographic information professional. The next chapter examines these critiques of the geoweb and outlines some of the problems – both reconfigurations of old ones and nascent new ones – that are emerging as the geoweb matures.

Further reading

Sui, D., Elwood, S. and Goodchild, M. (2012) *Crowdsourcing Geographic Knowledge: Volunteered Geographic Information (VGI) in Theory and Practice*. New York: Springer Science and Business Media.

5

Challenges of the Geoweb

Data Accuracy, Privacy, and Surveillance

 **Overview**

This chapter looks at:

- Privacy and surveillance in the digital age
- Digital breadcrumbs in a city of surveillance
- The power of algorithms
- Geodata inaccuracies in a spatially connected world

Each time you make a call on a mobile telephone, your voice is transmitted via radio waves to a nearby cell tower. The concept of breaking up geographic space into cells emerged in the 1970s as a way to minimize interference and maximize the reuse of the limited radio frequencies available for such calls. Ever since, the number of cell towers has been increasing rapidly as cellular networks have spread across the landscape, broadening the spatial extent of mobile communication networks. Given that a mobile phone communicates only with nearby cell towers, and that the radio communication varies in strength based on distance to each tower, triangulation and other methods of radiolocation can be used to identify the approximate location of a cell phone even if that phone does not contain a GPS receiver. As a phone moves about geographic space, the radio communication will switch towers in order to maintain signal strength (which, if ineffective, leads to the phenomenon of the "dropped call"), which in effect means that the phone must always broadcast its location in order to work.

Because of this, there is much more information produced by a single telephone call than the voice exchange between two individuals. This information, or "metadata," typically includes the time and duration of each call, the unique serial IDs of the phones involved, and other transactional data about the exchange. It also includes various types of location data, from the approximate location based on cell tower signal strength to the exact latitude and longitude of the phone based on GPS data. Such data are typically stored by network providers, and can also be made available to public service providers during emergency calls.

In 2009, the German politician Malte Spitz sued the telecommunications provider T-Mobile for access to six months of the metadata produced by his phone and saved by the company. Spitz received a disk containing 35,830 records that provided a detailed accounting of his mobile phone activity, including the time and duration of his calls and text messages, the individual cell towers he connected with, and the amount of time spent on the internet. It also contained a significant amount of geospatial information associated with that activity. When combined with other information that was produced and voluntarily shared by Spitz, such as Twitter posts and blog entries, the six-month period of Spitz's life could be chronicled in great detail (Cohen, 2011).

Spitz's discovery of the extent to which our mobile devices and other online behavior leave "digital breadcrumbs" across geographic space came just a few years before a much larger exposure of the scope and potential impact of large-scale metadata collection by the US government. As the geoweb has expanded to include more users and devices sharing all sorts of volunteered information – and, as Spitz has shown, plenty of information *not* voluntarily shared – concerns over who has access to our digital breadcrumbs and how this information might be used have grown. While we have seen in the previous chapter how voluntarily sharing geographic information can provide us with new tools and insights for better understanding our world, privacy advocates decry the appropriation of digital geodata for use by governments, advertisers, and media corporations and articulate legitimate concerns over the potential for misuse. This chapter examines some of the issues and concerns that are emerging as the geoweb expands to geolocate and network more people and things than ever before. Maps are power, as we have seen, and there is a growing concern that by utilizing the tools made possible by the geoweb, we are increasingly susceptible to being mapped by those whose interests do not necessarily align with our own.

PRIVACY AND SURVEILLANCE IN THE DIGITAL AGE

On June 5, 2013, the *Guardian* newspaper published an article revealing that the US National Security Agency (NSA) was requiring Verizon Wireless to submit records on every call in its system made each day (*Guardian*, 2013a). The court order, given to *Guardian* reporters by a former employee of one of the NSA's defense contractors, required Verizon to hand over electronic copies of all "telephony metadata" obtained from calls in the USA received domestically or from abroad. While this was not the first time that the indiscriminate, bulk collection of communications metadata by the US government was made public – the George W. Bush administration legalized "enhanced surveillance procedures" for monitoring domestic communications following the attacks of September 11, 2001 – it was the first indication that the Obama administration was continuing such widespread surveillance and reignited fears that privacy was a relic of the pre-internet age.

A day later, another story in the *Guardian* revealed that the level of surveillance being conducted by the NSA went far beyond the telephone metadata of a single network provider. A clandestine data surveillance system known as PRISM was being used by the NSA to collect vast amounts of digital communication, from search histories and file transfers to emails and live chats, that were being produced across several of the internet's largest companies, including Google, Apple, and Facebook. As the article stated, "the NSA is able to reach directly into the servers of the participating companies and obtain both stored communications as well as perform real-time collection on targeted users" (*Guardian*, 2013b). The fact that such revelatory information about a famously secretive and guarded organization was suddenly made public revealed two things: a whistleblower was at work, and he was providing evidence of digital surveillance on a much more comprehensive scale than anyone had previously envisaged.

As the world began digesting and reacting to this news, the informant Edward Snowden went public as he continued to unveil new revelations about the scope and extent of NSA surveillance activities. He released information on Boundless Informant, a data analysis and visualization tool that allowed the NSA to create global "heatmaps" of internet communications and track locations based on internet service provider (ISP) addresses. He revealed that the Government Communications Headquarters (GCHQ) in the UK also had access to data through PRISM. Other programs and tools for metadata surveillance were revealed by Snowden, including the program codenamed ShellTrumpet that collected more than 1 trillion metadata records and the FASCIA database containing trillions of device-location records. While digital surveillance by governmental organizations is not a novel concept – and particularly since 9/11 we have been aware of the enhanced appetite for intelligence, both international and domestic, by the US and other governments – the sheer volume of data collected, stored, and analyzed by the NSA was startling.

Some view the actions of the NSA as a necessity of our modern age, given the terrorist cells and cybercriminals who rely on digital networks to coordinate their activities. Others side with Snowden and argue that the level and extent of data collection by the NSA is overreach and demonstrates an invasion of privacy that goes far beyond what is necessary for the gathering of counter-terrorism intelligence. Either way, it is clear that in today's society individuals produce a significant quantity of geographic metadata, volunteered or not, that is of considerable interest to governmental organizations and is systematically being gathered and stored on a daily basis. Not long after Snowden's leaks, the United Nations issued a report on "The Right to Privacy in the Digital Age" which pointed out the ongoing lack of transparency by government agencies engaged in mass digital surveillance (United Nations, 2014). At the same time, the UK Data Retention and Investigative Powers Bill, which would expand the surveillance powers of the UK government, was being fast-tracked through the House of Commons.

Governments are not the only organizations interested in tracking geolocational metadata, however. While the NSA's work might represent one of the most comprehensive and far-reaching efforts to collect location information on a population, interest in personal geodata is also widespread among companies that recognize the value in being able to monitor the location and movement of individuals. As such, many of the software tools and applications that people commonly use include some form of mechanism for capturing geodata, and some software companies are entirely reliant on geodata for their very existence.

Here again, at issue is the extent to which individuals voluntarily share their locational data in exchange for some benefit. A mapping application on a mobile phone, for example, is a clear case of a tool that explicitly gathers geodata and compiles them with detailed road network data in order to provide the user with accurate directions. Similarly, social media apps often have the capability of identifying a user's location so that he or she can "check in" to a place and communicate that location to a group of friends. Fitness tracking applications use GPS data to monitor a person's speed and distance covered during a physical activity, restaurant review sites use location data to list establishments in order by proximity, and "digital assistants" like Apple's Siri or Google Now can send you alerts and reminders when you reach a specific geographic location. As we have seen in the previous chapter, voluntarily sharing our location data can provide us with a host of benefits.

It is when our location information is shared without our explicit intent that issues of privacy and surveillance resurface. In 2011, concerns arose when it was discovered that Apple's iPhone operating system, iOS 4, included an unencrypted file that collected location data over time without the direct consent of the end user. Instead of voluntarily sharing geolocation with specific software applications for specific purposes, iPhone users were unknowingly sharing their location information at all times and without clear benefit. As in the case of Malte Spitz and T-Mobile, a considerable amount of geographic metadata was being collected by iPhone users without their knowledge. A class action lawsuit was filed against Apple over this issue of background location tracking.

Apple was certainly not the only company embroiled in litigation over the collection of location data, however. Google launched its Streetview technology in 2007, which added panoramic street-level photos to its mapping software and gave users an unprecedented close-up look at many places across the world. Privacy concerns emerged soon thereafter, as everyone from an individual Frenchman caught urinating in his garden to the entire German government opposed the intrusion of Google's cameras. When it was discovered that the cars used to capture Streetview imagery had also collected personal data from unprotected WiFi networks, Google faced its own class action lawsuit.

One issue in the Google case was the question of to what extent imagery and geographic data collected from a public location (e.g., an urban street) could be considered an invasion of privacy. Another was whether or not the gathering of data from unencrypted wireless routers (which Google maintained was unintentional) was a violation of wiretapping laws and the Fourth Amendment. Technology law has had to adjust quickly as our actions have increasingly become trackable and our whereabouts have come under increasing surveillance. Recent US Supreme Court rulings have addressed some of the issues surrounding the right to privacy and unreasonable search in the age of mobile geodata: in 2012 the Court ruled that installing a GPS device on a car for the purposes of monitoring location was a search requiring a warrant, and in 2014 the Court unanimously ruled that accessing data on an individual's mobile phone without a warrant was a clear violation of the Fourth Amendment. In the latter case, Chief Justice John Roberts acknowledged the fact that historic location information found in a today's standard phone could be used to create a detailed reconstruction of an individual's geographic movements. Geodata that are captured and stored in a mobile phone, Roberts wrote, "can reconstruct someone's specific movements down to the minute, not only around town but also within a particular building" (Liptak, 2014).

DIGITAL BREADCRUMBS IN A CITY OF SURVEILLANCE

Despite the recent court rulings acknowledging the close relationship between locational data and privacy, it remains true that a vast amount of geodata is collected on unknowing individuals in many different ways. And, as Roberts noted in his Supreme Court decision, such data can be used to create a highly detailed map of those individuals' spatial patterns and geographic histories. A police search of a person's mobile phone might now be illegal, but there are still many ways that individuals can be mapped as they go about their daily lives. From surfing the internet to strolling across town, human behavior and activity are increasingly monitored, recorded, and mapped. Just as the emerging technologies of the geoweb can enable surveillance from below, as described in Chapter 4, they can also reinforce "top-down" surveillance by those entities with an interest in knowing the geographic patterns of populations. Those who argue that our new digital tools and decentralized networks empower users and democratize the production of data are countered by those who point to examples of ways in which power and control are being consolidated through the use of networked geodata.

We likely do not consider the extent to which our daily actions and behavior are geographically monitored, but most of us leave a significant trail of "digital breadcrumbs" or "digital exhaust" when we do everything from performing a web search to acquiring cash from an automated teller machine. When you log on to the internet and visit a website, your internet protocol (IP) address is available to that site's host and can be geolocated by city, time zone, telephone area code, or some other form of spatial reference. That same site might silently install a small piece of code, a "cookie," on your computer that can monitor your browser activity and share information with third party sites that you might not ever visit. Your search queries can be mapped by your ISP location as well as by the content of the query itself, and the path your query takes as it travels across the internet to Google can be easily tracked with a simple traceroute command. Similarly, your social media posts and browser history can be tracked, mapped, and shared with advertisers located near you who cater to your particular tastes. Without ever sharing your physical address or explicitly revealing your geographic location, your internet activity lets others know exactly where – as well as a good bit about how – you live.

This activity is not fleeting, nor is it forgotten. While we may refer to our daily use of the internet as "browsing" or "surfing," our digital behavior is intensely monitored, analyzed, and stored on servers in large data centers around the world. Your location and past internet activity serve to shape your window to your present and future internet, as everything from advertisements to news headlines is increasingly tailored to your personal geography and perceived preferences by internet algorithms – a phenomenon labeled the "filter bubble" by Eli Pariser (2011). Your physical location gets combined with the digital terrain you traverse to paint a very specific portrait of your internet presence. As these data get backed up and stored and shared with a multitude of other sites on the web, calls for a digital "right to be forgotten" have grown louder.

Your contribution of geospatial information to third parties does not end when you log off the internet. When you travel across town, your license plate might be digitally scanned by the police, or you might be captured on the digital video of a closed-circuit television camera (CCTV) owned by a municipal government or private corporation. CCTV surveillance has become widespread and facial recognition algorithms have improved to the point that CCTV footage has been used for everything from determining the cause of traffic accidents to identifying the suspects in acts of terror like the bombing at the Boston Marathon in 2013. London's so-called "ring of steel," for example, is one of the more comprehensive examples of a surveillance network, consisting of thousands of surveillance cameras scattered throughout the city. The London Underground subway network alone is watched by more than 10,000 CCTV cameras. The mere act of walking across town now means that your whereabouts can be quite extensively documented.

Any transactions you might make as you go about your daily life also produce a range of geospatial information. When you make a purchase with a credit card, the location of your purchase is recorded and stored. If you use a prepaid card to pay fees for toll roads or public transit, the time and location of your transportation are collected, and your speed might be monitored by radar from a parked police car or perhaps even an aircraft. Without giving it any thought, you are capable of generating a considerable trail of digital exhaust.

Bring your mobile device into the picture and the amount of geospatial data you produce is likely to increase exponentially as you broadcast your location both locally and to far-flung servers that are connected to the geoweb. Using technology called "geofencing," your mobile device might alert you when you are within a certain distance of a specific locale or notify you that a certain friend is at the coffee shop next door. Location-based software apps in your device take your location into account before providing you with search results, weather conditions, or traffic. Once again, this information may seem fleeting, but most of it is captured and stored across computers owned by the organizations and companies providing the hardware, software, and communication network that enable you to access such a tremendous amount of information from your handheld device. And while we have come to rely heavily on our mobile devices to tap the digital world so that we may better navigate the physical world, some fear we are becoming too reliant on algorithms and devices at the expense of some very important aspects of pre-internet human nature and cognitive ability.

"YOU ARE NOT A GADGET"

One day in early May 2010, the Dow Industrial Average of the New York Stock Exchange began to plummet. In a matter of minutes, the Dow lost 1000 points, and almost as quickly bounced 600 points back before the closing bell at the end of the day, resulting in one of the largest point swings in the history of the stock market. While several factors were blamed for contributing to the so-called "flash crash," from the European debt crisis to an overall volatility of the market at the time, it is undeniable that the crash would not have happened had it not been for high-speed computer trading and the use of "sell algorithms" to automate the trading of billions of shares each business day. These automated algorithms are programmed with instructions for buying and selling based on specific variables, then react to the market and execute trades without human intervention. The flash crash of 2010 brought to light the extent to which computer algorithms, running on complex supercomputers and moving share trades across fast fiber optic cable networks, were controlling the activity of the stock market – sometimes in spectacularly poor fashion.

The artist and former computer scientist Jaron Lanier has written books that examine the potential downsides of a world where internet collectivism and software algorithms are increasingly trumping individualism and limiting freedom of choice. "The digital hive is growing at the expense of individuality," he argues in his book *You Are Not a Gadget* (Lanier, 2011). Lanier points out that the design decisions of software engineers, the rules that make up the digital communications protocols of the internet, and the software algorithms that trigger decisions and actions without the need for human intervention are defining the limits of our behavior in cyberspace and having a very real impact on human society.

Computer algorithms are at play no matter what you do on the internet, contributing to your own personal filter bubble. Google returns the result from your search query, ranking a list of millions of results in order of how relevant they are likely to be to your search (making "search engine optimization" – helping companies and organizations improve the likelihood that their site will make the first page of search results – an important algorithm industry in its own right). When you visit an online shopping site, items you might be interested in automatically appear based on your shopping history and other information gathered about you. When you log on to Facebook, ads for products you examined at the shopping site might now appear next to your news feed and the status updates of your friends, which themselves are organized for you based on Facebook's algorithms that determine what posts are likely to be of most interest to you. When you send out a tweet or update your blog with a new post, your text is not only read by humans, it is also searched, scanned, and "scraped" by software algorithms that might automatically retweet your post to an entirely different network of individuals, add your post to an aggregated "newsletter" of posts on a related topic, or include words from your text in some sort of data analysis or visualization. There are more algorithms than eyeballs looking over your handiwork.

Just as the information on your social network apps is being tailored specifically for you based on how computer algorithms interpret your digital past, so too are the cartographic features found on the digital map you use on a web browser or mobile device. The new version of Google Maps released in 2013 included customized map features for each user based on that user's preferences and location history, so that a book lover's map, say, might look different than the map used by someone who frequents dining establishments or loves attending live concerts. The more you use the map, the more its underlying algorithms determine what becomes a cartographic reality on your individualized map. The map "learns" where you live and where you work. And every time you punch in a location or chart directions to a place, that information is stored and incorporated into the compilation of your digital location history that will help the application's algorithms fine-tune your personal map even further.

Other mapping algorithms use your location data and preferences to help monitor traffic patterns, road conditions, and several other variables in order to provide you with up-to-date driving directions. Many of us have become very reliant on GPS and digital maps to guide us around unfamiliar cities or tell us the fastest way to get from point A to point B. Recent research suggests that this outsourcing of spatial navigation – using our digital tools to tell us where to go instead of our cognition – could have a negative impact on brain function. In studies comparing brain scans of GPS versus non-GPS users, the GPS users were found to have a smaller hippocampus, which is the part of the brain that is believed to be important for spatial orientation and navigation (Edwards, 2010). Building our own cognitive maps, this research indicates, clearly requires more brain function than does acquiring navigation directions from GPS and digital maps.

Whether we are worried about reduced brain function or that our current digital maps increasingly reflect our past spatial behavior, it is clear that information flowing across the geoweb is changing the way that we perceive and navigate the world around us.

Information flowing across the geoweb, like much of the networked information we produce today, is being filtered and shaped for us before we receive it. We, in turn, produce and share our own collection of spatial information, from our geolocational history to our geographic search queries. As we have seen in the sections above, this information might be used to track our location and behavior by a government intelligence agency, or it might be used by mapping software and social networks to feed us news and advertisements that are refined by our geography. We live in a location-aware world, and progressively our locations and movement across physical space are being intertwined with our digital locations across the internet as algorithms shape our personal interactions on the geoweb. Given the growing relevance and importance of location as the geoweb matures, an important question arises: what are the implications and possible ramifications if location data are wrong?

GEODATA INACCURACIES IN A SPATIALLY CONNECTED WORLD

In 1999 the United States bombed the Chinese embassy in Belgrade, leading to heightened tensions between the two countries and days of protests from a furious Chinese populace. The bombing was a mistake, according to the US government, that was supposedly caused by outdated location information on the building targeted and incorrect GPS coordinates programmed into the bombs used in the attack. While many Chinese questioned this account, arguing instead that the bombing intentionally targeted the embassy, analysis of the event showed that, if not intentional, the attack could have certainly been avoided. What was argued to be a failure of geographical intelligence cost the lives of three Chinese reporters, a payment of $4.5 million from the United States to the families of those killed, and countless hours of effort to smooth diplomatic relations between two of the largest countries in the world.

While the accuracy of much of the spatial data now incorporated into the geoweb is improving daily, there are still many datasets that contain incomplete or faulty geographic information. The lack of accurate location data, as seen in the example above, can lead to deadly consequences. Further, the purposeful blocking or misdirecting of location information can be undertaken for various purposes, which also has the potential for disastrous results. As the geoweb continues to fill with volumes of geodata, much of which is produced by neogeographers who do not attempt to verify data accuracy, the threat of the accidental or purposeful use of erroneous geodata is of concern.

There are many types of error that can be introduced into spatial datasets, from imprecision due to poor GPS data or incorrect map projection to data inconsistencies due to multiple database users and conflicting information. The computational and mathematical issues behind the creation of data error are too complex to cover in depth in this book, though we will touch on these issues in later chapters. For now, it is important to recognize that no geographic dataset is perfect and some are rife with error. Placing blind trust in a single set of location data can often lead to problems, as in 2012 when Apple iPhone users began using the new Apple Maps product – a mapping product that was released so full of errors that it quickly became the butt of jokes and led to a letter of apology by company president Tim Cook.

While many found humor in the Apple Maps example, error in locational or directional data can be costly or even deadly. If emergency response systems such as 911 do not have access to accurate routing data to minimize response time, costly time can be wasted by impaired navigation. Similarly, if mobile devices used to report location by those caught in disaster conditions such as an earthquake or avalanche produce faulty data, search and rescue can take much longer. Miscalculating the units of measurement can also result in costly error, as in the famous case of the *Mars Climate Orbiter*, whose trajectory was inappropriately calculated due to unit conversion error, leading to the crash of the $125 million spacecraft.

In addition to human error, technical malfunctions or various sorts of interference and interruption can disrupt the availability or reliability of geodata. Satellite function is key to the Global Positioning System, yet these satellites sometimes have temporary failures and GPS signals can be scrambled by radiation emanating from solar flares. The snapping of an undersea internet cable or the temporary downtime of a large-scale internet provider can create large data traffic jams and result in widespread loss of access to location data (and the entire internet) for periods of time. Large storms and natural disasters can completely disrupt communication networks and the power grid in specific areas, disconnecting individuals in the region from the geoweb at a time it is arguably needed most.

Knowing that disconnecting access to the geoweb can wreak havoc, certain technologies have been developed to allow individuals to do exactly that. GPS jammers, small tools that emit an electromagnetic signal that interferes with cellular network and GPS signals over a limited area, are widely available and inexpensive. While illegal in many parts of the world, these small devices allow a user to block communications between mobile devices and nearby cell towers and/or the GPS satellites overhead. The result can range from amusing, as when someone uses a jammer to silence the phones of passengers in a public transit commuter car, to potentially devastating, as when North Korea was discovered jamming the GPS signals over two of South Korea's largest airports.

In addition to GPS jamming, other technologies can be used to disrupt satellite signals so that a GPS receiver shows location coordinates different from the actual location of the device. A group of researchers demonstrated an example of a form of this "GPS spoofing" when they were able to hijack the GPS signals being used for navigation aboard a 65-meter luxury yacht off the coast of Italy. Using a device built from scratch in response to a dare from the US Department of Homeland Security, the research team was able to take control of the ship's navigation and change its course without the ship's crew noticing. While this was merely a research exercise to demonstrate the feasibility of such actions, it made clear the need for stronger systems for protecting location and navigation data.

Given these techniques for tampering with geodata, it is understandable that emerging navigation technologies such as Google's self-driving car can make people nervous. These autonomous vehicles are equipped with an array of sensors that gather data on the car's immediate surroundings and compare them with its vast database of maps and location data. Using several technologies described in this book, Google's cars gather and process a tremendous amount of data letting them sense their surroundings in real time and adjust accordingly. They are seemingly a tantalizing promise of the evolving geoweb – a new technology that, by crunching geodata much faster than a human, will take over a task that we often find tedious and which at times we perform quite poorly.

Self-driving cars may indeed become commonplace in the coming years. And they have the potential for saving thousands of lives, since they will not get drowsy, drive under the influence, or become distracted by texting on a mobile device. Yet these vehicles, for all of their advanced technology, are ultimately running on software algorithms that contain a rulebook for appropriate driving procedures. So while the total number of lives per year might be reduced by a shift to autonomous cars, new ethical dilemmas arise. If an imminent crash is unavoidable, and a car's algorithms are designed to minimize total loss of life, might the vehicle choose to sacrifice one driver to save a van full of children? Would crash-optimization algorithms decide that in certain situations the best alternative was to purposefully wreck your own vehicle? And given the fact that GPS jamming and spoofing have been shown to be effective, can we devise new systems that will prevent autonomous vehicles from being tampered with or hijacked?

In a sense, the example of the self-driving car illustrates both the promise and the potential new problems of the geoweb. In a world where everything is connected and location aware, fantastic new possibilities await that will transform science fiction into scientific fact. At the same time, this new world ushers in a fresh set of technical, social, and moral complications. Our previous conceptualizations of many aspects of human nature, from privacy to free will, must be reassessed as we continue to knit together a world that has historically been far less connected. We are essentially creating a new geography. A new society must follow.

 **Chapter summary**

This chapter has demonstrated that the geoweb brings with it a new set of challenges as it continues to grow and mature. New technologies in mapping, tracking, and networking create new possibilities for social interaction and communication, while at the same time opening the doors to new forms of exploitation. As Edward Snowden has shown through his leaks of NSA documents, the US government has taken tremendous advantage of the geoweb as the surveillance net has widened to include many of these new location-based and networked technologies. Corporations take advantage of the large volumes of geodata

(Continued)

we produce as well, using location information to help construct a personalized internet that caters to our perceived interests and consumer needs. Computer algorithms make a growing number of decisions on our behalf, from telling us where to drive to deciding what social network posts and online advertisements we see. We now rely quite heavily on the geoweb for many aspects of our daily lives, from shopping to ship navigation to combat, even though the geodata we use might be inaccurate, incomplete, or even purposefully tampered with. The geoweb, like any new technology, is not yet fully understood and harbors the potential for misuse and abuse.

Like any new technology, the emerging geoweb provokes new anxieties about human nature and social relations. As connected technologies continue to infiltrate all aspects of society, from our cars to our homes to our mobile devices, there is understandably a great deal of human attention being paid to what all this means for us. Underneath our idolatry of shiny tech toys and the abundance of our social communication is a fear that technology is fundamentally transforming our society and even that the machines, perhaps, are beginning to take over. Yet, as Clive Thompson (2014) has pointed out, every new tool shapes the way we think, and every tool tends to improve as we come to understand its deficiencies and figure out ways to improve it. Instead of viewing the geoweb as the harbinger of a computer-controlled society that is stripping us of our privacy and freedom of choice, we should view it as an emerging collaboration between computers and humans that creates new ways of understanding and acting upon space and place. From this vantage point, the fear of the shrinking hippocampus, the danger of texting while driving, and the critique of our ubiquitous mobile phone use in public are all examples of how we as humans are messily trying to absorb and navigate our newly connected world. We are only just beginning to understand the power of the geoweb.

In Part Two of this book, we will examine some of the current tools and techniques for acquiring and visualizing geodata. From gathering location data from a GPS or list of street addresses to mapping Twitter data to visualizing data on a web mapping application, we can take advantage of a large and growing collection of new tools for examining geodata. As we do so, we can find entirely new ways of asking questions about society and hopefully find new answers as well. The geoweb is providing us with a platform for a new cartography as we begin to understand how these new tools and techniques can help us glean new insights into our world. By learning how to take advantage of the geoweb to collect and visualize geodata, we can truly begin to see the power of "where" in a connected age.

 **Further reading**

Greenwald, G. (2014) *No Place to Hide: Edward Snowden, the NSA, and the U.S. Surveillance State.* London: Metropolitan Books/Henry Holt.

Schneier, B. (2015) *Data and Goliath: The Hidden Battles to Collect Your Data and Control Your World.* New York: Norton.

6

Introduction to Geodata: Types of Geodata

How Do We Identify and Gather Location-Based Data?

 **Overview**

This chapter looks at:

- Absolute location
- Relative location
- Topological space
- Temporal data and time-space compression
- Structured and unstructured data
- Geodata types and tools – some examples

Suppose you receive a simple, three-word message from a friend – "where are you?" – on your mobile device. How might you respond to this query? You might simply reply with "at home" or "going to work." If you are traveling, you might mention the name of a city or a specific place. If you know your friend's location and are planning to meet them there, you might respond with "a couple of blocks away" or "10 minutes away." There are many ways to describe your present location based on the relative location of someone or something else. It is much less likely that you would respond to your friend by reporting your *absolute* location in terms of a pair of geographic coordinates. Texting "I'm at 35.5396° N, 82.5510° W" would likely elicit a quizzical reply and would not be as helpful as a simple description of your relative location.

The above scenario demonstrates three important points about location information that illustrate one of the main computational challenges of the geoweb. First, it reminds us that we as humans tend to rely on relative location as we navigate through our daily lives. Second, because the communication of relative location information is taking place through SMS over a cellular network, the scenario shows that we can be connected to our friends even when we are not in close proximity – a different sort of geography that we can define as *topological* space. And third, while we may prefer to use relative space in our everyday conversations, computers often produce and share geodata in terms of absolute space. The GPS chip in your phone, for example, receives data from three or more satellites to determine your absolute location on the face of the Earth. For the geoweb to function, then, requires that we have systems in place that can translate across these various types of space. The approximate location of your place of residence can be described in various ways, from your street address and postal code to its proximity to specific landmarks as well as its precise latitude and longitude coordinates. You may use one of these more than others, but they are all examples of the types of data you might come across on the geoweb.

This chapter describes the various types of geodata that can be captured and communicated via the geoweb, categorizing them by the three types of space mentioned above: absolute, relative, and topological. The chapter then addresses the temporal component of geodata, since time is so often crucial when we seek and use spatial information. Similarly, the chapter covers the concept of "time-space convergence," a term used to illustrate the ways in which geographic space is being reconfigured through our increasingly connected information networks. The chapter also covers the differences between "structured" and "unstructured" geodata and the challenges that these differences present to anyone seeking to capture and visualize geodata. Finally, the chapter briefly outlines the different ways we will work with geodata in the chapters ahead.

ABSOLUTE LOCATION

As shown in Chapter 2, the development of a globally agreed-upon system for calculating the location of any position on Earth has a long history. From the early grid system of Eratosthenes to the elimination of intentional scrambling of signals from GPS satellites in 2000, we have slowly developed the technologies that now make it possible for us to produce and acquire location data by generating geographic coordinates of latitude and longitude. The eventual combination of Euclidean geometry, Cartesian coordinates, and Newtonian ideas on the nature of absolute space led to a cohesive system for classifying location that, when coupled with the technologies behind the GPS, has given us an unprecedented ability to measure absolute location.

For a geographic coordinate system to work, a unified mathematical model of the size and shape of the Earth must be used by anyone accessing coordinate data. The Global Positioning System that we access today uses the World Geodetic System 1984

(WGS 84), which includes a standard coordinate system, a spheroidal model of the Earth's surface, and a geoid model that is used to estimate nominal mean sea level. Taken together, these standardized models allow for the interoperability of location data around the world, data available to anyone with access to a GPS receiver.

The implications of a global positioning system that uses a widely adopted geographic coordinate system are profound, since we now have in place a way to share and produce geographic information that is meaningful to anyone else using this same arrangement, no matter where they are in the world. If you have access to a Digital Earth browser such as Google Earth, you can simply type in a pair of latitude and longitude coordinates to locate any place on the surface of our planet and share that information with others. Typing "5,5" into the search bar of a digital globe, for example, will point to the spot where a line of latitude 5 degrees north of the equator meets a line of longitude that is 5 degrees east of the International Reference Meridian (which, due to refinements and improvements in geodesy, actually lies about 100 meters east of the famous Royal Observatory in Greenwich, England), putting you in the Atlantic Ocean just off the coast of Nigeria.

The ability to calculate absolute space is extremely important for navigation where the opportunity to use relative location is absent, such as on the open sea. Ships today rely on GPS to keep track of their ocean location, mapping the location of navigational hazards, and for search and rescue operations. Similarly, being able to identify your exact location when in a vast snowfield, in a dense rainforest, or in the midst of a natural disaster can potentially be life-saving. In North America, the 911 system for emergency reporting has been enhanced to allow authorities to access GPS information from mobile phones during an emergency response. And, given the origins of the technology, the military use of GPS to calculate absolute location is widespread, from monitoring potential targets (as we saw in the example of the Chinese Embassy in Belgrade) to identifying the whereabouts of downed pilots. In short, the geoweb would not be possible without our relatively recent ability to calculate with a fair amount of accuracy the location of almost anything or anyone on the face of the Earth.

It probably bears repeating here that an additional wrinkle emerges when we attempt to translate the geographic coordinates of our spheroidal model of the Earth into some form of projected model of the Earth as a flat surface. There are many different mathematical models for creating map projections, all of which by necessity must distort some combination of shape, area, distance, and direction. As we will see when working with projected spatial data in a GIS software application, we can run into problems if we attempt to overlay two sets of absolute location data that were created with different projection models. We also must pay attention to the different ways of reading the measurements of absolute location – you might come across a pair of coordinates written in degrees, minutes, and seconds (e.g., 48° 51' 29.1348" N, 2° 17' 40.8984" E) or in decimal degrees (e.g., 48.858093° N, 2.294694° E). While conversion between the different systems is certainly possible, they cannot be used interchangeably.

As mentioned, we do not tend to use coordinate pairs to describe location in our everyday lives, choosing instead to refer to more natural systems for describing features of geographic importance. We use street addresses, postal codes, telephone area codes, and other systems for classifying and distinguishing between locations all the time in order to make geographic sense of the world. Because of the importance and utility of the Global Positioning System, we are seeing tools and techniques for quickly and easily translating between these different ways of spatial description. You can now access vast databases that match the geographic coordinate pairs of all kinds of locations with the more conventional description of those locations that we use. You can type a street address into an online geocoding application, for example, and get back a coordinate pair of latitude and longitude for that address (see Chapter 8). Conversely, you can submit the current latitude and longitude of your mobile device and a software service might convert those coordinates to the name of your city or neighborhood.

RELATIVE LOCATION

Of course, the examples of absolute location described above are not of much use to us without also knowing something about relative location. Simply knowing the coordinates of a single ship is of little value unless we also know if the vessel is on course to make it to its destination and is a safe distance away from other ships and navigational obstacles. The coordinates broadcast from a mobile phone during an emergency call only supplement additional location data such as street network optimization and distance to the closest medical care. A single street address is worthless without knowing the transportation networks providing access to that address. One could even argue that there is no such thing as truly absolute location, since even a simple pair of geographic coordinates describes a place's location relative to the Equator and the International Reference Meridian. For the purposes of capturing and visualizing data from the geoweb, however, we will continue to refer to absolute location when we talk about location in terms of coordinate pairs.

Once we identify the absolute location of more than one entity we can begin to calculate relative location. We might measure relative location in terms of the physical distance between point A and point B, such as when we query a social network app to see which of our friends are nearby. Or we might determine relative location according to digital street map, which provides for us an optimal route to a location by incorporating information on current traffic conditions, speed limits, and other potential travel impediments that might widen the relative distance to our destination. We often include time as well as space into our calculations of relative distance, as the most typical use for relative distance is the calculation of how long it will take for two separate entities to come together in the same location.

In other words, relative location provides us with an understanding of *proximity*. Very often we query the geoweb in order to identify how close something or someone is to us at a particular time. In a matter of seconds, we can find out what recreation opportunities are nearby, which of our friends are close enough to meet up, how far away the coming storm cloud is, and what movie theaters are around in case we need to seek shelter from the rain. When we emerge from an unfamiliar subway station or travel to a different city, we can submit our absolute location to a host of software applications that are more than happy to provide us with information on our proximity to nearby attractions, restaurants, and hotels. As more devices and objects are connected to the geoweb, and as software algorithms for calculating proximity improve, our ability to obtain data on relative location is improving rapidly. We can easily track the current position and anticipated arrival time for most any commercial airplane, check river levels by accessing nearby river gauge data, or tap into the Twitter stream based on our current location to see what others are talking about in the vicinity.

Increasingly, relative location is harnessed by software algorithms to provide, or "push," data that we do not even actively seek out. Personal digital assistants such as Apple's Siri, Google Now, and Microsoft's Cortana include powerful analytical tools for geolocation and comparing that with other known data. These software tools can scan your email and let you know when you should leave for the airport or the bus terminal. They notice your surroundings and offer information on local weather and things to do nearby. They can remind you of your shopping list when you enter a specific store. They can even adjust the temperature and lighting of your home once you are within a specific range and send a text to a family member letting them know you are home.

These are just a few examples of how absolute and relative location can be used in combination to create powerful new tools and datasets across the geoweb. Powerful spatial databases, application programming interfaces, and visualization tools can now all interact in real time to generate proximity data and trigger any number of location-based applications and services. While this fact gives rise to some of the fears and concerns raised in Chapter 5, it also means that we have a wide variety of new datasets that can be gathered and visualized geographically. While we may be concerned with a loss of privacy based on the digital exhaust we leave in our daily lives, in aggregate these spatial data can be used for studying geographic information that has never before been accessible. We can map flows, identify clusters and "hot spots," reveal uneven geographic distributions, and uncover other sorts of spatial patterns and correlations that might otherwise go unnoticed.

For example, in his book *The Human Face of Big Data*, the photographer Rick Smolan placed GPS receivers on pizza delivery cyclists throughout Manhattan (Smolan and Erwitt, 2012). By tracking the movement of pizza deliveries across the city, Smolan created a beautiful visualization that revealed the patterns of transport and pizza consumption during a typical New York evening. The ingredients in the pizzas can also be tracked and visualized, since the delivery trucks used to bring them to distribution centers are also equipped with GPS receivers. We can begin to connect the very localized consumption of pizza in one city to a vast network of distribution and food production that connects one delivery person to a global web of food production. That the absolute and relative location of local pizza delivery is also connected to far-flung places that the customer might not even know about brings us to the third type of space of interest to us as we seek to understand the geoweb – topological space.

TOPOLOGICAL SPACE

Topology refers to a mathematical field of study that emerged out of geometry and has as its focus the study of shapes and the properties of space. While there are several variants of topology that are used for many different types of applications, for our purposes we refer to "topological space" as a measure of connection or connectivity between two or more nodes on the geoweb. Two places with a high level of connectivity would be considered to be in close proximity in terms of topological space, even if the two were fairly distant from each other in physical space. Likewise, two entities having little or no inter-action would be considered to be topologically distant, even if in physical space they were quite close.

Topological space provides us with a useful conceptualization of space in our contemporary "network society," since it is so often the flows of various phenomena between places and across the networks of the geoweb that are of interest to us. We analyze flows of all kinds in our efforts to understand everything from the movement of information across social network applications to the migration patterns of undocumented individuals from one country to another. We track diseases as they diffuse through a population and work to prevent an epidemic by disrupting the pathways for further spreading. We research the social interaction in an urban environment, noticing the ways in which physical proximity and social propinquity are often, but not always, correlated. We supplement our understanding of absolute and relative spatial relations, in other words, by incorporating a better understanding of the level of interaction, or flows, taking place.

In addition to borrowing the concept of topology from mathematics to help us formulate an understanding of connectivity, we can also use some of the concepts and tools of graph theory and social network analysis to help us begin thinking about how topological space might be examined across the geoweb. In graph theory, graphs are mathematical structures that help us model relationships between entities by examining the relationship between "nodes" that are connected with "edges" or lines. Typically visualized as a set of circles or dots connected by lines, graphs are used for the study of systems and networks across fields as diverse as biology, computer science, and linguistics. Given our definition of the geoweb as outlined in Chapter 1 – *a distributed digital network of geo-located nodes that capture, produce, and communicate data that include an explicitly spatial component* – you can begin to see how graph theory might be helpful to us in modeling the spaces and flows of networked geodata.

In this sense, we can begin to explore the geoweb using some of the theories and tools that have been developed in the field of social network analysis. Popular in sociology and other social sciences, social network analysis is the application of network theory to social graphs in order to understand the structure of and relationships between the nodes and edges of a given network. Considerable insight can be gained into a particular social network by analyzing the level and type of connectivity between nodes as well as the distribution and density of nodes across that network. Software tools can be applied to social network analysis in order to help us model and visualize these connections and structures.

While social network analysis dates back to at least the early twentieth century, the emergence and widespread adoption of the internet has provided a social network on an unprecedented scale. Millions of "nodes" in the form of computers have been connected via the "edges" of routing protocols and communication infrastructure to create an incredibly complex graph. Tools for facilitating communication across digital sub-networks on the internet have evolved into the social media applications, such as Twitter and Facebook, that we use today, providing a host of new network datasets for analysis and visualization. Applying the visualization tools of social network analysis can often help us more fully understand the topological space of a given network, which in turn can be incorporated back into the more traditional study of absolute and relative space to provide a more comprehensive understanding of spatial relationships across the geoweb.

All three types of space described above – absolute, relative, and topological – can be useful as we seek to use geography to help make sense of data and better understand the spatial relationships of various phenomena. Being aware of these different types of space can help us more robustly interrogate the geoweb as well as employ more tools for the collection and visualization of geodata. We must also be aware, however, of one additional aspect of space that is crucial to our understanding of the geoweb and geodata – time.

TEMPORAL DATA AND TIME-SPACE COMPRESSION

The temporal component of geodata can range from relatively unimportant and seemingly unchanging, as in the latitude and longitude of a city center, to crucial, as when you seek location information and directions on a GPS application while driving. If your car GPS receiver lags by even a single minute it loses a great deal of its value, since it is the ability to provide you with your exact location in relation to the surrounding street network, in real time, that makes it so useful. Similarly, all sorts of data that can be mapped, from weather or air quality to traffic and the location of your friends, are much more useful if there is a temporal component to them. The power of "where" often depends on the power of "when."

In cases where time is an important aspect of geodata, it is typically (but not always) used to help calculate proximity through relative location. The above example is an obvious one, since GPS-enabled driving directions would not be possible were it not for the real-time plotting of your location relative to your surroundings, but there are many other examples of geodata that need a temporal component (sometimes called "spatiotemporal" data) in order to be of any use. Companies use spatiotemporal data to track shipping trucks, optimize routes, and alert you as to the whereabouts and predicted arrival time of a product. Epidemiologists map the rate and direction of the spread of an infectious disease as they seek ways to prevent it from diffusing further. Participants in a social movement coordinate their actions over time and space by communicating with others over social media. Advertisers can send you coupons the moment you walk into a particular store. Any number of software applications let you track everything from your friends to the orbits of satellites and planets. By including data on time along with the absolute location data of something – referred to as "timestamping" – we can measure spatial relationships and patterns as they evolve and change.

Because of the geoweb, we also have the ability to send spatiotemporal data across digital networks to almost any place on Earth in an instant. Data on earthquake tremors, tweets about celebrity sightings, frequently updated aerial imagery – all are immediately available to anyone around the world with access to the internet. Information that was once confined to a local area, or that took weeks or months to spread across the globe, is now broadcast worldwide instantaneously. We have effectively removed the "friction of distance" for the spread of information and helped usher in an era of truly global communication networks. Known as "time-space compression," this new reality of instant global data mobility has fundamentally reshaped, and in many ways shrunk, the world we live in today.

Of course, the shrinking of the world through advancements in technology is not entirely new. Every improvement in transportation technology has reduced the time it takes to get from one place to another. Communication technologies, too, have steadily increased our ability to interact with others not in our immediate vicinity. The emergence of the telegraph in the 1800s – referred to as the "Victorian Internet" in a book by Tom Standage (1998) – provided the means for transatlantic communication in real time, leading one journalist to proclaim that time and space had been completely annihilated (Rosen, 2012).

Yet in some ways the geoweb does signify a transformative relationship between space and time. The internet has given us for the first time in history a communications medium that allows for both one-way and two-way communication between designated sub-networks without regard to distance or location. Whereas satellites and television brought us real-time broadcasts of audiovisual information, we did not have the means for choosing where the camera was aimed or limiting who could access those broadcasts. Telephone networks did allow for two-way communication in real time, but that communication is limited to a very small number of individuals in any one conversation. In contrast, the internet has given us a communication medium that allows for the transfer of all kinds of data to any number of various interconnected networks of individuals and groups who can now interact in both synchronous and asynchronous time-space. The very concept of globalization, one might argue, came about because of this newfound ability to connect immediately with precisely the people and places we choose. Couple this with the ability to tap into any number of location-based, real-time data collection networks and you have a truly revolutionary system for the communication and dissemination of spatiotemporal information.

The volume, velocity, and variety of data moving about the geoweb all continue to grow, making the twin jobs of capturing and visualizing such data a considerable challenge. In some cases, we have found ways to organize data in such a way as to facilitate our ability to represent them spatially, but in others there is not an organizational framework in place. In the remainder of this chapter, we will examine the differences between structured and unstructured data, look at some examples of each, and then turn to the types of data and some of the tools you will use as you begin to collect your own sets of geodata.

STRUCTURED AND UNSTRUCTURED DATA

Geodata can be considered to be *structured* if they are organized in a way that can be easily read and processed by a computer. The vector data model used in geographic information systems, for example, represents geographic features as discrete objects with points, lines, and polygons that can be stored in a relational database management system (RDBMS). Because vector data are structured in this way, they can be interrogated using Structured Query Language (SQL) and otherwise manipulated by an individual wishing to work with the data. The popular shapefile format of vector data, created by ESRI in the early 1990s, consists of several files of structured geodata including feature geometry, attribute information, and geographic projection. Similarly, GeoJSON is an open data standard that is used widely across GIS and web mapping applications. Geographic Markup Language and Keyhole Markup Language (KML) are also standardized formats for vector data.

Often, however, we come across various types of *unstructured* geodata that we nevertheless want to capture and visualize. Geodata can often be found in PDF files and other forms of textual reports but not formatted in a way that is easily read by a software program. Web pages, emails, and other forms of digital communication often include some quantity of geospatial information that is difficult to obtain as it has not been specifically formatted to fit a defined data model or be organized by an RDBMS. Unstructured data are not organized into a spreadsheet ahead of time so that they can later be queried and manipulated, but rather are created in such a way that breaking them down systematically can be difficult. As we will see in subsequent chapters, techniques for acquiring useful geographic information from unstructured data include geocoding, geoparsing, and geotagging. Given the amount of unstructured digital data being produced every day, it is important that we find ways to extract and visualize the geospatial information that is often embedded within them.

As we have seen so far in this chapter, there are different types of space to take into consideration when we look to the geoweb for spatial data. Our ability to acquire useful data depends on the questions we are asking (are we hoping to identify location, or proximity, or perhaps uncover a particular pattern of spatial distribution?), the temporal aspect of our questions (how frequently must data be generated to be of use to us?), and the ways in which the data we seek can be structured or manipulated for their capture and visualization. Returning for a moment to the "three Vs" of big data discussed in Chapter 3, we can see that one of our biggest challenges in effectively harnessing the geoweb is in finding tools for managing the volume, velocity, and variety of geospatial data that are being produced in ways that help us ask – and hopefully answer – pertinent questions.

The primary goal of this book is to help you identify tools and techniques for doing just that. While data science and geographic information science can be incredibly complex, it is assumed that your academic training falls outside these areas and that you are looking to identify ways in which the geoweb and basic forms of spatial analysis can supplement research in your own area of expertise. As such, the following chapters tend to focus on geoweb tools that can be used with no prior experience in computer programming.

All of the software tools used in the following chapters are available for free, and many of them are both free and open source. While powerful commercial packages for GIS analysis, imagery analysis, and other applications certainly exist, there are an increasing number of freely available tools that are just as powerful and at times more flexible than off-the-shelf proprietary software. Perhaps you have access to a specialized computer lab and expert consultants, or perhaps you are a student at a small institution with few resources to dedicate to the collection and visualization of geodata. Either way, leveraging free and open source tools for tapping the geoweb can be both philosophically and economically rewarding, as they often have behind them a community of enthusiastic developers and an ethos of created shared knowledge for the benefit of all.

GEODATA TYPES AND TOOLS – SOME EXAMPLES

The chapters in Part Two focus on the various types of geodata you may be interested in capturing and visualizing, along with some of the tools available for doing so. In some cases there might be dozens of available software alternatives for conducting similar types of data collection, in which case we will focus on one or two as examples. Some tools for acquiring geodata must be downloaded to a computer, while others are primarily web-based. In the case of the former, instructions on how and where to download the appropriate tools will be included. The world of the geoweb is evolving rapidly, but every effort has been made to include up-to-date software tools and exclude those that have been deprecated or discontinued. The companion website includes access to download links, example datasets, and, where applicable, updates to the list of software tools available. Some examples of the types of geodata and software tools you will see in Part Two are described below.

The first two chapters of Part Two focus on the collection of geodata representing absolute location. These data may be structured, such as the points or tracks collected by a common GPS receiver, or they may be unstructured, as when we attempt to extract geodata from a set of text documents. We will also see examples where structured and unstructured data are combined, such as when we organize a collection of photographs through the process of geotagging. We will examine the various ways in which absolute location can be obtained, along with the challenges of each. We will also examine different software tools for storing location data, from simple text pages on your desktop to cloud-based databases on the web.

Chapters 9 and 10 examine geodata generated by social media and the internet of things, respectively. Chapter 9 focuses on ways to capture geodata from Twitter, while Chapter 10 examines ways to tap into data generated by sensor networks as well as create an entirely new sensor node using the popular Arduino microcontroller. The latter chapter also includes an exercise with a particular technology – RFID – that has gained in popularity and is now used in everything from passports and animal tracking to asset management and inventory analysis.

Chapters 11–13 focus on the use of geographic information systems for mapping and analyzing geodata, with each chapter featuring a particular set of free and open source software tools: QGIS (Chapter 11), GRASS (Chapter 12), and the R statistical programming language (Chapter 13).

Chapter 14 then turns to the web, exploring several popular applications for mapping geodata online. From creating a simple Google Map to using the API for the OpenLayers JavaScript library, this chapter will provide you with an introduction to the rapidly evolving world of web mapping.

 Chapter summary

In this chapter, we have expanded our understanding and definitions of the different types of space of interest to us as we investigate the geoweb. In addition, we explored the relationships between time and space that are crucial to our ability to interrogate the geoweb and which are changing as we see the continued growth of a network with a growing number of nodes that are location aware. We have also made a distinction between structured and unstructured data and looked at the ways in which they pose challenges to us as we seek ways to collect and store them. Finally, this chapter has charted a map for Part Two, discussing some of the data types and analysis tools we will employ as we begin to collect geodata.

The remainder of this book can be read in two different ways. Those with a general interest in the many ways to collect and visualize data from the geoweb should feel free to continue reading in a linear fashion. Others might be interested in employing a specific set of tools or type of visualization to meet an immediate research need; those readers are welcome to jump ahead to the chapter(s) that are most relevant to the

(Continued)

specific questions at hand. Each chapter will include examples, instructions on downloading and using software, and simple exercises for you to try so that you can get comfortable with the various types of geodata and the ways to explore them. Feel free to use the sample datasets provided on the companion website or use your own datasets as you orient yourself to these tools.

As the geoweb continues to grow in size and complexity, organizing and visualizing data spatially will continue to present its share of challenges. The volume, velocity, variety, and veracity of location data will continue to drive the need for new approaches and tools, and demand that we look for new ways to find meaning in the messy world of "big geodata." The opportunities for scientific understanding that the geoweb promises are indeed great enough that we need to rise to this challenge. Spatially integrating the sciences by harnessing the power of "where" has tremendous potential, and we are only now beginning to understand the many ways in which a web of location-aware connected devices is giving us an entirely new way of seeing the world. Let us jump in.

 **Further reading**

Bray, H. (2014) *You Are Here: From the Compass to GPS, the History of How We Find Ourselves.* New York: Basic Books.

PART TWO

Capturing and Visualizing Geodata

7

Capturing Absolute Location with the Global Positioning System

 **Overview**

This chapter includes:

- Geolocation with trilateration
- Five practice exercises on GPS data on the internet

This chapter is the first of several in which you will begin working with geodata. Each of the remaining chapters in Part Two will introduce new tools for collecting absolute and relative location and will provide examples of how these tools can be used to incorporate geodata into your research. Links to the necessary software downloads, sample datasets, and examples of online data repositories will be provided. In this first "hands-on" chapter, we will briefly examine how absolute location data are produced by the Global Positioning System and look at some of the ways in which such data are transmitted and stored across the geoweb. We will then use sample sets of geodata to explore some of the ways in which geodata can be stored and manipulated with a mix of web-based and downloadable software tools. We will also generate and store our own GPS data in order to see how we might use such data in our own research.

GEOLOCATION WITH TRILATERATION

As mentioned in Part One of this book, the end of "selective availability" – the intentional degradation of satellite signals from the Global Positioning System – by Bill

Clinton in 2000 marked the beginning of a new era in geolocation. Location information could now be determined, with great accuracy, with a simple handheld device. The ease with which we could now collect our absolute location as a simple pair of coordinates belied the centuries of advancements in mathematics, aeronautics, computer science, and many other fields that were necessary precursors to this wondrous new capability.

The key components of the GPS are the more than two dozen satellites that orbit our planet. These satellites continuously send out radio signals that can be captured with any device containing a GPS receiver chip, such as a dedicated GPS receiver or your mobile telephone. Signals from at least four of the GPS satellites are accessible at all times at any point on Earth, which means that enough information is available for a GPS receiver to calculate current latitude and longitude using geometrical *trilateration*.

Trilateration refers to the point at which three circles (in two dimensions) or spheres (in three dimensions) meet. GPS receivers perform trilateration by calculating the distance from the receiver to the satellites, an extremely complicated affair requiring atomic clocks on each satellite, information on the location of each satellite based on its flight path, and myriad corrections for slight errors due to gravitational pull and the impact of our atmosphere on the speed of radio waves. By adjusting for all of these factors, a GPS receiver can then use the location of the satellites and the differential in the time it took for the satellite signal to be received to calculate the three "spheres" needed for trilateration (though often more than three satellite signals are used – "multilateration" – in order to improve accuracy). The result is an (X, Y) coordinate pair that can be used to mark absolute location on the WGS 84 datum surface. To the end user, the result is one's latitude and longitude.

Trilateration can also be used to calculate the location of a device on a cellular network by using the location of three cell towers instead of GPS satellites. If a device's radio signal is broadcast to at least three cell towers, the same general principle of combining the known location of the towers and the differential in time it takes for the signal to reach each tower can be applied. While typically not as accurate, such terrestrial-based trilateration does make it possible to geolocate a device even if it does not contain a GPS receiver.

Determining geolocation is becomingly increasingly sophisticated, as location data obtained from GPS and cell tower trilateration are often combined with other locational datasets (trilateration based on WiFi hotspot locations, for example, or even acoustic triangulation based on a device's microphone sensor). For our purposes, it suffices to say that we now have the technological infrastructure in place that allows for the production and collection of absolute location at a high level of accuracy and precision. Because of this, we are now able to generate a tremendous amount of spatial data that has become the fabric of the geoweb.

GPS DATA ON THE INTERNET

Latitude and longitude coordinate pairs can be found online in a wide variety of applications and in several different formats. Sites like FlightAware.com and Vesselfinder.com let you track commercial air and sea traffic in real time, while applications like Waze inform you of current traffic conditions based on crowdsourced GPS data from other users. Social media applications like Twitter allow users to embed geolocation information in the log file of each tweet. Tools such as OpenStreetMap let you upload and download GPS data in the form of individual points or in connected "tracks," so that a hike, bike route, or boat trip can be stored and overlaid on top of a digital map.

Location data generated with GPS take many different forms, some of which are easier to capture than others. Some coordinate datasets are organized into rows and columns, making them easily accessible in spreadsheets and databases. Others might be structured in formats such as KML, the popular encoding structure for files used in online mapping applications such as Google Maps and Google Earth, or as a shapefile or GeoJSON file, two additional formats for storing geographic data that are frequently used. A good bit of GPS-generated data is not specifically organized into structured datasets, however, and can take much more effort to acquire. "Scraping" geodata from websites and extracting coordinate data from a collection of social media posts are additional approaches to data capture that range in difficulty from using a ready-made online tool to writing sophisticated code.

Below are five exercises that will give you an opportunity to download different types of coordinate datasets and examine them using a few types of software tools. First, we will download a simple dataset that is formatted as a comma-delimited (CSV) file and view it in a text editor and a spreadsheet. Second, we will generate and store our own location data using a simple software application for smartphones. A more sophisticated approach to collecting our own location data is explored in the third exercise as we customize our own data collection tool with OpenDataKit. We will then download coordinates that were collected and strung together as a "path" by someone using a handheld GPS unit and examine this dataset using both an online tool (GPS Visualizer) and a downloadable program (GpsPrune). Finally, we will download a file of average daily traffic counts throughout the city of Chicago and create an online database using Google Fusion Tables. This final exercise will also include our first attempt at mapping coordinate data using the mapping capabilities of Fusion Tables.

Before we begin, it is important to remember that absolute location can be expressed in different formats. One common expression is the degrees–minutes–seconds format, which looks like this: 41° 54′ 10″, 12° 29′ 10″ or 41N 54′ 10″, 12W 29′ 10″. These coordinates, you will recall, mark a particular place based on its relative location from the Equator (latitude 0°) and the Prime Meridian (longitude 0°). This same location can be expressed in the decimal degrees format, which is more suited to data analysis with a computer: 41.9, 12.5. Negative numbers can be used for locations south of the Equator and west of the Prime Meridian (e.g., −35.55, −70.62). While some software applications can read the degrees–minutes–seconds format, you should typically use the decimal degrees format when working with location data.

Exercise 1: Download a structured file of GPS data

Let us take a look at an example of a structured data file that contains geodata. On the internet, navigate to the Africaopendata.org website and enter "Health facilities master list" in the search box. Look for the entry labeled "Health Facilities Master List (working data)" and click on the little "CSV" box to get some basic information about this dataset (Figure 7.1; CSV stands for "comma-separated values" and is a very

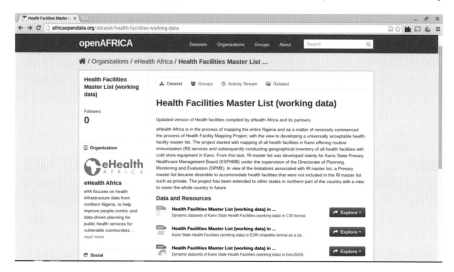

FIGURE 7.1   Links to health facilities data on the Africaopendata.org website © openAFRICA

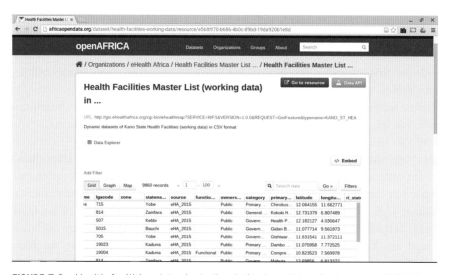

FIGURE 7.2   Health facilities data, including latitude and longitude © openAFRICA

common data format). Clicking on the name of the file should then take you to a preview screen that allows you to look at the information found in this dataset. The file contains records on health facilities and has several columns of attribute data that provide information about each facility, including the name, type of health care provider, whether it is public or private, and more. If you scroll to the right you will notice two columns labeled "latitude" and "longitude" that contain absolute location coordinates in decimal degrees (Figure 7.2).

You can quickly test this data by selecting one of the coordinate pairs and entering them into the search box of an online mapping application such as Google Maps or OpenStreetMap. Let us enter the first coordinate pair (12.064155, 11.662771) into OpenStreetMap to plot the location (Figure 7.3). The search results return the coordinate pair and the location "Yobe, Nigeria." Hovering over either of these will place a symbol on the map that represents the coordinate pair you entered.

You can also download this dataset for use in other programs on your computer. After downloading, try opening the file in a text editor of your choice (such as Notepad or TextEdit) as well as with a spreadsheet program such as Excel, LibreOffice Calc, or Google Sheets. Depending on the program you choose, you might see the data separated by commas, by spaces, or by columns (see Figure 7.4). No matter what program you use, however, you now have a structured dataset where each row represents a health facility and its associated attribute data (including geodata).

There is a tremendous amount of geodata structured in this away across the internet, often freely available for download. But you also might have a very specific set of data points you would like to collect on your own. For that, we will turn to devices with GPS receivers on board that let us generate our own geodata.

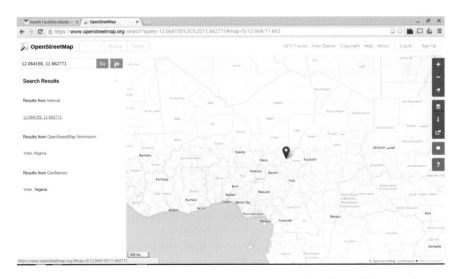

FIGURE 7.3   Coordinate pair search on OpenStreetMap © OpenStreetMap contributors

(Continued)

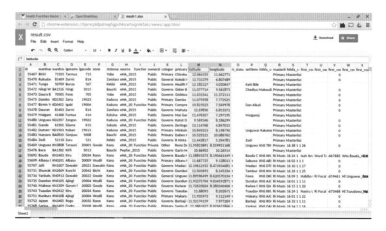

FIGURE 7.4 Downloaded health facilities dataset in CSV format

Exercise 2: Creating and storing GPS data using smartphone applications

As mentioned in previous chapters, the merging of the GPS and mobile communication networks has meant an enormous increase in the amount of geodata being produced by handheld devices. GPS devices are increasingly networked, meaning that location data can easily be captured, stored, and instantly shared. And while professional grade GPS receivers are still necessary for capturing a very high level of location accuracy, the GPS technology now found within the typical smartphone is capable of generating a level of accuracy that is good enough for most needs. As such, the smartphone is increasingly the GPS receiver of choice for those wanting to collect mobile geodata.

The three main smartphone operating systems – iOS, Android, and Windows – all provide an application programming interface (API) to the GPS receiver embedded in phones running them. This means that you can create a software application that accesses the location information provided by a phone's GPS, or you can take advantage of the dozens of apps that have already been developed. Each of the existing apps has its own set of features and limitations, but there are several that allow you to capture, store, and share geodata directly from the device.

For this exercise, we are going to use one such app (Geo Tracker for Android) to collect a set of latitude and longitude coordinates, save it, and export it as a file that can be used in other applications. This app is for Android and can be downloaded from the Google Play store. Apps with similar functionality can be acquired for iOS (MyTracks) and Windows (GPX Viewer). Again, there are many apps available that have various features and capabilities, so you may want to download a few different ones to see what works best for your needs.

Once you have the application downloaded and installed, start the app and click on "Add new empty map." This will take you to another screen where you can enter a name for your new map and any description you would like to include. Click "Add" once you've completed entering this information. Geo Tracker will now access your device's GPS and begin collecting location data. You can also mark specific places by clicking the pushpin icon. This feature gives you the coordinates for your current location, your approximate elevation, and a timestamp. You can also edit this information to include a name and a more detailed description.

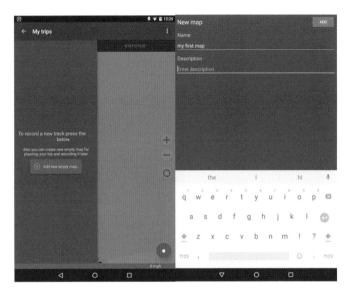

FIGURE 7.5   Geo Tracker for Android © Google

FIGURE 7.6   Exporting using Geo Tracker for Android © Google

(Continued)

Spend a few minutes marking several different locations. After you have completed your "trip," press the stop button and save the file. Once saved, you will now see your newly collected data under "My Trips" and several options for sharing and editing. Here you can easily export your data in other formats such as GPX, KML, and KMZ, which can be easily viewed in various software tools and web applications (including many of those covered in the upcoming chapters of the book).

As you can see, mobile applications such as Geo Tracker make it quite simple to collect a basic set of geodata. Latitude and longitude coordinate pairs are easy to capture, some basic attribute data for the coordinates can be entered, and the resulting table can be downloaded and shared for further analysis. Yet these types of apps tend not to be very customizable. So if you wanted to include additional attributes, say, or include audio and video files with your coordinates, or allow multiple users to add points to the same database, you will typically find off-the-shelf mobile apps wanting. It is in cases like these that you might be interested in developing a more customizable application for geodata collection without resorting to building software from scratch. This is where OpenDataKit fits in.

Exercise 3: Customizing your geodata collection application with OpenDataKit

OpenDataKit (ODK) is an open source software application developed for the Android operating system that lets you build custom forms for data collection, share those forms, and aggregate collected data on a central server. Setting up OpenDataKit for collecting geodata is more complicated than simply downloading an app, but the increased functionality and flexibility can make the effort well worth it. In this exercise, we will first download the ODK application for mobile devices, view an existing form that has been built for demonstration purposes, collect some data, and view the data on the aggregated database. After that, we will build our own custom data collection form and set up a server to store our data.

Collecting and viewing sample data

To use ODK, you will need access to a smartphone or tablet running the Android operating system. First, access the Google Play store and search for "open data kit." Download and install the ODK Collect application.

Once you have installed and opened the application, you will see a basic menu of choices (Figure 7.7).

Click on "Get Blank Form." You should then see several forms that have been created as demo applications (Figure 7.8).

Select "Geo Tagger v2." Now back at the main menu, select "Fill Blank Form." Click on the Geo Tagger v2 form.

You are now at the default opening screen for data collection forms (Figure 7.9).

From here you can swipe back and forth on your screen to see the various input prompts. This basic form asks that you capture an image, record your location, and enter a description of your image and location. These have been set as optional, so you do not necessarily have to enter an image. Skip this page.

On the next page, click on "Record Location." The application will now access the GPS on your device to acquire your approximate location. This might take a few minutes. Once it looks like your GPS has acquired your location, click on "Record Location." Your latitude, longitude, altitude, and location accuracy will then be listed. Swipe to the next screen to enter a basic description. Keep it simple and take note of exactly what you enter here, as you will need this text later to filter out your data from the rest of the sample data collected by others using this form.

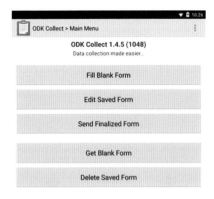

FIGURE 7.7 OpenDataKit (ODK) menu © OpenDataKit

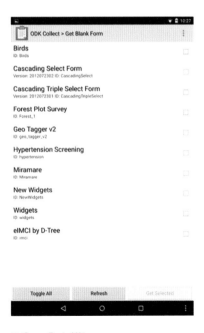

FIGURE 7.8 ODK forms © OpenDataKit

(Continued)

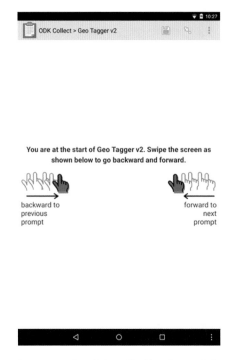

FIGURE 7.9 ODK opening screen for data collection forms © OpenDataKit

Swipe to the final screen and click on "Save Form and Exit." You have now saved a record to your device. Back at the main menu, click on "Send Finalized Form." You can now send your data to the online server at opendatakit.appspot.com. Check the box by "Geo Tagger v2," then click on "Send Selected." You have now uploaded your data to the server.

On a web browser, navigate to opendatakit.appspot.com. Here you will seek the ODK page for aggregated form data. In the dropdown menu in the upper left corner, change the form selection from "Birds" to "Geo Tagger v2." You will see a list of data collected from other users of the form (Figure 7.10). Under "Filters Applied," click on "Add Filter." In the dialog box that appears, you want to display only those rows that match the description you entered in your form. Change "DeviceId" to "Description," then type the exact text you entered from your form. Click on "Apply Filter." If you entered your text correctly, you should now see only the data you collected with your copy of the Geo Tagger form (sometimes it takes a few minutes to upload the data from your form to the server, so you might have to try this a couple of times before your entry appears).

If you see your data entry, you can now click on "Visualize." Change the type from "Pie Chart" to "Map," then click on "Map It." A Google Map with a placemark representing your location should appear in the window. Click on the marker and you will see the data that you collected with the Geo Tagger form.

The "Geo Tagger v2" form is a very basic form for recording location, but there are many other input prompts that can be built with ODK. You can ask users to select from a list, record audio or video, input the date and a timestamp, scan a barcode, and more. You might want to take a look at the "Birds" form or one of the other example forms included on the opendatakit.appspot.com site to get an idea of the possibilities.

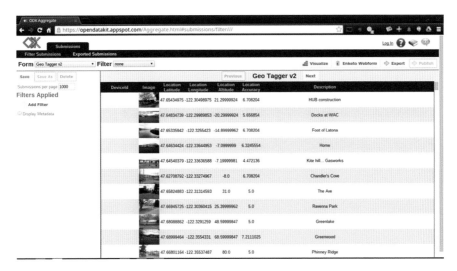

FIGURE 7.10 Geo Tagger form © OpenDataKit

Next, we will turn to creating our own ODK form and setting up our own site for data aggregation so that we can control what data we collect and who can access our collection form.

Creating your own ODK form

The first step in developing our own data collection system is to build a form. To begin this, go to build. opendatakit.org and click "Don't yet have an account" in the sign in dialog box. Here you can enter a user-name and password along with an email address to create an ODK account. Once you have done this, you will see an empty screen labeled "Untitled Form."

Let us build a simple "Litter Mapper" application that will allow us to describe, map, and photograph litter that we find in a given area. At the bottom of the ODK Build window, add a new "text" block to your form. You should see a large block appear in the main window, along with several properties along the right-hand side of your screen. Let us change the data name to "Litter" and the caption to "What type of litter did you find?" The remaining properties are optional, so for now let us just leave them as they are.

Next, try creating a page for recording the location of your identified litter. At the bottom of your form, add a new "location" tool to the page. A new block appears along with a new set of properties. Let us change the data name to "Location" and the caption to "Please record your location." Finally, we will create a prompt for the user to take a photograph of the litter. Add a media tool to your form, change the data name to "Photo" and the caption to "Please take a photograph of the litter" (Figure 7.11). Note that the default type of media in the properties window is "image," which is what we want, but that audio and video recording options are also available.

You can now save the form, naming it "Litter Collector" or something similar. You now have an ODK form that you can access any time you return to the build.opendatakit.org site. Before we can use the form, how-ever, we have to establish a place to host the form and a database for storing all of the data collected with

(Continued)

FIGURE 7.11   ODK Build menu © OpenDataKit

the form. In the Geo Tagger example above we used opendatakit.appspot.com, but for our own applications we will need to set up a new location. You can also choose to store your collected data locally or on another cloud service such as Amazon AWS. Detailed instructions for each type of data aggregation can be found at https://opendatakit.org/use/aggregate/. For our example, we will install our ODK Aggregate database on Google's App Engine.

Setting up ODK Aggregate

In order to set up your ODK Aggregate database, you will need a Google account and a Google App Engine account. App Engine provides a free quota of data usage, so unless you are building a large-scale data collection application you will not have to pay for the service. Once you have logged in to your App Engine account, you can select "create project" and enter a new project title and application ID. You will need to remember this information once you begin building your project in ODK Aggregate.

Before proceeding, make sure that your operating system is running Java 1.7 or higher. Once you have confirmed this, go to opendatakit.org/downloads and select the appropriate ODK Aggregate installer from the list. Download the file, run the installer, and accept the license agreement. When asked to choose platform, select Google Apps Engine.

Next, create a new instance name for your ODK Aggregate server. In the Google AppEngine application ID dialog box, click the link appengine.google.com to see your App Engine application names, or if you already know it you can enter it directly. The installer then configures ODK Aggregate. Once the setup wizard has finished configuring ODK Aggregate, you can launch the installation script. You will be asked to enter the email and password of the email account that created your App Engine instance. Click on "upload." This might take some time.

Note that if you use two-step verification for your Google account, you will need to set up an application-specific password in order to connect (refer to ODK documentation for details).

If the upload to Google App Engine is successful, you should see "END-SCRIPT-SUCCESS" at the bottom of the upload dialog box. Close the window. Now, back in build.opendatakit.org, make sure your "Litter Collector" form is open and then choose **File > Publish to Aggregate**. You should now have a form available on the instance you created in App Engine.

In a new browser window, type in the name of your instance followed by ".appspot.com" (e.g., mynewlitter collector.appspot.com). This takes you to the ODK Aggregate site that looks very similar to the one used to download the Geo Tagger form we used previously, but now you should see your new "Litter Collector" form as a choice in the form dropdown list. There is nothing here yet since we have not collected any data.

Open up the ODK Collect application on your phone or tablet. Open the General Settings menu, then select "Configure platform settings." Click on the URL to edit it so that it matches the one on your browser (e.g., mynewlittercollector.appspot.com). Return to the main menu in the ODK Collect app. Click on "Get Blank Form." Your new litter collection form should be available for download.

Now you are ready to collect some data! Select "Fill Blank Form" and choose your litter form. You should then see the swipe screen that is the default opening screen for forms. Swipe through the screens to add data, location, and a photograph. Once you have completed all of the steps, save your finalized form.

Back at the main ODK Collect menu, select "Send Finalized Form." Select the litter form you just filled out, and click on "Send Selected." You can now return to your ODK Aggregate site and check to see if your data appear. As we saw in the Geo Tagger example, this might take a few minutes. Once you have confirmed that your data have successfully been uploaded, you can share the appspot URL with anyone using the ODK Collect application. They can then download your new form, collect data, and upload it back to your ODK Aggregate site. This can prove quite useful, as you now have the tools for crowdsourcing geodata collection among several users.

Exercise 4: Downloading and analyzing a GPS track

At times you might be interested in collecting absolute data in the form of pathways or tracks rather than points. A researcher might be interested in tracking a specific set of animals, or mapping the movement of people throughout a particular city, or examining immigrant pathways over time based on historical records. Each of these examples requires that we collect and visualize more than a simple set of discrete points.

For this exercise, we will first examine sets of GPS tracks, or traces, that have been created and uploaded to OpenStreetMap. These traces are public and freely available for download. In a web browser, go to www. openstreetmap.org/traces to see a list of recently uploaded GPS paths (Figure 7.12). You will notice that most of these files have the .GPX extension, which is an open and quite common format for GPS track data. Scroll through the list, find one of interest (some include labels and descriptions to help you identify the track), and click on the link. This takes you to a page that provides additional information on the trace you selected. To simply see a map of the general area where the trace was recorded, click on "map" next to the start coordinate listed. To save the file for use in other applications, return to the previous page and select "download." You now have a copy of the file on your computer.

(Continued)

FIGURE 7.12   Public GPS tracks ("traces") on the OpenStreetMap website
© OpenStreetMap contributors

Next, navigate to www.gpsvisualizer.com (Figure 7.13). GPS Visualizer is a popular website for working with GPS data (including geocoding, which we will look at in the next chapter). Let us upload our GPS trace and visualize it. In the green box on the main page, upload the GPS file that you downloaded from OpenStreetMap. You can then select your output format. To see the trace on top of a map, select Google Maps as your output format. To see an elevation profile of the trace, select elevation profile.

FIGURE 7.13   GPS Visualizer homepage © Adam Schneider

There are also software tools that you can download to your computer in order to work with GPS track data. One good example that is free and open source is GpsPrune, which is available at activityworkshop.net/software/gpsprune/download.html. For this part of the exercise we will examine our downloaded GPS trace using GpsPrune on our desktop.

After downloading and installing GpsPrune, click on the "Open File" icon to open your downloaded .GPX file. You should see the GPS trace and an elevation profile (Figure 7.14). From here you have several options. You can view the trace on top of a basemap, plot a 3D view of the trace, add audio or video clips, and even get Wikipedia articles on places nearby. You can also export the data in a variety of formats.

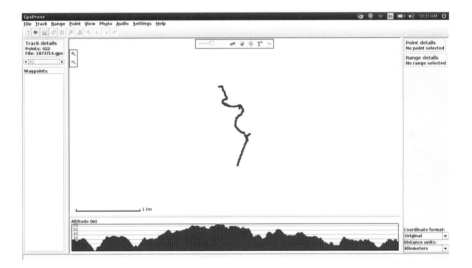

FIGURE 7.14   Downloaded GPS file viewed in GpsPrune © Activity Workshop

GpsPrune is one example of a simple software program that lets you easily view and manipulate GPS traces. If you are working with larger and more complicated datasets, you will probably want to turn to a more full-featured software program for managing geographic information. We will cover the use of geographic information systems in Chapters 11–13. Somewhere in between is another web-based application from Google called Fusion Tables, which lets you store, query, and visualize geodata.

Exercise 5: Download a structured file and create a Google Fusion Table and map

For our final exercise working with absolute location data, we will download a structured data file and create a simple database using Google Fusion Tables. The Fusion Tables web application has some basic database functionality which allows us to select subsets of data based on particular attributes and visualize data on a basemap.

(Continued)

First, navigate to the City of Chicago's website at www.cityofchicago.org. From here you can search "traffic count" and select the first search item returned. Here you will see a table with information on traffic volumes at various points throughout the city as measured on various dates in 2006 (Figure 7.15). The site includes its own visualization tools for mapping the data, but we are going to download this dataset and work with it in Fusion Tables. Click on the red menu button and select "Download." Download the file as a CSV file (you do not need to select "CSV for Excel").

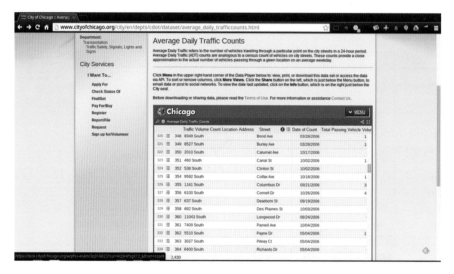

FIGURE 7.15 Average daily traffic counts at www.cityofchicago.org

You now have a copy of the traffic count dataset. If you wish, you can open it in a text editor or spreadsheet software to see the data. Note that the dataset includes both street addresses and coordinate pairs.

Your next goal is to upload the data into a Fusion Table. Navigate to tables.googlelabs.com (or, if you use Google Docs, you can add a Fusion Tables app to your set of applications) and select "Create a Fusion Table." Next, import your traffic count file by selecting "Choose File" from your computer. This is a comma-delimited dataset, so you can accept the default and click on "Next." You should now see a portion of your dataset in the browser window. Choose "Next" again to give your file a name and any descriptive information you would like to include. Click "Finish." You now have the Chicago traffic count data uploaded into a Fusion Table, viewable as spreadsheet rows, cards, and a map. Click on the "Map" tab to visualize all of the traffic count locations on a street map of Chicago (Figure 7.16). Click on any point to access the information on that location from your Fusion Table.

Let us suppose that you only want to see traffic count locations where the traffic volume was very high. While still in the map view, click on the "Filter" button and then select "Total Passing Vehicle Volume." We can now enter a range that we would like to query out. To see only those locations where the traffic count surpassed 100,000 vehicles, type in "100,000" in the first box. We can see in our filter view that the highest value in this column is 165,200, so we will enter that value in the second range

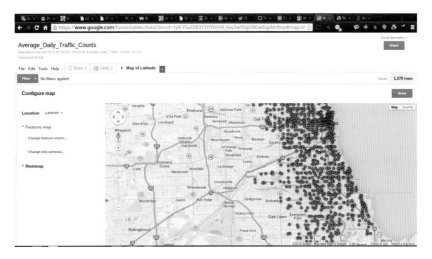

FIGURE 7.16 Chicago traffic count data uploaded into a Fusion Table and visualized on a street map © Google

box (Figure 7.17). Click "find." You will now see only three points on the map, all located on Lake Shore Drive. Clicking on the northernmost point on the map shows us that 1550 S Lake Shore Drive had the highest vehicle volume in our dataset.

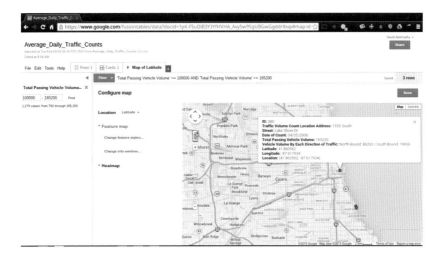

FIGURE 7.17 Filtered view of the Chicago traffic count data © Google

Close the filter box to return to the map of all of the data points. In addition to querying out subsets of data, we can also change the look of the entire dataset according to traffic count.

Under the "Feature Map" options, select "Change feature styles." Instead of using a single symbol and color for all of our traffic count locations, we are going to differentiate by vehicle volume. Under "Map Marker

(Continued)

Icons," choose "Buckets." We will divide our data up into three different ranges, so choose "Divide into 3 buckets." Choose "Total Passing Vehicle Volume" for the column name. Divide your data range into three categories: 700–25,000; 25,000–50,000; and 50,000–165,200. Select a green marker for your lowest range of values, a yellow marker for your middle range, and a red marker for your highest range (Figure 7.18).

FIGURE 7.18   Changing map feature styles © Google

Select "Save." You should now see your data symbolized according to the ranges of traffic volume you created (Figure 7.19). We can now quickly identify areas where traffic volume seems highest.

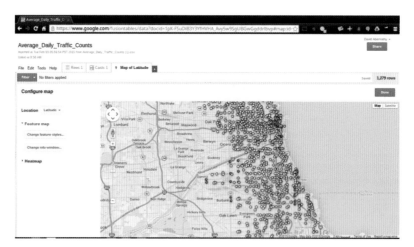

FIGURE 7.19   Chicago traffic count data symbolized according to range of traffic volume © Google

As you can see, Google Fusion Tables provides some basic database functionality for manipulating your spatial data. We will return to more robust approaches to data query and visualization in later chapters.

Chapter summary

This chapter introduced the primary building block of the geoweb – absolute location data. Geolocating data in physical space using coordinate pairs of latitude and longitude is an exceptionally common way of spatially referencing all kinds of data, from traffic counts and airline flights to social media posts and photographs. The chapter also provided an overview of some free and easily accessible software tools for working with absolute location data. Whether you are collecting your own location data or acquiring an existing dataset, there are several tools available for gathering, storing, manipulating, and visualizing absolute location data.

Despite the seeming ubiquity of absolute location data, however, much of the spatial information that humans use in their daily lives is not conveniently structured in a comma-delimited file of latitude and longitude data. Rather, we tend to navigate our world by "place" rather than "space." We read books and news articles that reference specific countries, regions, or cities. We look up restaurants not by latitude and longitude, but by street address. We imagine our town as a collection of neighborhoods, not individual data points.

The next chapter looks at these types of unstructured geodata and examines some tools and techniques for capturing and analyzing them. From geocoding street addresses to geoparsing spatial information from written text, being able to convert relatively unstructured spatial data to a structured dataset along the lines of those discussed in this chapter is an important skill.

Further reading

Xu, G. (2007) *GPS: Theory, Algorithms and Applications.* New York: Springer.

COMPANION WEBSITE

Visit https://study.sagepub.co/abernathy for:

- Links to the websites and free software packages discussed in this chapter
- Downloadable versions of all datasets presented in this chapter

8

Geocoding, Geotagging, and Geoparsing

 **Overview**

This chapter includes:

- Three practice exercises on geocoding
- Two practice exercises on geotagging
- Three practice exercises on geoparsing

As we saw in the previous chapter, absolute location data in the form of coordinate pairs are an essential building block of the geoweb. By providing us with a universal language of space (translatable, but consistent, across many different map projections), the geographic coordinate system gives us the ability to pinpoint a location on Earth quickly and easily. The increasing ubiquity of GPS receivers and the wide variety of software applications that can interpret and map coordinate pairs mean that more and more of the data we generate include some type of geolocation information.

Yet there is also a large amount of geospatial information we generate that has not traditionally been structured in the format of geographic coordinate pairs. You might read novels or guidebooks about a place before traveling there for vacation, identify the street addresses for your hotel and a nearby café when riding in a cab, and take photos of popular sites to help you remember your trip. While all of these are inherently spatial activities, they have not typically been formally recorded and structured for subsequent analysis. Such data are considered to be unstructured data, as they are not formatted according to a specifically defined data model.

Unstructured does not mean unimportant, of course. A collection of photographs from a vacation that helps you reminisce about your travels does not necessarily require a more structured geography, nor would a news article you read about current events taking place in your hometown. But you might imagine scenarios where being able to more specifically geolocate these photos and articles might be useful, particularly if these data were subsequently combined with other datasets that were similarly geolocated.

In the previous chapter, we learned how we could use OpenDataKit to capture a photo and link it to the geographic coordinates of the mobile device used to take it. In fact, most mobile devices today have the capability of automatically embedding geolocation into the metadata of any photo or video taken with the device. Latitude and longitude can be stored in the EXIF (exchangeable image file format) data of a digital photograph alongside the more traditional tags such as aperture, exposure, and focal ratio. This means that even if the user of a mobile device does not intentionally capture the geolocation of a photo with a tool such as OpenDataKit, the photo is still very likely to contain location data which can easily be extracted and mapped.

A vivid example of how such information can prove extremely useful occurred at the 117th running of the Boston Marathon. On April 15, 2013, two bomb blasts tore through a crowd of people who were watching runners approach the finish line. Within 24 hours, the Federal Bureau of Investigation had amassed more than 10 terabytes of data, much of it photos and videos that had been voluntarily submitted by those present at the bombings. Since most of these photos and videos were taken with mobile devices containing GPS units, location information had been automatically timestamped and embedded in the images themselves. Turning photos and videos into structured data allowed investigators to create a detailed spatiotemporal reconstruction of the day's events and search for important clues as to the bombing's suspects.

A very different example of how tying geolocation to unstructured data can reveal new information is the extraction of spatial data from texts – a process known as geoparsing. Translating text into geographic information is a much more difficult proposition than simply assigning a coordinate pair to a photograph. Nevertheless some interesting and useful tools for geoparsing have begun to emerge in recent years. CLAVIN (Cartographic Location and Vicinity Indexer) is one such tool that can be used to extract geolocation data from unstructured text, allowing for a more explicit engagement with the geographic components and spatial relationships embedded in text documents.

All sorts of data can now be geotagged in this way, allowing us to spatialize contemporary phenomena in ways that we were not able to before the emergence of the geoweb. In addition to photos and videos, we can now geotag our text messages, our tweets, our recorded audio, and more. But what about data generated before the emergence of the geoweb? Can we extract spatial information from old news articles, or perhaps our favorite novel? How do we translate between street addresses and geolocation? In short, how can we add an explicit spatial structure to data that do not already have it in order to mesh it with the geoweb?

This chapter will introduce you to some of the basic tools for translating semi-structured and unstructured place-based information into spatial information that can more readily be incorporated into the geoweb. Three distinct approaches will be covered: geocoding, geotagging, and geoparsing. *Geocoding* refers to the process of assigning geographic coordinates to places that are typically described with a different type of geographic nomenclature, such as the name of a city, postal code, or street address. *Geotagging*, while related to geocoding, refers more generally to the process of adding geographic coordinates to the metadata found in a variety of digital data formats. A digital photograph might contain location data, as mentioned in the example above, as might an online news article, digital music file, blog, or social media post (given the large and growing presence of social media across the geoweb, this will be covered separately in a later chapter). *Geoparsing* is the most difficult approach to acquiring geodata, as it refers to the extraction of geodata from unstructured text. While street addresses and digital photos have some level of structure (street addresses often have numbering systems to help identify location and direction, and digital images typically have a structured header file containing metadata), the spoken and written word quite often do not. Yet extracting geodata from a novel, speech, or historical news article can allow for new types of analysis and visualization, and we are starting to see tools emerging to assist in this process.

GEOCODING

In the previous chapter we plotted a map of points representing traffic count locations throughout the city of Chicago. The delimited text file we downloaded to create this map already had structured data in the form of latitude and longitude coordinates for each traffic count location. But what if we did not have those data, and instead only had the street address of each location we wanted to map? This is where geocoding comes in: we must find a tool for converting semi-structured street address data into a structured dataset of geographic coordinates.

Chances are you geocode data on a fairly regular basis. When you enter an address into a mapping application in your web browser or on your mobile device, you expect the application to return a point at the approximate location of the address you entered overlaid on a map; in other words, you want to geocode that address. You likely take this for granted as it has become a commonplace occurrence in everyday life, yet the computation happening "under the hood" of your address query is managing a fairly impressive feat of translation. Today's geocoding applications are surprisingly good at returning accurate results, even if you type "Rd" or "Road" when it should be "Lane," leave off a postal code, or in some other way enter an address slightly off from its appropriate label.

Our ability to geocode addresses given this problem of data entry has steadily improved but remains imperfect. While a full history of geocoding is beyond the scope of this book, a brief look at early efforts at structuring data such as street addresses is important as it illustrates the inexact science of translating semi-structured descriptive locations into structured geodata. More recent efforts to develop geocoders have led to more sophisticated and accurate translations, but no geocoder is foolproof (an important point to keep in mind when you begin conducting your own batch geocoding, as we will see below).

In the United States, the Census Bureau began creating a data model for geocoding street addresses back in the 1970s, and by the 1990s this model had developed into the comprehensive "Topologically Integrated Geographic Encoding and Referencing" (TIGER) system. TIGER continues to be updated and remains a key source of street data in the USA. The TIGER data model structured streets in such a way that a specific address could be approximated through interpolation. Street segments in the TIGER data had designated left- and right-hand sides, each having both a starting and an ending address number.

Once street segments were encoded in this way, each segment had a designated street name as well as a beginning and ending numerical address value. These values could then be matched with their latitude and longitude. Then querying a street address somewhere between the beginning and ending numerical values was simply a matter of interpolation. This approach to geocoding made it possible to predict the approximate location of street addresses, but was also prone to error.

A preferable approach to geocoding would be to construct a database where every address had a known latitude and longitude rather than an interpolated one. As you might imagine, such databases would be much larger and are more difficult and time-consuming to build than a database built on the street segment/interpolation model described above. But we increasingly see databases where individual homes, buildings, parcels, postal codes, or other geographic phenomena have been assigned a specific geolocation, which improves the accuracy of address geocoding.

Another challenge when attempting to translate a street address into a coordinate pair is in the parsing of the address text. As mentioned above, there are different ways to write out a given address. For example, if you live at a house numbered "100" on a street named "Oak," you might see your address as "100 Oak Street," "100 Oak St," "100 Oak Str.," or perhaps just "100 Oak." In addition, someone might incorrectly write "Road" or "Lane" instead of "Street." Early geocoding software packages had difficulty with such ambiguity and often returned incorrect results. Today's geocoding services are vastly improved, but users should still carefully examine geocoded output and be on the lookout for errors.

Below are some exercises for you to practice geocoding street addresses and places using online geocoding tools. There are many different geocoding services available; here we will focus only on those services that are available at no charge. Be aware that geocoding services, like other online sites, can come and go with little warning. These services also have their own terms and limitations, use different databases for their reference data, and place limits on the number of addresses you are allowed to geocode. In addition, some services will return the actual coordinate values for your geocoded addresses, allowing you to then input those data into some other analysis tool, while others will only return a map of the geocoded results. That said, geocoding services are continuing to improve and are valuable tools for assigning specific geolocation data to places whose geography is typically more ambiguously defined.

Exercise 1: Geocode a single address

We will begin by entering a single street address into different online geocoding tools to see what output each generates. Note that we will focus only on locations in the UK and the USA for street address geocoding, as geocoding tools are less robust for other parts of the world. Databases containing place names and postal codes are more globally comprehensive, so we will look at geocoding outside of the USA and UK in Exercise 3.

As mentioned previously, you are essentially geocoding when you enter an address into an online mapping tool. So to start, let us do a quick address query in OpenStreetMap. Navigate to openstreetmap.org and type "10 Downing St" into the search box. You should see two options appear on the left-hand side of your browser – one listed as an attraction in London and one listed as a pub in India. Click on the link for the attraction to zoom in to the location in London, which should take you to a map in London with the appropriate building highlighted (Figure 8.1).

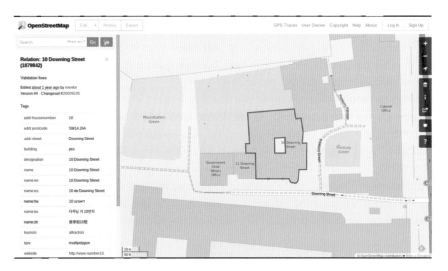

FIGURE 8.1   10 Downing Street in OpenStreetMap © OpenStreetMap contributors

Note that some data about the building at 10 Downing Street are located in the left-hand column of your browser, including the site's postal code, its name in several languages, and links to a website and Wikipedia entry for the location. If an address has a name associated with it you can search by that attribute without knowing the specific street address. Typing "The White House" in the OpenStreetMap search box returns the same results as entering "1600 Pennsylvania Avenue, Washington, DC" (Figure 8.2).

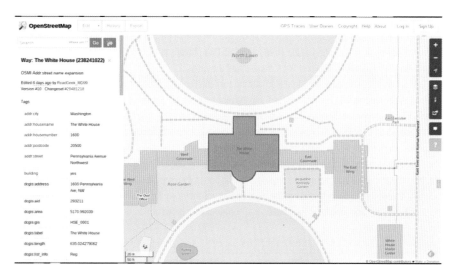

FIGURE 8.2 The White House in OpenStreetMap © OpenStreetMap contributors

We do not automatically see the latitude and longitude coordinate for the address, but that information is available for some of the individual map features within OpenStreetMap. On the right hand side of the map, you will notice several icons in a vertical black bar. Click on the "Layers" icon to pull up options for your base-map type and two checkboxes for "Map Notes" and "Map Data." Checking the box for "Map Data" highlights the individual features that have been created in OpenStreetMap by its contributors. We can now highlight the flagpole feature at the White House to return a latitude and longitude of 38.897718, −77.0365482 (Figure 8.3).

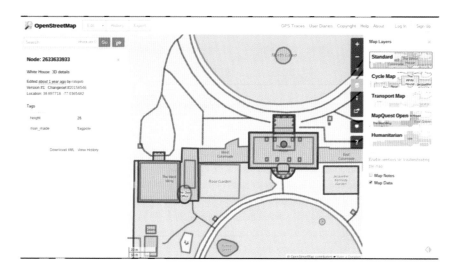

FIGURE 8.3 Checking for "Map Data" in OpenStreetMap © OpenStreetMap contributors

(Continued)

You can verify this coordinate pair by returning to the main OpenStreetMap page or any other online map-ping service and entering the latitude and longitude into the search bar. You should see a map zoomed in on the White House and a listing of the street address. This process is known as reverse geocoding, since you are translating a coordinate pair back into a street address.

As you may have noticed, OpenStreetMap lists the service(s) used to geocode your search when results are returned. When we entered "The White House" into the map browser, the first set of results come from something called OpenStreetMap Nominatim. Nominatim is the geocoding service maintained by OpenStreetMap for search queries on the site, and it can also be accessed directly at nominatim.openstreetmap.org.

Let us return to our first address query of "10 Downing St" and enter it directly into the Nominatim search box. The map returned (Figure 8.4) looks almost identical to the one we retrieved from the OpenStreetMap site, but note the additional information provided. In addition to the map, you can see the latitude and longi-tude coordinates for the bounding box of the map, and as you move your mouse across the map you can see the specific latitude and longitude coordinates in a corner of your browser.

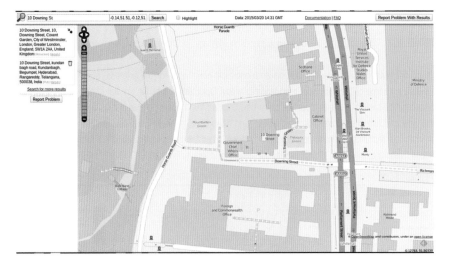

FIGURE 8.4   10 Downing Street in OpenStreetMap Nominatim © OpenStreetMap contributors

Nominatim is a free and open source software service, so in addition to accessing it via OpenStreetMap it can also be downloaded and installed locally for batch geocoding.

The second set of returns on our query are provided by a service called GeoNames, which is another geographical database containing more than 9 million unique features. These features are categorized into more than 600 different feature codes, including various types of landmarks, natural features, and building types. GeoNames does not actually geocode street addresses like Nominatim, however. Entering "The White House" into OpenStreetMap will give you a GeoNames result, but only because it has a building feature code within the database. Entering "10 Downing St" or your own address will return no GeoNames results. GeoNames is an excellent service for geocoding non-address features, however, and as such we will return to it in Exercise 3.

One last example of a single-address geocoding tool is GPS Visualizer, which we examined briefly in the previous chapter. As you might summate from its name, GPS Visualizer is an online service that provides tools for working with data collected with a handheld GPS receiver, including mapping GPS waypoints and tracks. But the site also provides access to geocoding services, allowing you to geocode an individual address or a batch of addresses. We will geocode an individual address here, then move on to batch geocoding in Exercise 2.

Navigate to GPSVisualizer.com and select "Geocode addresses" in the top portion of the page. From there, choose "Geocode a single address" which will take you to GPS Visualizer's Quick Geocoder page. Note that you have two different geocoding services to choose from in the dropdown box: Bing and Google. You also have several different basemap options to choose from in the map window.

The three geocoding services might return slightly different results, so it's worth experimenting with each. Try typing in our "10 Downing St" search again and note the results each geocoding service gives (Figure 8.5). Each service can successfully identify our address and geocode it, but they each have slightly different latitude and longitude coordinates. This should not typically be a problem unless you require extremely accurate location information, but be aware that different geocoders may return slightly different results.

FIGURE 8.5   10 Downing Street in GPS Visualizer © Adam Schneider

This exercise has demonstrated a couple of simple ways to quickly geocode a single address in order to obtain a pair of geographic coordinates and/or see the location of an address on a basemap. If you would like to geocode an entire batch of addresses, however, the approaches used above will be slow and cumbersome. Fortunately, some additional geocoding services are available that allow you to geocode a set of addresses all at once. This is known as "batch geocoding," which we will examine in the next exercise.

Exercise 2: Geocode a batch of addresses

Batch geocoding applications work the same way as individual address geocoding applications, with the added functionality of letting the user upload an entire list of addresses all at once. As before, we will look at a couple of different batch geocoding applications to see what types of output they produce.

First, let us download some address data. Navigate to the web page for the California Department of Education (www.cde.ca.gov) and select "Data & Statistics." Now select "Downloadable Data Files" from the list of available links. Download the most recent data file for private schools in California, which includes names and addresses for all of the private schools in the state. Open the dataset using a spreadsheet software program and take a look at the data. Note that the spreadsheet includes separate columns for address, city, and state.

Now return to the GPS Visualizer home page. We will once again select "Geocode addresses" at the top of the page, but this time we will then choose "Geocode multiple addresses" instead of the single address geocoding option we chose before. Note that you are extremely limited in terms of the number of addresses you may geocode on this site unless you have accessed a key to a geocoding service. Steps for accessing a MapQuest key are included here, and you can also access keys for Google and Bing geocoding services. If you prefer not to access a key right now, you can test the batch geocoding on GPS Visualizer by just entering five addresses or fewer (when using the MapQuest geocoder), as we will do next.

Accessing a MapQuest Key: You can begin accessing a key to MapQuest by clicking on the link just above the input box on the batch geocoding page of GPS Visualizer, or by navigating directly to developer.mapquest.com. From there you will be taken to the MapQuest developer's site where you can create a free developer account. A popup window will walk you through the remaining steps. Be sure to select the checkbox when asked if you would like to use an AppKey. It might take some time before your account is activated.

Go to the private school dataset and copy the column names and first five schools under the columns "School," "Street," "City," and "State." Now paste this subset of the school data into the batch geocode window of GPS Visualizer, as shown in Figure 8.6.

Underneath the input box, choose "tabular" for type of data (since you are including column names as your first row of data), use "MapQuest Open" as your geocoding source, and choose "tab" as the field separator between your columns. You should now see your addresses appear one by one in the results box, along with the geocoded latitude and longitude processed by MapQuest. Note that one of your five addresses was not successfully geocoded (a good reminder that no geocoding service is perfect, and some manual geocoding is usually required to improve results). You can click on the "Draw a map" button beside your raw output to quickly map your data, or you can just copy and paste the output for use in some other software application.

Now let us try geocoding our private school data using a different batch geocoding service. Navigate to www.findlatitudeandlongitude.com, scroll down to the menu box, and select "Batch Geocode." Copy and paste your same five schools from before, using a "tab" delimiter as before (Figure 8.7).

Output similar to what you geocoded in GPS Visualizer (but not exactly the same coordinates!) should appear in the Output window. Note that the first school in your list was geocoded in this instance – you might

FIGURE 8.6 Entering multiple addresses in GPS Visualizer © Adam Schneider

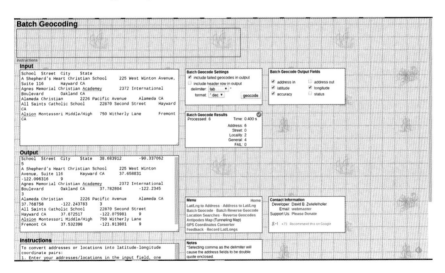

FIGURE 8.7 Batch geocoding at www.findlatitudeandlongitude.com © David B. Zwiefelhofer

want to enter the given latitude and longitude coordinates in a separate mapping application and see if it accurately geolocated the school.

The findlatitudeandlongitude.com geocoder does not give you the ability to map your data on the site – instead you will need to copy and paste it into another application in order to map the data. The site does, however, let you enter more addresses than GPS Visualizer without the need for a key. To test this, try copying and pasting 25 or 30 of your school addresses and running the geocoder again.

Batch geocoding tools are useful for quickly generating latitude and longitude coordinate pairs for sets of street address data. We have taken a look at two examples here, but there are other geocoding services available online. Such geocoding services have varying limits on the number of addresses you are allowed to input, use different geospatial databases for coding addresses, and sometimes disappear from the web without warning, so tread cautiously.

Exercise 3: Geocoding places

Compared to street addresses, which have different systems in different countries and can be difficult to parse, place names are more straightforward and simpler to geocode. Yet some of the same limitations of address geocoding – limits on number of places coded, different latitude and longitude coordinates for different databases, and the uncertainty of whether or not a given service will remain accessible – still apply when attempting to geocode particular places. As before, we will take a look at a couple of examples of place geocoding using some of the currently available online applications.

Historically, collections of information about places that included geographical reference data were called *gazetteers*. Many online gazetteers now exist that include specific geolocation information for thousands of places in specific regions or across the entire globe. From gazetteers of historical places (like the China Historical Gazetteer) to newer databases storing location information on a growing number of places around the world (like Google's Places or OpenStreetMap's Nominatim), there are many available online resources for geocoding place names.

Place name databases are included in most online mapping applications, meaning that you can search by place in addition to searching by street address. As we saw in the first example above, we can search for

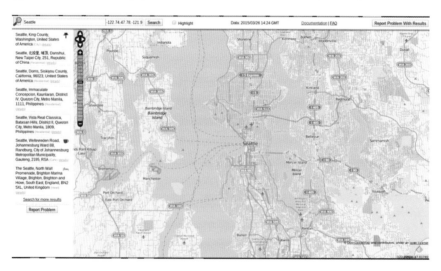

FIGURE 8.8   Search results for "Seattle" in OpenStreetMap Nominatim
© OpenStreetMap contributors

"The White House" and get the same results as when we search for "1600 Pennsylvania Avenue." Let us return to OpenStreetMap's Nominatim to search for some additional places.

Go to nominatim.openstreetmap.org and enter the name of a city or town with which you are familiar. You should be taken to that place on a map. Recall that the return includes the latitude and longitude coordinates for the map's bounding box, and you are also given the exact coordinates for your mouse as you move about the map. A search for "Seattle," for example, returns the map in Figure 8.8.

You can also enter place name searches into online gazetteers such as the Gazetteer of British Place Names or the US National Geospatial Intelligence Agency's GeoNames WMS Viewer. Navigating to www. gazetteer.org.uk and entering a place name will give you a list of matches. Entering "Nottingham," for example, gives only one result (Figure 8.9), and when clicked returns some information on the place, including a map and the latitude and longitude coordinate pair for the place.

FIGURE 8.9   Search results for "Nottingham" in the Gazetteer of British Place Names © The Association of British Counties

Likewise, navigating to geonames.nga.mil/gns/html/ takes you to a comprehensive database of places outside the USA that is searchable by text (Figure 8.10) or by map. Searching the database should return a list of results that you can subsequently view on a map viewer that includes the place's latitude and longitude.

You probably noticed that none of these services offer batch geocoding options. As with street addresses, most services limit the number of searches you can submit and also restrict your searches to one place at a time. If you want to geocode multiple places at once, try returning to the batch geocoding tool from findlatitudeandlongitude.com that we used before. In the input box we can enter multiple place names and get geocoded output, as in the example in Figure 8.11.

(Continued)

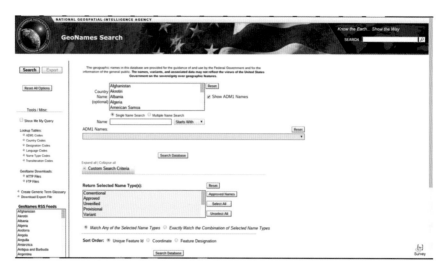

FIGURE 8.10   GeoNames Search © GEOnet Names Server

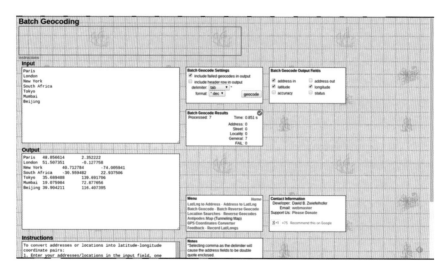

FIGURE 8.11   Entering multiple place names in the batch geocoding tool © David B. Zwiefelhofer

As we will see in later chapters, once you have successfully geocoded addresses or places you then have structured data that can be analyzed and visualized with other software tools, such as GIS software or a digital globe. But there are many other phenomena besides addresses and places that you might be interested in geocoding. For these, we turn to our next approach to converting data to geodata: geotagging.

GEOTAGGING

Geotagging, like geocoding, is a method used to add structured geographic attributes to existing information so that it can be incorporated into the geoweb. Much of the digital data we produce today – from audio files to photographs – includes embedded information, called metadata, that describes various aspects of the data itself. A digital photograph, for example, can have very detailed metadata on the type of camera used, the exposure time, whether or not a flash was used, and the time and date the photograph was taken. Geotagging, then, is the process of adding geographic coordinates to the metadata of a digital file of some sort.

Much of the data captured by mobile devices today has some sort of geographic metadata included, whether that information is explicitly used or not. Some software applications allow you to choose whether or not you would like to collect location metadata when using them and whether or not you will make that information publicly available. You can choose, for example, whether or not to capture location data with the photos you take on your mobile device or with the posts you share on social media. And as we saw in Chapter 5, other applications often geotag your data without your knowledge or consent, resulting in ongoing concerns over privacy in the digital age.

Despite the increasing amount of geotagged data being produced today, there are still plenty of datasets that do not automatically include geographic metadata. While photographs captured by mobile phones tend to be geotagged today, those captured with stand-alone digital cameras still tend to not include geodata. Likewise, audio data recorded with digital devices – from formal concert performances to ambient street noise – often do not include any explicit geographic metadata. In cases like these where there is no digital header file containing geodata, the data must be geotagged manually.

The exercises below will familiarize you with the basics of geotagging. You will examine the existing geographic metadata of a digital image using online tools and a downloadable software package as well as manually geotag data files that do not contain such metadata. Like the geocoding examples above, these exercises will help you create structured data that can be analyzed and visualized with other software tools that we will explore in later chapters.

 Exercise 4: View EXIF data using online tools

As mentioned above, most digital images captured with mobile phones (and, increasingly, with stand-alone digital cameras) include geographic coordinates as one component of the digital metadata associated with those images. Metadata for digital images are formatted in the exchangeable image file format (EXIF), which includes a standard for geolocation information. Several online tools exist that allow you to enter the URL for a photograph or upload your own and view the EXIF data contained within the image. For this exercise, we will use one popular online tool called Jeffrey's EXIF Viewer. You will either need your own photo containing EXIF geodata or the URL of a photo that includes geographic metadata.

(Continued)

Navigate to regex.info/exif.cgi. You will see a very simple interface for examining EXIF data. Here you can choose to upload your own image or enter a link to an existing photo online. In Figure 8.12 you can see a URL entered that directs the tool to an image of the CN Tower in Toronto.

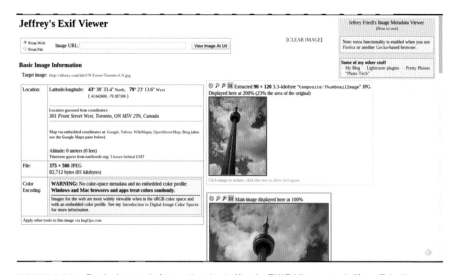

FIGURE 8.12 Jeffrey's EXIF Viewer © Jeffrey Friedl

Once you have selected the photo to examine, click on the appropriate "view image" button. All available EXIF metadata are then presented in a set of tables. Geographic coordinates are included in one or more of the tables (Figure 8.13), and a Google Map of the location is included as well.

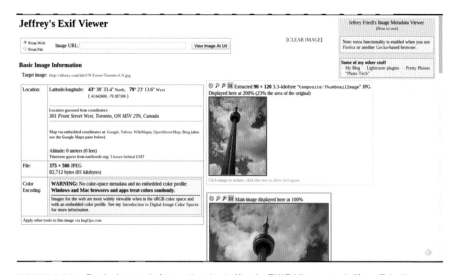

FIGURE 8.13 Basic image information in Jeffrey's EXIF Viewer © Jeffrey Friedl

Exercise 5: Using EXIFTool

EXIFTool is a popular free software tool that can be used to read and write metadata for digital files. You can obtain the software download here: www.sno.phy.queensu.ca/~phil/exiftool/.

The screenshots below are from the Windows version, but you can also install EXIFTool on Mac and Linux systems.

Once the software has been downloaded and installed, you can use the command line in a terminal to examine the metadata of your digital files (note that in Windows you will need to rename the .exe file to exifile. exe in order to do this, then type "cmd" in the Start menu search box to access a terminal). Make sure that you are working in the same directory as the one where you installed the tool, and also make sure that any images you want to examine are also in that same directory. To quickly see metadata for a single digital image, simply type "exiftool image.JPG", replacing "image.JPG" with your file name and type. You should see all of the image's available metadata, including geographic coordinates if they are included in the EXIF file (Figure 8.14).

```
C:\Windows\system32\cmd.exe                                          _ □ X

GPS Date Stamp             : 2015:03:27
Compression                : JPEG (old-style)
Thumbnail Offset           : 1172
Thumbnail Length           : 5580
XMP Toolkit                : XMP Core 5.1.2
Image Width                : 4320
Image Height               : 2432
Encoding Process           : Baseline DCT, Huffman coding
Bits Per Sample            : 8
Color Components           : 3
Y Cb Cr Sub Sampling       : YCbCr4:2:0 (2 2)
Aperture                   : 2.4
GPS Altitude               : 0 m Above Sea Level
GPS Date/Time              : 2015:03:27 14:00:12Z
GPS Latitude               : 35 deg 36' 34.78" N
GPS Longitude              : 82 deg 26' 33.28" W
GPS Position               : 35 deg 36' 34.78" N, 82 deg 26' 33.28" W
Image Size                 : 4320x2432
Megapixels                 : 10.5
Shutter Speed              : 1/58
Thumbnail Image            : (Binary data 5580 bytes, use -b option to e
act)
Focal Length               : 4.5 mm
Light Value                : 6.4

C:\Users\Default User.WWCXXXXX\Downloads\exiftool-9.90>
```

FIGURE 8.14 An image's available metadata, including geographic coordinates

EXIFTool also supports batch file processing, so you can quickly access metadata for multiple files at the same time. Simply place all the images you want to process into a directory, make sure it is in your exiftool directory, and run the `exiftool` command on the directory just as you did on the single image. For example, to access the metadata for a set of images in the directory named "Images," you would run `exiftool Images`. Metadata for all of the images in the directory will be included in the output.

While the examples above demonstrate the use of EXIFTool for extracting metadata from a digital JPG image, the tool works across a wide variety of digital file types, including audio and video. A list of supported file types can be found on the website where you downloaded the tool.

(Continued)

EXIFTool can also be used to manually add geodata to a digital file or batch of files. In the example in Figure 8.15, a PDF map of Asheville, North Carolina has been downloaded from the web. Running EXIFTool, we see that there are no geographic metadata included in the file.

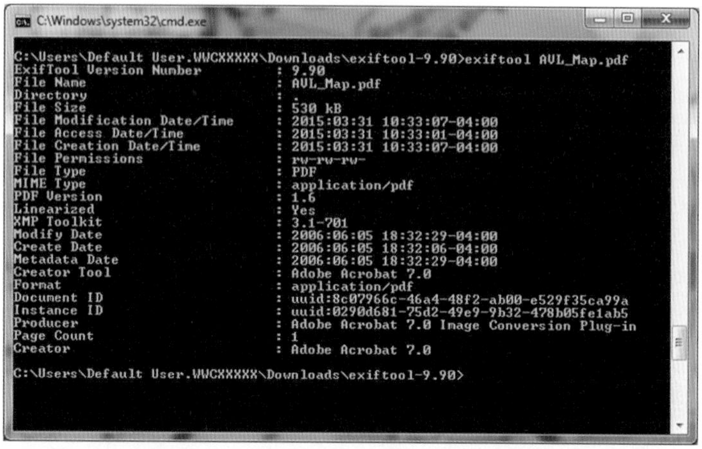

```
C:\Windows\system32\cmd.exe
C:\Users\Default User.WWCXXXXX\Downloads\exiftool-9.90>exiftool AVL_Map.pdf
ExifTool Version Number         : 9.90
File Name                       : AVL_Map.pdf
Directory                       : .
File Size                       : 530 kB
File Modification Date/Time     : 2015:03:31 10:33:07-04:00
File Access Date/Time           : 2015:03:31 10:33:01-04:00
File Creation Date/Time         : 2015:03:31 10:33:07-04:00
File Permissions                : rw-rw-rw-
File Type                       : PDF
MIME Type                       : application/pdf
PDF Version                     : 1.6
Linearized                      : Yes
XMP Toolkit                     : 3.1-701
Modify Date                     : 2006:06:05 18:32:29-04:00
Create Date                     : 2006:06:05 18:32:06-04:00
Metadata Date                   : 2006:06:05 18:32:29-04:00
Creator Tool                    : Adobe Acrobat 7.0
Format                          : application/pdf
Document ID                     : uuid:8c07966c-46a4-48f2-ab00-e529f35ca99a
Instance ID                     : uuid:0290d681-75d2-49e9-9b32-478b05fe1ab5
Producer                        : Adobe Acrobat 7.0 Image Conversion Plug-in
Page Count                      : 1
Creator                         : Adobe Acrobat 7.0

C:\Users\Default User.WWCXXXXX\Downloads\exiftool-9.90>
```

FIGURE 8.15 An image without geographic metadata

We can add the latitude and longitude of Asheville to the file with the following command:

```
exiftool -GPSLongitudeRef=E -GPSLongitude=-82.565 -
GPSLatitudeRef=N -GPSLatitudeRef=35.538 AVL_Map.pdf
```

When we now run the `exiftool` command again, we see the geographic coordinate information included in the metadata (Figure 8.16)

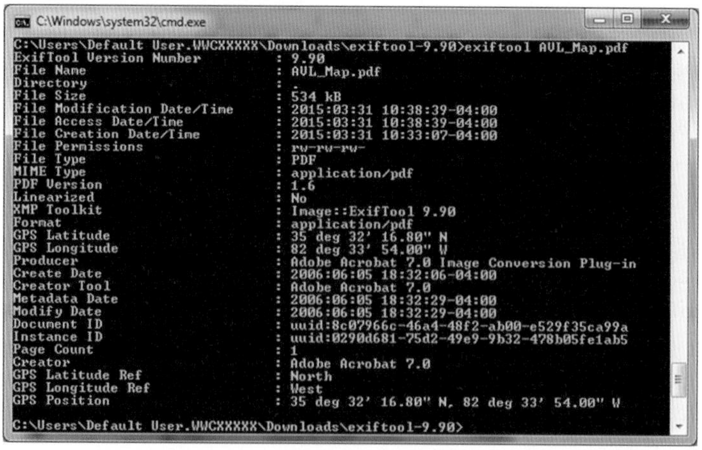

```
C:\Windows\system32\cmd.exe
C:\Users\Default User.WWCXXXXX\Downloads\exiftool-9.90>exiftool AVL_Map.pdf
ExifTool Version Number         : 9.90
File Name                       : AVL_Map.pdf
Directory                       : .
File Size                       : 534 kB
File Modification Date/Time     : 2015:03:31 10:38:39-04:00
File Access Date/Time           : 2015:03:31 10:38:39-04:00
File Creation Date/Time         : 2015:03:31 10:33:07-04:00
File Permissions                : rw-rw-rw-
File Type                       : PDF
MIME Type                       : application/pdf
PDF Version                     : 1.6
Linearized                      : No
XMP Toolkit                     : Image::ExifTool 9.90
Format                          : application/pdf
GPS Latitude                    : 35 deg 32' 16.80" N
GPS Longitude                   : 82 deg 33' 54.00" W
Producer                        : Adobe Acrobat 7.0 Image Conversion Plug-in
Create Date                     : 2006:06:05 18:32:06-04:00
Creator Tool                    : Adobe Acrobat 7.0
Metadata Date                   : 2006:06:05 18:32:29-04:00
Modify Date                     : 2006:06:05 18:32:29-04:00
Document ID                     : uuid:8c07966c-46a4-48f2-ab00-e529f35ca99a
Instance ID                     : uuid:0290d681-75d2-49e9-9b32-478b05fe1ab5
Page Count                      : 1
Creator                         : Adobe Acrobat 7.0
GPS Latitude Ref                : North
GPS Longitude Ref               : West
GPS Position                    : 35 deg 32' 16.80" N, 82 deg 33' 54.00" W

C:\Users\Default User.WWCXXXXX\Downloads\exiftool-9.90>
```

FIGURE 8.16 The image metadata of Figure 8.15, but now with geographic coordinate information included

Note that EXIFTool also created a file with the _original suffix that preserves your original file. As with the `exiftool` command, you can quickly geotag a batch of images by running the above code on a directory instead of a single file.

EXIFTool can also be used to remove all metadata from digital files. Since many mobile devices can automatically geotag digital files, such as photographs taken with the camera on a mobile phone, EXIFTool is often used to strip out geographic metadata by those preferring not to share location information when sharing files.

On the other hand, there are many cases where mapping digital files is purposeful and quite useful. Several crowdsourced mapping applications allow users to upload digital images or sounds and manually geotag them. Panoramio, for example, is a photo-sharing website that allows users to upload and geotag photos to Google Maps and Google Earth. Other applications, such as The Sound Around You project begun at the University of Salford, allow users to upload and geotag audio files to help create sound maps. As digital applications such as Meerkat, StoryCorps, and Twitter's Periscope make it even easier to capture the sounds and images of the world around us, we will continue to see new crowdsourced geotagging projects emerge.

GEOPARSING

The final approach to capturing geodata we will examine is geoparsing. As mentioned earlier in this chapter, geoparsing refers to the extraction of geographic information from unstructured text, the interpretation of that information in terms of geographic location, and the subsequent formatting of that information into structured geodata. A great deal of the textual information we generate each day, from books to news articles to blog posts, comes in an unstructured format; geoparsing tools can help us uncover the spatial dimensions of unstructured data and convert them to something more useful for further analysis and visualization.

The process of linking location information with text is part of a larger effort to categorize and structure text known as named entity extraction. Named entity extraction might be used to identify the names of individuals or organizations in a text, or specific dates, or some other type of categorical information of interest. This requires two distinct computational steps: the detection of words that potentially meet the specified criteria, and the classification of those words based on a predetermined set of possibilities.

Extracting such categorical information from text is a fairly easy activity for adults, but can be quite a difficult task for computers. This is because we categorize specific terms based on their context, which is a more nuanced task than simply categorizing a single word. If we see the number '2000' in a text we cannot tell if it is a date or simply an amount without looking at the words around it. Entity extraction algorithms must do the same thing. They flag words that seem to have the potential for meeting the extraction criteria, then further analyze those words to see if they seem to be a good enough fit.

Geoparsing tools, then, often look for clues that signify place or location, regardless of whether or not those words match a preconstructed gazetteer of place names. Words or phrases like "near," or "traveling to," or "hometown" might signify that a nearby word is a potential place name. That word can then be flagged and compared to an existing list of place names that includes associated geodata. Then the geoparser must undertake another round of disambiguation, since many places share common names. If "Greenville" is identified as a place name, for example, the geoparser might compare this to other identified locations in the text to see if this common place name can be further narrowed to a specific location. The final step the geoparsing tool takes is to then assign geographic coordinates to the place name.

As you might imagine, this is an inexact process and geoparsers often return incorrect results. But geoparsing algorithms are constantly being improved, and given the value of being able to accurately extract location information from unstructured text, there are companies devoting a lot of time and effort to developing geoparsing products to sell. In the examples below, however, we will look at two geoparsing tools that are free and easy to use.

Exercise 6: Extract geodata from text using CLAVIN

One free and open source tool for geoparsing is the Cartographic Location and Vicinity Indexer (CLAVIN). This tool combines the open source Named Entity Recognizer developed by Stanford University and the GeoNames gazetteer, adding its own algorithms for resolving place name ambiguities. The source code and an online demo are available at clavin.bericotechnologies.com.

To test out the code with the online demo, go to clavin.berico.us/clavin-web/ and paste some text into the text window. To see an example of how CLAVIN uses contextual clues to determine place location, let us enter "Washington" in the text box (Figure 8.17) and click on "Resolve Locations."

FIGURE 8.17 Cartographic Location and Vicinity Indexer (CLAVIN) © Berico Technologies

CLAVIN returns a map and the geographic coordinates of 47.50012, −120.50147, which is the coordinate pair assigned to the US state of Washington in the GeoNames gazetteer. However, if we type "Washington, Smithsonian" into CLAVIN we get a different result (Figure 8.18).

FIGURE 8.18 A CLAVIN search for "Washington" and "Smithsonian" © Berico Technologies

CLAVIN now returns the coordinates for Washington, DC, based on the context provided by the word "Smithsonian."

Exercise 7: Ad hoc search using Frankenplace

Another interesting tool that attempts to provide structure to unstructured text is Frankenplace.com (Adams et al., 2015). This site analyzes text input and attempts to produce heatmaps of the text based on where it is most likely to appear. At the time this chapter was being written, Frankenplace drew from 1.6 million articles from the English-language version of Wikipedia and a collection of online travel blogs. More data sources are planned to be included in the future.

Frankenplace acts as a geoparser of sorts, though instead of providing structured geodata on unstructured place names it attempts to provide a structured set of document returns that are associated with places. For example, if we navigate to Frankenplace.com and enter the place name of "Chile" into the search box, we get a heatmap that is probably not all that surprising (Figure 8.19).

Now let us zoom in closer to Chile to get a better look. Click on an area near the capital city of Santiago. You now see a few Wikipedia and travel blog entries on the right (Figure 8.20).

(Continued)

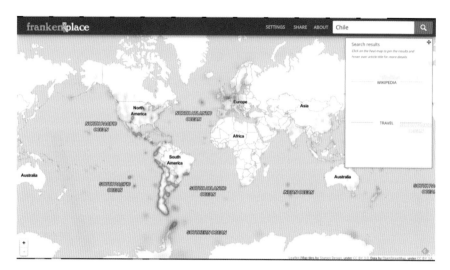

FIGURE 8.19 Search for "Chile" in Frankenplace.com © Frankenplace

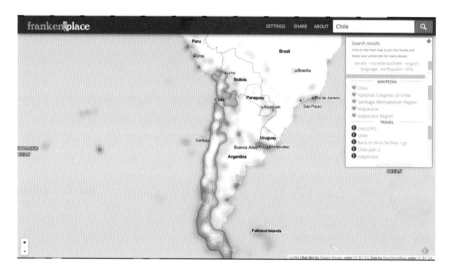

FIGURE 8.20 Zoomed-in look at Chile with Wikipedia and travel blog entries
© Frankenplace

Hovering over those article entries will give you a preview pane of the document. You can also click on "Settings" to move a slider closer to either Wikipedia or travel blogs.

Frankenplace does more than attempt to connect documents with specific place names – it can also be used as a tool to connect key terms or phrases to locations on a map. For example, we can enter a phrase like "Arab Spring" into the search bar without including any specific place names, and the resulting heatmap looks like the one in Figure 8.21.

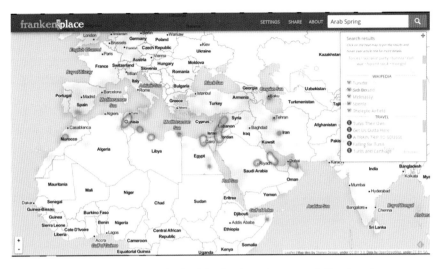

FIGURE 8.21   Search for "Arab Spring" in Frankenplace.com © Frankenplace

Frankenplace is one example of the sorts of tools that are being developed to provide a layer of geographical structure and organization to data that historically have not had such structure. While much of today's information is digitally produced, often with geo-data automatically created and embedded as metadata tags, the vast amount of information produced prior to the digital age is much more difficult to organize geographically. Yet new digital tools are providing us with new abilities to do just that, and opening up new avenues of research and new ways of understanding information in the process. One tool that allows us to read texts in a new way by combining the power of geoparsing and geotagging is GapVis.

Exercise 8: Exploring GapVis

GapVis is a beta software project being produced as part of the Google Ancient Places project. As described in the project overview, GapVis is a digital interface for exploring texts that reference ancient places and accessing those places with visualization tools. You can read more about the project and access a link to the site at googleancientplaces.wordpress.com/gapvis.

The GapVis interface allows you to select one of the listed texts, learn more about the ancient places referenced in that text, and then move back and forth between a map and the text itself. For example, we can select Livy's *The History of Rome* (in an edition published in 1797) from the list of accessible texts, and a page with a map and a list of most-referenced places is returned (Figure 8.22).

(Continued)

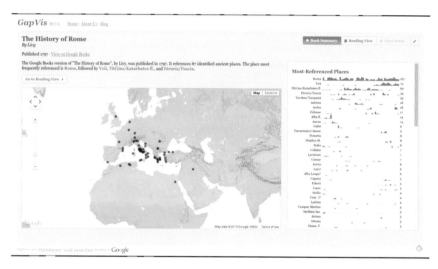

FIGURE 8.22   Search results for Livy's The History of Rome in GapVis © Nick Rabinowitz

We can now interact with those places by zooming in on the map, accessing the "Reading View" to see those places in the text itself, and learn more about how places interact in the text by clicking on individual place names. If we click on the place most frequently referred to in this text, Roma, we get a detailed view of Rome's location, its connection to other places in the text, and a collection of photos associated with Rome from the photo hosting site Flickr. In the Reading View we can even animate the text's timeline so that we can see places appear on the map as they arise in the text.

While limited in scope, GapVis provides one example of a digital tool that attempts to connect spatial information to places written about long before our current global system of classifying geographic information was developed. We will undoubtedly see new and better tools arise as our abilities to geoparse unstructured text improve.

Chapter summary

This chapter has explored ways to add spatial structure to unstructured data so that such data can be more systematically examined with digital tools. The three main approaches we have covered – geocoding, geotagging, and geoparsing – all help us make more geographic sense out of information and often help us create structured datasets that can be used with additional software tools for analysis and visualization.

We have seen, however, that no approach to adding geographic information to unstructured data is completely effective or reliable. While there are some increasingly powerful tools for each of the approaches we have examined, we must always anticipate coding errors and incomplete results. In short, creating structured geodata can be often be a difficult task. Even data created in the digital age, particularly when privacy issues are of concern, can be difficult to structure spatially.

On the other hand, some individuals are increasingly willing to volunteer their location information along with all sorts of other data that are openly shared. The rapid rise of social media tools, combined with the increase in mobile communications devices, has led to a whole new era of volunteered geographic information. The following chapter addresses the increasing volume of geodata being generated via social media and explores some tools for capturing such data.

Further reading

Hill, L.L. (2006) *Georeferencing: The Geographic Associations of Information.* Cambridge, MA: MIT Press.

COMPANION WEBSITE

Visit https://study.sagepub.co/abernathy for:

- Links to the websites and free software packages discussed in this chapter
- Downloadable versions of all datasets presented in this chapter

9

Social Media Geodata

Capturing Location-Based Twitter Data

 **Overview**

This chapter includes:

- Twitter 101, and the anatomy of a tweet
- Exercise 1: Basic queries using the Twitter Search API via the web interface
- Exercise 2: Using TAGS for querying and storing Twitter search results
- Exercise 3: Using the R programming language for accessing Twitter data

Twitter, the microblogging service that allows users to send short messages to groups of online "followers," exploded in popularity at the South by Southwest Interactive Festival in 2007. Attendees of the festival used the service to keep up with each other and comment on the various events taking place, while the founders of Twitter posted televisions throughout the festival venues that streamed live "tweets." While some ridiculed the service as merely a platform for posting trivial, pointless information, Twitter won the festival's Web Award and gained momentum as an important new tool for digital communication across social networks.

A year later, in November 2008, ten Islamic militants carried out a series of coordinated bombing and shooting attacks in Mumbai, India. Well before the news media could organize and deploy to cover the attacks, Twitter users were posting news and information throughout the city. Hashtags had caught on as a way for Twitter users to track information on specific topics without having to follow those posting that information, and #mumbai quickly emerged as a way for Twitter users to track news about the attacks as they unfolded in real time. While Twitter at the time did not have a tool for capturing geolocation, users nevertheless could communicate about the location of events by describing where they were and what they saw. Those following the Twitter feed online began piecing together a web map of events and constructing a dedicated Wikipedia page. The ability to quickly gather and share information in real time across a decentralized network was recognized as an important development in digital communication, and would soon be seen again during the 2009 Iranian presidential election protests, the 2010 Haiti earthquake, and the uprisings of Occupy Wall Street and the Arab Spring.

Yet this powerful new communication tool also had its downsides. The immediate and unfiltered nature of Twitter meant that news could not be verified, and many of the tweets during the chaotic first hours of the Mumbai attacks contained misinformation. In addition, the terrorists themselves were rumored to have followed events on Twitter, and the Indian government reportedly asked Twitter users to stop posting information about the events so that police actions would not be disclosed. When the tools for digital communication are ubiquitous, and when every consumer of information can also be a producer, the old rules for the dissemination of news do not apply.

Geolocation provides another double-edged sword for Twitter data. On the one hand, there are myriad examples of how the ability to geolocate tweets proves invaluable, whether it be responding to a natural disaster, conducting a sentiment analysis of a consumer brand across a region, or mapping out the location of respondents to a Twitter poll. On the other hand, revealing one's location via Twitter brings to mind issues of privacy and surveillance as discussed in Chapter 5. Recognizing this, Twitter provides tools for geolocation of tweets but gives users control over whether or not they would like to share their specific latitude and longitude coordinates, and most tweets do not contain coordinate data. That said, the Twitter API provides access to a large database of places and powerful geocoding tools, meaning that coordinate data can quite often be generated for tweets.

In this chapter we will explore ways to collect public Twitter data and organize them spatially. First, we will examine the basic search functions that can be employed directly from the Twitter web interface, allowing us to explore what people are saying *about* places and what they are saying *from* those places. Next, we will turn to a free script for Google Sheets that provides some useful tools for collecting and organizing tweets based on queries to the Twitter Search API. Here we will search for tweets that specifically include latitude and longitude data, use the Twitter geocoding tools to search for tweets within a specified radius of a particular coordinate, and then see how we can quickly make a basic map of our collected tweets using Google Fusion Tables. Finally, we will turn to the very powerful open source programming language of R to examine some of the free packages available for working with Twitter data. While you must always use caution when trying to geolocate Twitter data, the examples below will hopefully introduce you to some of the ways we can glean useful information when we organize volunteered social media geographically.

Before we jump into the exercises, however, it is worth spending a few moments going over some of the basic functions of Twitter and the structural components of an individual tweet. If you have not used Twitter or have only used it via the web interface or on a mobile application, you have only seen some of the data created each time a tweet is posted to the network. A quick peek under the hood will help you understand a bit more about the data flowing across the service and how we can harness a small amount of that data with the tools covered in the exercises.

TWITTER 101, AND THE ANATOMY OF A TWEET

As mentioned in the introduction above, Twitter has gained enormous popularity as a new communication medium since it first caught on in 2007. Designed as a social communication tool that would allow users to share information through the standard communications protocols of SMS (short message service, widely used for sending text messages via mobile devices), Twitter required that individual messages, or "tweets," be no more than 140 characters in length. Subsequent versions of the application allowed users to include photos and web URLs in their tweets, and other advancements such as URL shorteners allowed Twitter users to maximize the amount of information that could be included within the constraints of the character limit.

Twitter's utility as a "microblogging" tool was a great fit for the emerging era of mobile computing, as it allowed users to quickly and easily send short bursts of information from a mobile device and follow each other's activities while on the go – the ambient intimacy mentioned in Chapter 1. Additionally, Twitter did not require users to follow back those who followed them (unlike Facebook at the time), meaning that the application could also be used to follow celebrities and other famous people, and popular Twitter users soon found that the tool was an effective channel of communication.

Yet it was the emergence of the hashtag that arguably propelled Twitter from a mere social communication tool to a "cultural barometer" of sorts. Hashtags allow users to add the '#' symbol to words or phrases that can then be tracked and monitored by Twitter users everywhere without those users having to follow those creating the posts. The use of the hashtag to denote special characters or meaning pre-dates Twitter, but it was Twitter that gave it its prominence and global recognition, and the word was added to the *Oxford English Dictionary* in 2014. Key world events today quickly give rise to a hashtag or set of hashtags that allow those events to be followed as they unfold, as in the #mumbai example above; other well-known examples include #OccupyWallStreet and #ArabSpring. Twitter monitors the most popular hashtags at any given moment and provides lists of "trending topics" worldwide and by various geographic regions. When coupled with Twitter's geocoding services, hashtagged tweets provide a rich dataset that we can tap into spatially, as we will see in the exercises below.

Twitter has a rich API that provides multiple ways for a user to access the service. Most users access Twitter with a mobile application, commonly referred to as a Twitter client

(Twitter has its own, but there are also many other varieties, including Fenix, Seesmic, Hootsuite, and TweetDeck), or via a web browser. These interfaces provide users with a view of several important components of individual tweets, including the author's username, approximate time posted, and the contents of the post including any pictures and URLs. A search for "global" on Twitter's web interface in June 2015 provided the image in Figure 9.1, which also includes information on trending topics and popular Twitter users to follow.

FIGURE 9.1 Twitter search results for "global" © Twitter, Inc.

Individual tweets contain much more information than typically provided in client inter-faces, however. Additional information that is normally hidden in Twitter clients can be gleaned when we use other tools for capturing Twitter data. The number of followers a tweet's author has, the number of times a tweet has been "retweeted" and "favorited," an author's listed hometown and short biography, the language spoken, and much more can be uncovered in Twitter data. Crucially, tweets may also contain various forms of geodata, from time zone to hometown to specific latitude and longitude coordinates recorded from GPS. If a tweet contains coordinate data, for example, it will include a piece of code like this:

```
"coordinates":
{
        "coordinates":
        [
            -75.14310264,
            40.05701649
        ],
        "type":"Point"
}
```

It is this particular set of data that we want to capture in order to incorporate Twitter into our work with the geoweb. For more on the Twitter API and a "field guide" to tweets, see https://dev.twitter.com/overview/api/tweets.

Exercise 1: Basic queries using the Twitter Search API via the web interface

We will begin our exploration of Twitter data as geodata by conducting some simple searches directly from the Twitter web interface. The simplest search operators allow us to examine recent tweets that include place names as part of the text. In a web browser, navigate to www.twitter.com/search and enter a place name and examine the tweets that Twitter returns. If you are not logged in to a user account, Twitter will return two categories of search results: "top" and "all." "Top" tweets are those that Twitter deems most influential based on the number of retweets, favorites, and size of follower base. "All" tweets provides a list of some of the most recent tweets that include your chosen search term. If you are logged in to a user account your search can be organized and filtered in additional ways; you can search for user accounts containing your search term, or only tweets containing photos, and more. In every case, however, you will note that you only receive a relatively small number of tweets returned on your search.

You may notice that many of the tweets returned in your search are not relevant to the actual place you searched. Entering the term "Panama" into the Twitter search bar in hopes of seeing some tweets from Central America, for example, instead returns tweets that are about a recent musical performance by the rock band Van Halen and an invitation to follow another music group with the username @panamatheband (Figure 9.2).

FIGURE 9.2 Twitter search results for "Panama" © Twitter, Inc.

Switching from "top" tweets to "all" tweets provides a somewhat better return, but there are still several tweets about music as well as some tweets about Panama City, Florida. In order to narrow our search results to the actual country of Panama, we can employ the geocoding features built into the Twitter API.

One way to geographically filter your Twitter search is by including the "near:" parameter in your search request. Entering the search "Panama near:Panama" returns a different collection of tweets than does "Panama near:Florida," since Twitter recognizes most place names that you would find in a gazetteer like GeoNames. Note that Twitter has an advanced search that also lets you search according to location, as well as providing additional tools for narrowing your search according to language, date ranges, specific user accounts, and more (Figure 9.3).

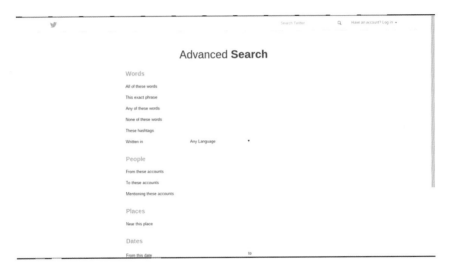

FIGURE 9.3   Twitter Advanced Search © Twitter, Inc.

The Twitter API also lets you search tweets by entering a pair of geographic coordinates and a search radius. A quick visit to findlatitudeandlongitude.com provides a coordinate pair that can be entered for Panama City, Panama. To search for tweets within a 15-kilometer radius of that location, enter the following search:

```
Panama geocode:8.952451,-79.536074,15km
```

The returned tweets should now be much more associated with the desired geographic location than those where the only search parameter is a place name. Be sure to include no spaces in the geocode search phrase, otherwise the geocode data will be searched as individual terms.

Several third-party applications and websites take advantage of the geocoding tools in the Twitter API to provide added geographic functionality to Twitter data. Websites such as trendsmap.com provide a web mapping interface to geolocated Twitter data, though functionality can be limited without a subscription or registered account. Entering "Panama" into the trendsmap.com search bar quickly returns multiple locations so that returned tweets can be focused on the geographic region of interest (Figure 9.4).

(Continued)

FIGURE 9.4   Trendsmap search results for "Panama" © Trendsmap Pty Ltd.

Other sites are geared more towards alerting users that their Twitter activity can be tracked and mapped, often with much greater specificity than one might suspect. A website called "Please Rob Me" gained notoriety in 2010 when it used the geodata embedded in tweets to show how Twitter users were broadcasting their locations. Similarly, the site geosocialfootprint.com allows a Twitter user to enter a username and see what geodata can quickly be accessed and mapped from that account, all in the name of educating users about the location intelligence that can be accessed from public Twitter data.

Privacy issues are certainly a concern, as was discussed in Chapter 5. But given the importance of Twitter as a real-time communication system with millions of users, the ability to geographically capture and organize Twitter data also provides us with powerful new ways to ask questions about the social world around us. This book certainly does not advocate invasions of privacy or the location intelligence tracking of individuals, but rather seeks to examine ways to organize Twitter data spatially in hopes that by doing so we may gain a better understanding of the geographical nature of our networked society.

The search tools outlined above can help us identify Twitter data relevant to particular places, but the results returned in the Twitter web interface are difficult to work with. Converting the individual tweets into something more organized, like a spreadsheet or database, would be difficult and extremely time-consuming using the web interface alone. Fortunately, there are other tools we can use to help gather Twitter data in a more structured and useful way. These tools also give us additional geocoding functionality so that we can further examine the spatial patterns of Twitter data. The next tool, called TAGS, provides a script for Google's online spreadsheet program (Google Sheets) that greatly enhances our ability to collect and organize data returned from a Twitter search.

Exercise 2: Using TAGS for querying and storing Twitter search results

The Twitter Archiving Google Spreadsheet (TAGS) is a tool developed by Martin Hawksey for Twitter data collection and visualization. While listed as a "hobby project" on Hawksey's informational page (https://tags.hawksey.info/) about the tool, it nevertheless provides an easy-to-use but powerful means for organizing Twitter search results. Installing the TAGS script for Google Sheets and giving the tool access to a Twitter account allows the user to collect and store an archive of thousands of tweets on a given search term. The resulting spreadsheet can then be further analyzed with additional tools in Google's suite of applications (like Google Fusion Tables) or exported as a structured file that can be incorporated into other tools much more easily than the more unstructured search results found directly on the Twitter web interface.

To begin using TAGS, you must first have an active Google account and access to the Google Sheets online spreadsheet software. If you do not yet have access to Google Sheets, you can get started at www.google.com/sheets/about/. The next step is to get a copy of the TAGS spreadsheet and make a copy for your own use. Navigate to tags.hawksey.info/get-tags/ and click on the "TAGS (New Sheets)" button to open the tool in Google Sheets. Then in Google Sheets, select **File** > **Make a copy** to save your own version of TAGS in your Google Drive.

Now that you have your own copy of the TAGS spreadsheet, you can customize your menu so that you have access to the various TAGS tools. In the Instructions section of your TAGS sheet, click on "Enable

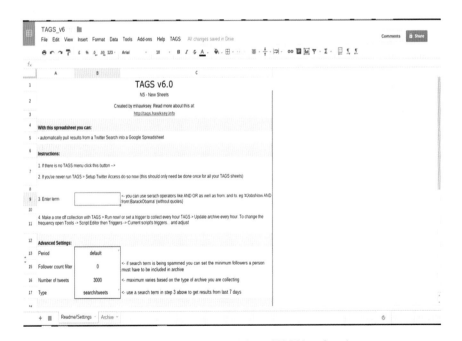

FIGURE 9.5 Twitter Archiving Google Spreadsheet (TAGS) © Google

(Continued)

129

custom menu." You should get a prompt saying that authorization is required to continue. Select "Continue," then click on "Allow." You should now see a "TAGS" menu item at the top of your Google Sheet, right next to the "Help" dropdown menu (Figure 9.5). You should also see two tabs at the bottom of your screen representing two separate spreadsheets. The first tab is the "Readme/Settings" sheet (the one that should currently be open on your screen) and the second tab is the "Archive" sheet. The first sheet provides some tools for setting up and tailoring your Twitter search to your needs, and the second sheet is the repository for the set of tweets gathered when you run a search.

Before you can begin running searches, you will need to link TAGS with your Twitter account. To do this you will need to set up a new Twitter application and authorize TAGS to access your existing Twitter account. To begin, click on the "TAGS" dropdown menu in your spreadsheet, then select "Setup Twitter Access" to begin linking your Twitter account to TAGS. You will need to register for a Twitter API key by following the link provided. You will then be prompted to enter your name, a brief description of your application, and a URL (or placeholder), and agree to the Twitter Developer Agreement. Click on "Create your Twitter application" to complete the process. (*Note*. This assumes you already have set up a working Twitter account. If you do not yet have a Twitter account or would like to create a new one, go to twitter. com and click on "Get Started.")

You should now see a Twitter application management page that shows the settings for your new application. Select "Keys and Access Tokens" to see both your Consumer Key (API Key) and your Consumer Secret (API Secret). Copy and paste both of these keys into the appropriate boxes back in your TAGS sheet and click on "Next." Click on "Next" again to authorize your app with Twitter.

You can now enter search terms into TAGS and collect Twitter data. Let us try a basic search to see how TAGS operates. In the search box on the Readme/Settings sheet, enter the word "Olympics." We will keep the default settings as they are in the "Advanced Settings" section for now, but note that you can change some parameters on your search, including setting TAGS to collect tweets every hour for a specified duration. Under the TAGS dropdown menu at the top of your spreadsheet, select "Run Now!" to run the TAGS script and begin capturing Twitter data. Click on the "Archive" tab and watch as your spreadsheet is populated with data (this might take a few minutes).

Depending on the level of Twitter activity at the time of your search, you should now have a large collection of tweets, one for each row of your Archive spreadsheet (Figure 9.6). Take a minute to examine the different column headings to see what data you have collected. Note that in addition to the username and text of each tweet, you have information on the day and time each tweet was posted, the preferred language and number of followers of each poster, a URL for profile photos, and more. Also note that there is a column marked "geo_coordinates," but that this column is largely blank. That is because TAGS only labels those accounts whose users have explicitly authorized Twitter to capture latitude and longitude data for tweets. Since this is a feature of Twitter that requires users to opt in, the vast majority of Twitter users do not have this feature activated.

In order to capture more geographic data on a set of Twitter data, we will need to include the "geocode" search parameter that we used back on the Twitter website. This allows us to access Twitter's geocoding tools so that we can hopefully identify meaningful location data on tweets posted by users who have not activated location services. Let us conduct another search in TAGS that includes the geocode parameter to see if we can improve upon our ability to capture geodata.

First, remove the archive of data you collected on your previous search. Under the TAGS dropdown menu, choose "Wipe Archive Sheet." Now back in your TAGS search box, enter a search term along with the required geocoding parameters of latitude, longitude, and radius. Remember to have no spaces in your

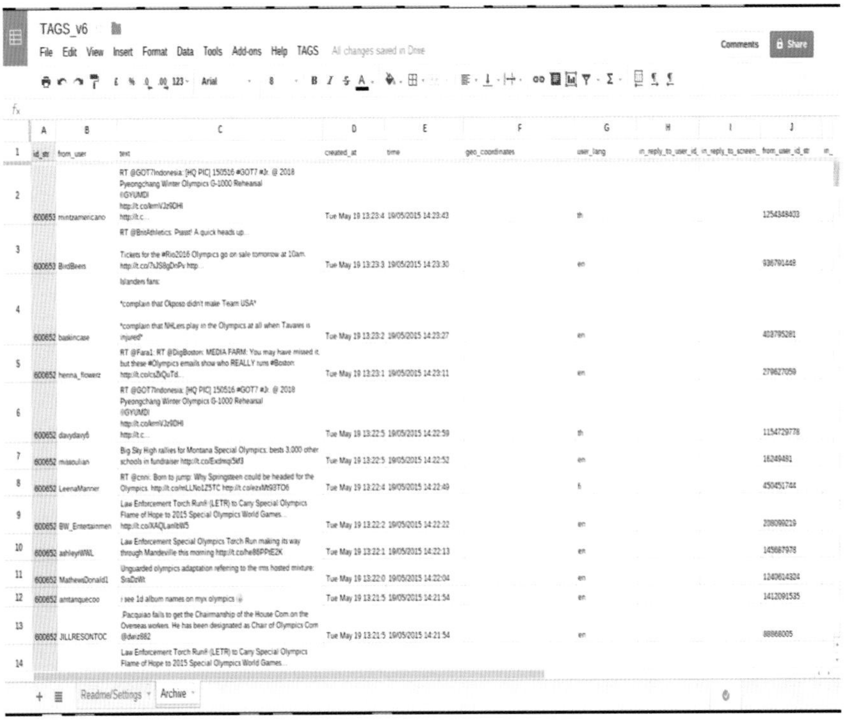

FIGURE 9.6 TAGS spreadsheet showing a large collection of tweets © Google

geocode line, but do include a space between your search term and your geocode parameter. For example, you could enter something like this in your search:

```
Nepal geocode:27.754732,85.274319,1000mi
```

As we saw in our web-based example in Exercise 1, this line will attempt to identify recent tweets posted within a 1000 mile radius of Nepal. In addition to looking for explicit latitude and longitude coordinates embedded in tweets, the Twitter geocoder will also look for place names and other clues to attempt to provide coordinate data for as many results as possible. After running the TAGS script on this search, we can see that the resulting archive includes location data for many (but certainly not all) of the tweets returned (Figure 9.7).

In this example approximately 700 of the almost 3000 returned tweets included location data. (*Note.* At the time these searches were run, Twitter was undergoing a shift in its search API, so your results may vary.)

Your spreadsheet can now be exported for use in another application, such as a GIS (see Chapters 11–13). But you can also make a quick visualization of your dataset by importing it into Google Fusion Tables and creating a map similar to the one we made back in Chapter 7. Let us create a map of the geocoded Twitter data from our "Nepal" search to see what the distribution of tweets looks like.

(Continued)

131

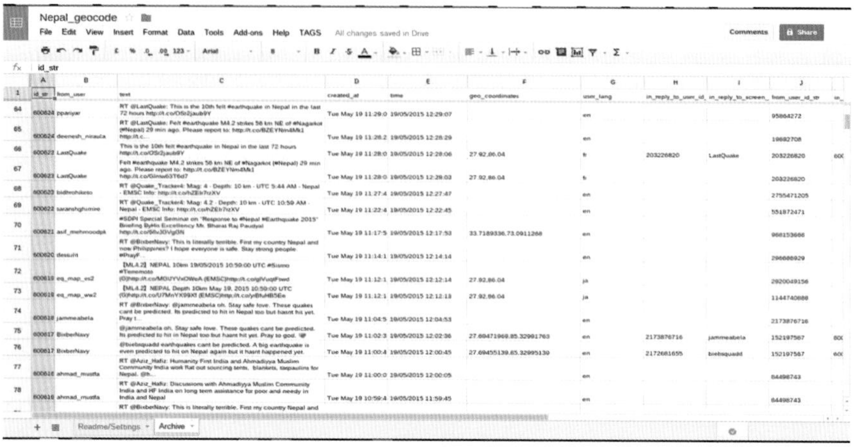

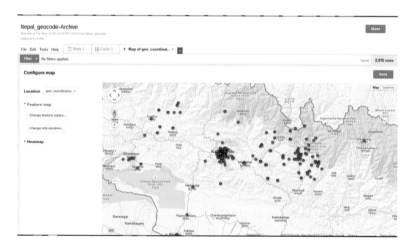

FIGURE 9.7   TAGS spreadsheet showing location data for many of the tweets © Google

Save a copy of the file and give it a name like "Nepal_geocode." Before importing into Fusion Tables, we need to clean up the geolocation column in the spreadsheet so that only the latitude and longitude are included (otherwise the Google geocoder will not be able to read the data in the column). While on the archived data page of your Nepal_geocode spreadsheet, Select "Edit" and then "Find and Replace." In the "Find" box, enter "loc: " and leave the "Replace" box blank. This will remove the "loc: " prefix from our location data so that only coordinate data remain. We can now import the file into Fusion Tables.

In Google Drive, create a new Fusion Table, then choose to import a file from Google Sheets. Follow the prompts until your table is created, then click on the "Map" tab. You should see a map of your geocoded Twitter data (Figure 9.8). This search was conducted not long after the major earthquakes in Nepal, so there is a cluster of tweets around Kathmandu. Clicking on any point on the map brings up the associated tweet.

FIGURE 9.8   Map of geocoded Twitter data © Google

TAGS also includes a couple of experimental visualization tools you can use to explore your dataset: TAGSExplorer and TAGS Archive. Toward the bottom of your Readme/Settings sheet you will see a "Make Interactive" section that provides links to the two tools. Clicking on the TAGSExplorer link will take you to a visualization of your search results that includes each individual tweet and connections between users. You can also select one of the dropdown menus to quickly graph the top users and most popular hashtags (Figure 9.9). The top hashtag for the Nepal data, for example, is #earthquake.

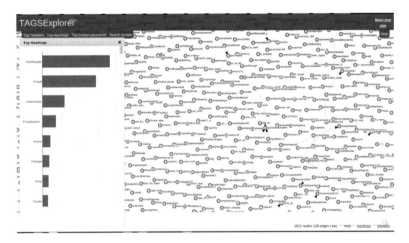

FIGURE 9.9 TAGSExplorer visualization of search results © Google

The TAGS Archive link takes you to a new web page that lists your search results in a format similar to the Twitter web interface, but includes some additional search functionality that allows you to search your data by tweet, username, or a plotted timeline.

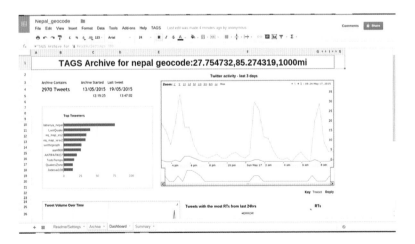

FIGURE 9.10 TAGS Archive summary graph © Google

(Continued)

You can also obtain some summary information by adding two additional tabs from the TAGS dropdown menu. Choose **TAGS** > **Add Summary Sheet** to get some summary data on your dataset, and choose **TAGS** > **Add Dashboard** to get some summary graphs (Figure 9.10).

The TAGS script for Google Sheets taps into the Twitter API to provide a useful tool for searching and organizing Twitter data. Power users can examine the source script and make changes or add new functionality (select **Tools** >**Script Editor** to see Martin Hawksey's script).

TAGS is only one of a number of ways to access the Twitter API and collect data. Another tool that is rapidly gaining popularity in the world of data science is the R programming language. While it has a steeper learning curve than a ready-made script for Google Sheets, the flexibility and power of R make it an extremely useful tool for analyzing and visualizing data. In the next exercise, we will explore two specific packages for R that can be used for capturing Twitter data. For those not working inside the Google ecosystem or those who just want more control over their software tools, R is an excellent tool to add to your geoweb toolkit.

Exercise 3: Using the R programming language for accessing Twitter data

While many consider it to be software for statistical analysis, R is actually a robust programming language that is suitable for a wide range of computational tasks. An implementation of the S language developed at Bell Laboratories, R is a free and open source software environment that emerged in the late 1990s and has grown to become one of the most popular programming languages for data science and analysis today. One of the key strengths of R is that it is *extensible* – users can create and submit individual packages that can be downloaded and implemented in R to take on specialized problems or provide additional data analysis tools. At the time of this writing there were more than 6670 packages available for download on the Comprehensive R Archive Network website (cran.r-project.org). In this exercise we will examine two packages that can be used to collect Twitter data, twitteR and streamR. Additional packages that are useful for mapping and GIS will be introduced in later chapters. Before examining these packages, however, we will first take a brief look at the R programming interface. Additional information on R, including instructions for download and installation, can be found on the companion website.

The R command line

Once R has been downloaded and installed, you can run the software from a terminal by simply entering the letter R at the command line. Doing so should give you something like Figure 9.11.

R commands are written on the command line, or you can string together multiple R commands and save them as a file. Below are some examples of the basic functionality of R to help you get familiar with the command line before we move on to our required packages. This is a very brief overview of the

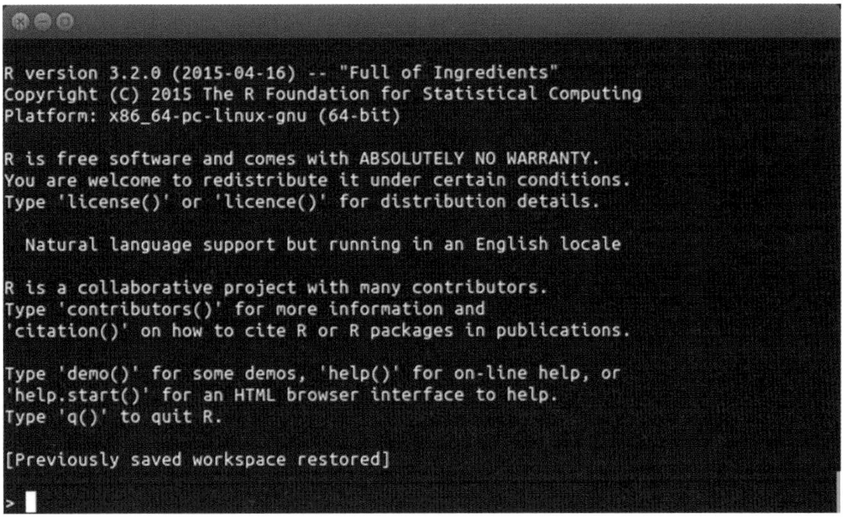

```
R version 3.2.0 (2015-04-16) -- "Full of Ingredients"
Copyright (C) 2015 The R Foundation for Statistical Computing
Platform: x86_64-pc-linux-gnu (64-bit)

R is free software and comes with ABSOLUTELY NO WARRANTY.
You are welcome to redistribute it under certain conditions.
Type 'license()' or 'licence()' for distribution details.

  Natural language support but running in an English locale

R is a collaborative project with many contributors.
Type 'contributors()' for more information and
'citation()' on how to cite R or R packages in publications.

Type 'demo()' for some demos, 'help()' for on-line help, or
'help.start()' for an HTML browser interface to help.
Type 'q()' to quit R.

[Previously saved workspace restored]

>
```

FIGURE 9.11 The R command line © The R Foundation

R command line – for more detailed examples and documentation you should visit the main R website at www.r-cran.org. A good overview and introduction manual can be found at cran.r-project.org/doc/manuals/r-release/R-intro.html.

First, note that you can use R for conducting simple mathematical operations:

```
>  1 + 1
[1]  2

> 10 * 5
[1]  50

> sqrt(64)
[1]  8
```

R also allows you to create *objects*, or data structures, and assign them variable names. A key data structure in R is the numeric *vector*, which is an ordered collection of numbers. The simplest example of a vector assignment is:

```
> x <- 1
>x
[1]1
```

Here we assigned a single numeric value ("1") to x using the <- symbol. (In more recent versions of R you can also use the = symbol, so x = 1 should give you the same result. Nothing happens after you create this

(Continued)

135

object, but if you then type x at the command line you will get [1] 1 as a result. The [1] refers to the first item in your vector, and the 1 after that shows the value assigned to that item. A vector of five numbers, then, might look something like this:

```
> x <- c(1,3,5,7,9,11)
> x
[1]  1  3  5  7  9  11
```

The `c()` command is a function that tells R to concatenate everything within the parentheses into one vector called x. To see the third item in the vector, you can type:

```
> x[3]
[1]  5
```

You can also perform mathematical operations on vectors:

```
> x * 2
[1]  2  6  10  14  18  22

>sum(x)
[1]  36
```

Another important data structure used in R is the *matrix*. To create a matrix, you designate the number of rows and columns for your data. To create a matrix of numbers from 1 to 25 ordered in 5 rows and 5 columns, for example, you can input:

```
> m <- matrix(1:25,5,5)

       [,1]  [,2]  [,3]  [,4]  [,5]
[1,]     1     6    11    16    21
[2,]     2     7    12    17    22
[3,]     3     8    13    18    23
[4,]     4     9    14    19    24
[5,]     5    10    15    20    25
```

Again, we can perform mathematical operations on matrices just as we did with vectors:

```
> m*10

       [,1]  [,2]  [,3]  [,4]  [,5]
[1,]    10    60    110   160   210
[2,]    20    70    120   170   220
[3,]    30    80    130   180   230
```

136

```
[4,]    40   90  140  190  240
[5,]    50  100  150  200  250
```

You can name your columns and rows with the `colnames()` and `rownames()` commands:

```
> colnames(m) <- c("Mon", "Tues", "Wed", "Thurs", "Fri")
> rownames(m) <- c("Bob", "Jim", "Sue", "Ted", "Kim")
> m

    Mon Tues Wed Thurs Fri
Bob   1    6  11    16  21
Jim   2    7  12    17  22
Sue   3    8  13    18  23
Ted   4    9  14    19  24
Kim   5   10  15    20  25
```

To quit your R session, type `q()` at the command line. R will prompt you to save your workspace image, which enables you to keep the objects you have created for a future work session.

This section has given you a very preliminary introduction to the R command line. Next, we will use R to download and install two packages that can be used to collect and store Twitter data: *twitteR* and *streamR*. The twitteR package for R allows users to access Twitter information and retrieve recent tweets, while the streamR package provides the user with the ability to monitor Twitter in more or less real time.

Collecting data with the twitteR package

The twitteR package for R provides much of the same functionality we saw when using TAGS in the previous exercise. Once a connection to Twitter has been established, we can run a search on recent tweets using a search term and any additional parameters, such as a pair of coordinates and a search radius, that we wish to specify. In the example below, we will install the twitteR package, set up the necessary objects in R to establish a connection to Twitter from R, and then run some searches to see what data are returned.

To install the package from R, type the following at the R command prompt:

```
> install.packages("twitteR")
```

R will then prompt you to select a CRAN mirror site from which to download the software. Once you have selected a mirror, R will then download and install the package. To make sure you have correctly installed the package and to make it available for use, type the following:

```
> library(twitteR)
```

If nothing happens, or if additional libraries are loaded but no error message is returned, you are ready to go.

As in the TAGS example in Exercise 2, you must establish a "handshake" to Twitter so that you can authorize twitteR to access data through your Twitter account. Since you already created a Twitter application in the previous exercise, you should have the necessary access information. Navigate to apps.twitter.com and

(Continued)

login to with your Twitter username and you should see the application you developed for the TAGS example. If you do not yet have a Twitter app listed there you can create a new one.

Click on the name of your app to see the details, including an information tab for "Keys and Access Tokens." Click on this tab to see your Consumer Key (API Key) and Consumer Secret (API Secret) codes. You will need these to establish a connection to Twitter from within R.

Further down the page, you will see a section called "Your Access Token." You may not yet have access tokens, so if not go ahead and generate them now. After doing this you should now have two additional codes: an Access Token and an Access Token Secret. We will also use these codes in establishing our Twitter connection.

Returning to the R console, type the following line at the command prompt, replacing the placeholder "yourkeyhere" with your actual codes (but do keep the quotation marks).

```
> setup_twitter_oauth(consumer_key="yourkeyhere",
consumer_secret="yoursecret",access_token="yourtoken",
access_secret="youraccesssecret")
```

If you are able to successfully connect to Twitter, R will return the following:

```
[1] "Using direct authentication"
>
```

You are now connected and are able to use some of the functions built into the twitteR package to gather Twitter data.

First, try conducting a quick search using the `searchTwitter()` function. Simply enter a search term in quotes and the number of tweets you would like returned, as in the following example:

```
> searchTwitter("BBC", n=100)
```

The results from your query will be output directly to the R console, which is rather unwieldy. We will save our search results as an object that we can export as a spreadsheet file shortly, but first let us recall how we can narrow our search results by including a coordinate pair and search radius:

```
> searchTwitter("Asheville geocode:35.55,-82.55,20mi", n=100)
```

To store our search results as an object, you can enter something like:

```
> avl <- searchTwitter("Asheville geocode:35.55,
-82.55,20mi", n=100)
```

Entering `avl` at the prompt will now give you the results from your geocoded search. But this is still messy and difficult to deal with. We can take our results and save them as a *data frame*, which is another data structure used in R. From there we can save the file as a CSV file and open it with a spreadsheet application.

First, convert your data to a data frame by entering the following:

```
> avlDF <- twListToDF(avl)
```

This converts our search results into the structure of a data frame and saves it in the object `avlDF`. Now we can write our data frame to a CSV file with the following command:

```
> write.csv(avlDF, "TestFile.csv")
```

This function takes our data frame and outputs it as a file called "TestFile.csv" in our current working directory (Figure 9.12). You should now be able to open the new CSV file from within a spreadsheet application of choice.

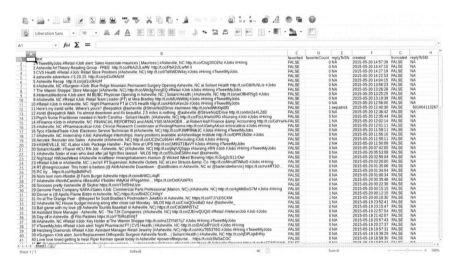

FIGURE 9.12 CSV file showing data collected through the twitteR package

The resulting output looks a lot like the spreadsheets we created with TAGS. Note that each row contains the text of a tweet, information on retweets and favorites, a timestamp, and – crucially for us – latitude and longitude coordinates.

You can also use twitteR to identify what is currently "trending" on Twitter in a specific location by using Yahoo's Where On Earth ID, or *woeid*. You can look at the all of the places around the world that have a woeid by entering the following at the R prompt:

```
> availableTrendLocations()
```

This will return a list directly in the R terminal. You could also save this function to an object, convert it to a data frame and save it as a CSV file as we did above if you would like to view the list in a spreadsheet.

(Continued)

You can also find the woeid for any places near a particular latitude–longitude coordinate pair. To find the woeid for New York City, for example, we could enter:

```
> getClosestLocations(40.736881, -73.98887)
```

which will return:

```
    name           country    woeid
1 New York  United States  2459115
```

Let us use the woeid for New York to collect data on what is trending in New York. Follow the steps below to capture the data and create a CSV file of your result. In this case we do not need to convert our output to a data frame, so you only need to write the following two lines in R:

```
> ny <- getTrends(2459115)
> write.csv(ny, "NYtrends.csv")
```

You now have a file you can open with a spreadsheet program that gives you the top ten trending hashtags in New York.

There is more you can do with Twitter data using the twitteR package in R. For a complete listing of all of the available functions in twitteR, go to the package's reference manual at cran.r-project.org/web/packages/twitteR/twitteR.pdf.

Collecting data with the streamR package

The streamR package for R allows you to "dip into" the real-time flow of Twitter data by accessing Twitter's streaming API. The authorization "handshake" with Twitter and the commands for search are different than with twitteR, but our goals are the same: to gather geolocated Twitter data and store them in a CSV file.

To get the package and prepare it for use, do the following:

```
> install.packages("streamR")
> library(streamR)
```

Connecting to your Twitter application is a little more complicated in this example, as you must conduct it each time you run a search. To make this a little easier, we can create an object that stores the consumer key and access token for our application. We can then call this object into our search commands. Below are the steps for setting up your authorization. Use the consumer key and consumer secret from your own Twitter app back on the apps.twitter.com page.

```
> library(ROAuth)
> requestURL <- "https://api.twitter.com/oauth/request_token"
> accessURL <- "http://api.twitter.com/oauth/access_token"
> authURL <- "http://api.twitter.com/oauth/authorize"
> consumerKey <- "xxxxxyyyyyzzzzzz"
```

```
> consumerSecret <- "xxxxxxyyyyyzzzzzzz111111222222"
> my_oauth <- OAuthFactory$new(consumerKey=consumerKey,
    consumerSecret=consumerSecret,
    requestURL=requestURL, accessURL=accessURL,
    authURL=authURL)
> my_oauth$handshake(cainfo = system.file("CurlSSL",
    "cacert.pem", package = "RCurl"))
```

You can now use the object `my_oauth` when you begin a search of real-time Twitter data.

Next we will test some of the features of streamR. We will use the `filterStream` function to search a set number of tweets and store them in a file. Let us suppose, for example, that you would like to collect 50 tweets containing "breaking" and "news" and store them in a CSV file. The streamR package lets you store your collected Twitter data in a JSON file, which can then be parsed and saved as a data frame.

```
> filterStream(file.name="news.json", track="breaking news",
    tweets=50, oauth=my_oauth)
```

streamR will then run until 50 tweets are collected. Once complete, you can parse the data, store the tweets in a data frame, and then write that data frame to CSV:

```
> news.df <- parseTweets("news.json")
> write.csv(news.df, "breakingNews.csv")
```

We can now open our CSV file in a spreadsheet to see the tweets we collected (Figure 9.13).

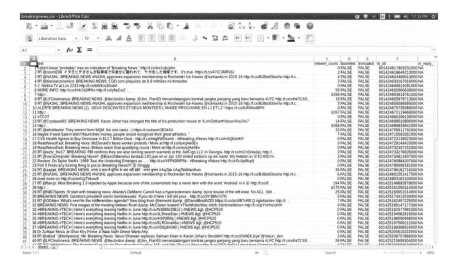

FIGURE 9.13 CSV file showing data collected through the streamR package

(Continued)

You can also set streamR to run for a set period of time instead of limiting it to a specified number of tweets. If you wanted to collect tweets on "breaking news" for a specified time period – say, 1 hour – you could enter the following:

```
> filterStream(file.name="news.json",
track="breaking news", timeout=3600,
oauth=my_oauth)
```

Filtering data from specific geographic locations works a little differently with the Twitter streaming API. Instead of setting a specific location and search radius, we instead establish a geographic *bounding box* by setting southwest and northeast pairs of latitude and longitude coordinates. The data returned will be limited to those tweets geocoded by Twitter inside the rectangle formed within those two points. To limit our search for breaking news to London, then, we would enter the following:

```
> filterStream(file.name="LondonNews.json",
    track="breaking news", locations=c(-
    0.684469,51.297209,0.398669,51.702928), tweets=10,
    oauth=my_oauth)
```

Note that the correct format for entering coordinates to define your bounding box in this case is longitude first, then latitude.

The streamR package has a few additional parameters you can use to structure your data collection. You can choose to limit your search results to a specific language or to only those tweets coming from specific user accounts. To retrieve 100 tweets from Mexico in Spanish we could run the following search:

```
> filterStream(file.name="Mexico.json", language="es",
    locations=c(-118.652,13.411,-85.428,31.353),
    tweets=100, oauth=my_oauth)
```

To collect tweets from an individual account you can search using a specified Twitter identification number. To monitor tweets coming from the official account of the White House during an hour-long press conference, for example, we could run:

```
> filterStream(file.name="whitehouse.json",
    follow="30313925", timeout=3600, oauth=my_oauth)
```

We can also do an open search on a particular geographic region to see what people there are saying on Twitter. To collect 200 real-time tweets from Barcelona we simply run:

```
> filterStream(file.name="barcelona.json",
    locations=c(1.977,41.29,2.27,41.46), tweets=200,
    oauth=my_oauth)
```

Hopefully you are now comfortable searching Twitter data using both the twitteR and streamR packages in R and understand how you can use Twitter's geocoding tools to help provide some spatial reference to social media. In later chapters we will examine some ways to visualize Twitter data through various mapping applications.

A note on API limits: it is important to note that using these tools does not give you access to the full stream of data on Twitter. Each access token on Twitter has limits on the number of search requests that can be made during a given 15-minute window. These limits are maintained by Twitter in order to avoid abuse and are subject to change. When using twitteR you can run a check on your current use limits by entering the following command in R:

```
> getCurRateInfo()
```

For more on rate limits and Twitter's APIs, go to the Twitter developer website at dev. twitter.com.

 **Chapter summary**

In this chapter we have examined several ways to tap into the flood of information on the Twitter social media platform and collect spatial information on collections of tweets. Non-existent just over a decade ago, Twitter has emerged as an important communication platform for people around the globe. The mind-boggling number of tweets being posted during any given moment provide us with a new window on our contemporary zeitgeist and demonstrate an unprecedented expression of networked communication. From sporting events to social movements to emergency response, Twitter provides us with a tool for organizing our behaviors and activities across our network society.

Harnessing the geographic dimensions of Twitter is no easy task, but attempting to do so can give us important and fascinating new ways to study the spatiotemporal dynamics of human sentiment, activity, and interaction. The Twitter APIs give us access to this novel form of networked communication, and Twitter's geocoding services can help us order it spatially as we ask questions and seek answers about the social world around us. With more than 300 million people now active on Twitter and more than 500 million tweets being sent per day – mostly on mobile devices – uncovering the spatial aspects of this social network is crucial to our understanding of the geoweb.

It is not only human beings who are active on Twitter, however. All sorts of devices – from sensors that monitor environmental systems to vending machines to household pets – are connected to Twitter via its APIs and are actively tweeting across the network. Each day, entities that previously operated in relative isolation – from home thermostats to cars to skyscrapers – are becoming networked and integrated across the internet and can communicate on platforms like Twitter. Known as the "internet of things," this growing interconnectedness of the physical world will transform the geoweb.

(Continued)

The next chapter examines some of the spatial aspects of the coming internet of things. From RFID to wireless sensor networks, much of the data generated by the nodes across the internet of things will have important spatial components. As we see more and more aspects of our lives being incorporated into the geoweb, the power and importance of "where" will become increasingly apparent.

Further reading

Mejova, Y., Weber, I. and Macy, M.W. (2015) *Twitter: A Digital Socioscope*. Cambridge: Cambridge University Press.

COMPANION WEBSITE

Visit https://study.sagepub.co/abernathy for:

- Links to the websites and free software packages discussed in this chapter
- Downloadable versions of all datasets presented in this chapter

10

Mapping the Emerging Internet of Things

 Overview

This chapter includes:

- The internet of things on the geoweb
- Three practice exercises on viewing and capturing spatial data from the internet of things
- Four practice exercises on creating sensor data using Arduino

A quick browse of the aisles of almost any electronics retailer makes it quite clear that the age of the "connected home" is upon us. Your home's thermostat, lighting, security system, and some appliances can be linked to your internet router and controlled wirelessly from a computer or smartphone. You can monitor the soil moisture of your houseplants or garden, receive an alert when motion is detected inside your house while you are away, and arrange to have your home set the temperature, lighting, and music to your taste when you are within a couple of kilometers of returning. The increasingly "smart" home promises convenience, comfort, and cost savings as once isolated and "dumb" components of a typical residential dwelling are connected and can react to external stimuli. If the transition from an internet that mainly resided on wired computers to one that is increasingly wireless and mobile represents one major internet revolution, we are told that the next revolution is one where the internet is increasingly embedded in all aspects of the physical world around us. The lines between physical and digital will blur as we continue to transition into this emerging world of the *internet of things* (IoT).

But what if your house gets hacked? Or your self-driving car? In 2015, a hacker and founder of a cybersecurity firm claims to have made an airliner climb and shift sideways after he hacked into the flight controls from the in-flight entertainment system

(Foster, 2015). Many home network routers have been shown to be easily hacked, giving the intruders access to any smart device and any information passing along the network (including more than one documented case of hackers taking over a baby-monitoring webcam). A study released by Hewlett-Packard in 2014 estimated that around 70 percent of devices on the IoT were vulnerable to hacking (Hewlett-Packard, 2014). As more and more information flows between an ever-growing number of connected devices, new threats to our safety, privacy, and wallets will emerge and new tools for thwarting potential attacks will emerge in response.

Nevertheless, it does seem likely that the IoT will continue to infiltrate many aspects of our lives. Home automation is merely the tip of the iceberg, as everything from earthquake monitors to urban transit systems to wearable heart monitors will be internet-enabled. And for many (if not most) of these devices, *geography* will be of paramount importance. Tracking components moving along a manufacturing supply chain, monitoring the flow of traffic and the availability of open parking spaces in a city, controlling the amount of water and fertilizer needed on large farms, measuring ambient noise and crowd flow inside a conference center – all of these are examples of not just an internet of things, but a *location-aware* internet of things.

This chapter explores the emerging location-aware IoT as it becomes an increasingly important component of the larger geoweb. After examining some current examples of, and challenges to, the IoT in more depth, we will turn to some hands-on exercises. The first set of exercises will focus on ways to access data being generated by the IoT, including data from weather stations, transit systems, and sensor networks that are monitoring ecosystems. The second set of exercises will provide an introductory look into developing your own "thing" to collect data and share it over the internet. In these exercises we will use the Arduino open source electronics prototyping platform to develop a temperature sensor and a radio frequency identifier (RFID) tag reader. These basic exercises will demonstrate some of the fundamentals of networked sensor data and hopefully provide you with some ideas about how you might implement similar technologies in your own projects.

THE INTERNET OF THINGS ON THE GEOWEB

Many of the "things" being connected to the internet today have an explicitly spatial component. Data on traffic congestion, seismic activity, weather, or urban air quality are not all that useful unless we can connect those data to a particular locale. The current average global temperature might be of interest to climate scientists, but you are probably more inclined to find out the present temperature in your specific city or town. Similarly, you are likely to be concerned only with data being generated by traffic sensors between your present driving location and your destination, not what is happening miles behind you. In addition, relative location information is often used to generate new data or trigger certain actions on the geoweb. A package scanned at a shipping distribution center might update the tracking status and estimated delivery date for your order on Amazon. com. You might receive an alert on your mobile device when a train is on its way or a coupon when you pass by a particular shop. Or, as in the home automation example above, your house might turn up the thermostat and turn on some lights once your car is within a specified distance.

The data being generated by a wide array of networked sensors are increasingly being incorporated into software algorithms that can analyze how these streams of data might interrelate. Digital "voice assistants" like Apple's Siri, Microsoft's Cortana, and Google Now can search your calendar for an upcoming event and, based on your location and current traffic conditions, alert you when you need to begin traveling in order to reach your destination on time. They can track your upcoming airline flight information, notify you of any delays or gate changes, help you rebook your flight if necessary, and provide information on the weather and nearby hotels and restaurants at your travel destination.

This level of coordination and synthesis will likely be much more sophisticated in coming years, but as yet there is no common operating system or set of software protocols for the IoT. While there are emerging standards for geospatial data and sensor observation sites, as we will see below, presently there are many different organizations and companies vying to be the standard-bearer for the software backbone of the IoT. We clearly do not yet have an integrated IoT, but we are beginning to see ways in which our growing ability to stitch together multiple datasets across different smart networks is increasing the power of the geoweb. Below are just a few examples.

SMART CITIES: SENSING THE BUILT ENVIRONMENT

More than half of the global population now lives in cities, and in the USA and UK more than 75 percent of the population resides in urban areas. As cities continue to grow and evolve, there is considerable interest in ways to plan and manage urban infrastructure in a way that promotes economic efficiency, good quality of life, and environmental sustainability. Proponents of "smart cities" argue that by connecting many aspects of our built environment to the IoT we can better understand and manage a host of urban processes, from traffic and parking problems to stressors on environmental health.

You can think of the idea of a "smart city" as the "connected home" example extended to a metropolitan scale, with a similar mix of possibilities and threats. Cities have had bits and pieces of a smart city for some time, if you include such technologies as traffic sensors, CCTV surveillance systems, and skyscrapers whose systems of power, waste management, and mobility can all be monitored and managed from a "dashboard" on a computer screen. The idea of the smart city, then, is that such systems are increasingly networked and further embedded into the social and physical worlds of urban life.

Knowing where smart city sensors are located and how the data they generate vary over geographic space can assist decision-makers (often computers rather than humans, as much of the data flowing over smart city networks is from machine to machine rather than from machine to human) in allocating resources and managing infrastructure needs. Traffic sensor data can show which roads are busiest at what time of day. Water quality sensors can identify areas of impaired waters and potentially isolate point-source pollution locations. Automatic lighting systems can show which areas tend to draw pedestrian traffic and at what times, helping urban planners understand the "live" and "dead" social spaces of a particular city and alert police to areas that may require additional officer presence at certain times of the day.

In short, knowing *what* is happening *where* and *when* at any given moment in a city gives us the potential for maximizing efficiency by allocating resources to where they are needed most. The smart city could well be a place that is more functional, more sustainable, and more conducive to a good quality of life than cities that do not incorporate these technologies. On the flip side, however, some are concerned that such systems might increase the tendency toward a surveillance society, where the actions and behaviors of others are increasingly monitored and controlled. Further, some see smart cities as potentially widening the economic disparities in cities by limiting access and control to a small minority of the total urban population.

SMART FORESTS: BUILDING AN ECOSYSTEM "MACROSCOPE"

The James Reserve is an ecologically rich plot of land in the San Jacinto Mountains of southern California and contains a diversity of ecosystems and wildlife. Managed by the University of California at Los Angeles, the reserve is a designated Federal Research Natural Area and houses facilities for biologists and other scientists conducting field research. Starting in 2002, the reserve also became home to an almost bewildering array of sensors designed to collect environmental data. Sensors were deployed by researchers from the Center for Embedded Network Sensing to capture everything from soil moisture and rainfall to audio and video from bird boxes (Hamilton et al. 2007). Moreover, many of these individual sensors were connected to each other and the internet wirelessly, meaning that they could be deployed over a wide swath of terrain. By combining data being collected at spatial and temporal scales that were not possible before, it was hoped that this *wireless sensor network* would serve as a sort of terrestrial "macroscope," giving us new ways to "see" ecosystems that were previously invisible.

The sensor network on the James Reserve is but one example of a growing network of embedded and connected sensors that are giving us more data on our terrestrial, aquatic, atmospheric, and social systems than we have ever had before. From the Ocean Observatories Initiative to the Polar Earth Observing Network to the Global Seismographic Network, humans are actively monitoring and collecting data on a variety of environmental variables. We are building a sort of "nervous system" for the planet that is increasingly interconnected and integrated into the geoweb.

Such sensor networks are routinely incorporated into our daily lives, often without our giving them much thought. Checking a weather app on your phone, for example, can provide you with a regional forecast that is based on the analysis of data collected by terrestrial and satellite weather monitoring systems. River gauge and tidal monitoring systems can help you plan your aquatic activities. The United States Geological Survey is working on an earthquake early warning system that will translate seismic event data recorded by the California Integrated Seismic Network into public warning alerts that can be instantly transmitted across mobile communication networks and the Wireless Emergency Alert system of the Federal Emergency Management Agency. The ability to quickly disseminate data from one sensor network across the broader internet, and then tailor those data to a specific set of needs for particular places, is a growing strength of the global geoweb.

SENSING PROXIMITY: RFID, GEOFENCING AND THE LOCATION-AWARE IOT

Many of the smart city and environmental sensors described above are deployed *in situ* – they are each positioned in a fixed location in order to continuously record data for that location. The geographic coordinate pair for each sensor node can easily be recorded and included with the collected data for subsequent mapping and spatial analysis. Datasets collected in a fixed place over time are vital to many of the analyses of our natural and built environments that are described above. This is one example of what it means to have a "location-aware" IoT.

But location awareness also requires that we have the capability to monitor phenomena that are not fixed in place. Very often we seek information that is based on geographic relationships that are not absolute, but rather are questions about relative location and proximity: how long will it take for the next bus to arrive? How many of my friends are nearby? What are the spatiotemporal patterns of wildlife populations in certain ecological habitats? Could studying the dynamics of human mobility in certain places help us understand the diffusion of infectious disease? These are all questions that have been asked before, but now the IoT provides us with new opportunities to capture data on relative location and proximity and to share such data across the geoweb.

As we have seen in earlier chapters, the ubiquity of GPS receivers and our increasingly comprehensive databases of geocoded places mean that collecting a geographic coordinate for most anything is fairly simple. As both the size and cost of GPS receivers have shrunk, we have been able to equip all sorts of things with them, not just mobile phones. GPS has been used to track patterns of animal movement (both domestic pets and wildlife), the location of shipping containers, and the driving activity of a fleet of police cars. Combined with some form of radio communication, such trackers provide near-real-time location data that can be made immediately accessible on the geoweb.

Geofencing is another common way that proximity data can be gathered. Geofencing allows us to go a step further than just collecting data on individual entities; it allows us to measure data on the geographic relationship between two or more things as they move throughout space. By setting a perimeter, or fence, at a set distance from a known coordinate pair, geofencing establishes a form of territorial boundary around that point. If the location of some other phenomenon falls within the territory set by the geofence, some sort of event or notification can be triggered.

For example, you might set your mobile device to remind you to purchase milk when you drive by your local grocery store. An urban transit system might employ geofencing to notify passengers when a bus is getting close to a particular stop. A wildlife research scientist could employ geofencing to alert herself if a tracked animal gets too close to populated areas or to monitor the movement of certain species through a wildlife corridor. As long as the absolute location for two or more things can be captured, relative location and proximity can also be measured.

Another technology for capturing proximity is radio frequency identification. One advantage of RFID over GPS is the extremely small size of the chip, or tag, used for tracking. Another is that the chip can be passive, meaning that it does not require a power supply and can instead be powered by an RFID reader. Combined with the very low cost of individual RFID tags, these attributes have helped make RFID technology widely adopted across a range of uses.

RFID tags have been embedded in a wide variety of things for tracking, from books in a library to clothing in a retail store to pets whose owners are worried that they may stray. Shipping companies use RFID technology to track packages, hotels embed tags in room keys, and governments issue them in passports. Walt Disney World gives every visitor to its theme parks an RFID-equipped wristband – a "MagicBand" – that can be used for everything from entering the park to purchasing food and souvenirs. These bands provide convenience (and facilitate spending) for park visitors, and also give Disney a great deal of data on wait lines for attractions, traffic flow, and spending behavior throughout the park.

RFID, geofencing, and GPS tracking are all used to provide geographic context to the IoT by capturing both absolute and relative location data. We can track location data on individual things as well as measure the proximity of one thing to another. The spatial interaction of objects on the IoT can trigger any number of activities across the internet – from financial transactions to police alerts to shifts in production that reverberate down a manufacturing supply chain. As our physical surroundings increasingly become integrated with our digital networks, understanding the geographical relationships across the IoT will only increase in importance.

Yet as mentioned above, the IoT is still in its infancy, and as such there is no one underlying software or hardware platform serving as an infrastructure backbone. Several large companies see the growing importance of the IoT and are working to develop infrastructure platforms that they hope could emerge as the industry standard (Canonical's Snappy Core,

Google's Brillo and Weave, and Samsung's Artik chips are all efforts to shape the hardware and software components of the IoT, while companies such as Cisco and General Electric are working on creating the IoT's network infrastructure). This can make working with data generated by the IoT a daunting and confusing task. In the exercises below, we will take a look at just a few of the many different ways to engage the geospatial internet of things, recognizing that this layer of the geoweb is in tremendous flux and evolving rapidly. The exercises will certainly not make you an expert, but hopefully after completing them you will have a better sense of how to further explore the networked geodata being generated by this increasingly interconnected world of things.

VIEWING AND CAPTURING SPATIAL DATA FROM THE IOT

 Exercise 1: Viewing sensor network data online

Given that there are currently no widely agreed-upon platforms for sensor networks across the IoT, there is no central place you can visit online to access data from a full variety of networked sensors. We have already seen sites that let you tap into a particular category of geodata, such as an airline tracking site that lets you locate all airborne flights, or a similar shipping map that lets you see the current state of oceanic transport, or a Twitter "sentiment" map that gives you a peek into the current mindset of individuals across a specified landscape. Weather Underground uses a combination of official and crowdsourced volunteer weather station data to give "hyperlocal" conditions and forecasts. And of course traffic and transit maps help us keep track of mobility and transport information in a particular city or region.

There have been some recent efforts to combine multiple networks of sensor data into one application. One website that is attempting to combine the various static and near-real-time transit network datasets is the Transit Visualization Client, or TRAVIC, a collaborative project between the company geOps and the University of Freiburg. By combining published transit data from transit operators around the world and overlaying the data on OpenStreetMap, the site provides a useful visualization of the estimated location and departure/arrival times of many networks of buses, trains, and ferries.

You can view the interactive website at tracker.geops.ch (Figure 10.1). Try navigating to the site and then selecting one of the many transit feeds on the map. You can speed up time with the navigation bar at the bottom of the map to see transportation vehicles move around the map, and you can select individual bubbles on the map to see retrieve information on the particular vehicle, its route, and estimated arrival times at specific stations.

Another site that attempts to combine multiple sensor networks is called Thingful (Thingful.net), a web service that calls itself "a search engine for the internet of things" (Figure 10.2). On the site you can access multiple sensor networks on one map interface, from air traffic to personal weather stations to tagged sea turtles. Thingful also lets you search for sensors near your current location, as well as tag specific sensors to track over time.

(Continued)

FIGURE 10.1   Transit Visualization Client (TRAVIC)

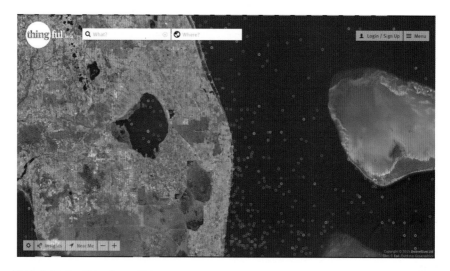

FIGURE 10.2   Thingful © Thingful Ltd.

The camera is perhaps our most ubiquitous sensor, and as we saw in Chapter 8 today's digital images often have geographic coordinates embedded in the EXIF metadata attached to them. Several online mapping applications allow you to view and upload digital images that will automatically be geolocated on a map, while other sites give you access to webcams positioned around the world. Earthcam.com, for example, lets you access live webcams from its world map interface, while Google's Views lets you see images and 360-degree panoramas that have been submitted by users and located on Google Maps and Google Earth. Google also makes its Street View imagery – panoramic imagery stitched together from streets around the world – available on its digital mapping applications so that users can go on virtual "drives."

Street View, in particular, has been criticized by privacy advocates and others who prefer not to have their houses, faces, and activities captured and mapped online. Google has agreed to blur faces and homes, remove certain images, and even suspend its data collection in certain countries in response to such criticism. Privacy advocates have also been critical of the amount of imagery taken in public places with closed-circuit television cameras, which are used for everything from traffic monitoring to crime surveillance. Several online mapping sites provide location data on CCTV monitors around certain urban areas to inform citizens about the location – and extent – of digital surveillance. As digital streaming services like Meerkat and Periscope gain popularity there will undoubtedly be attempts to geolocate and map live streams being taken with mobile devices, and digital maps showing real-time satellite imagery are on the horizon – meaning that issues of privacy on the geoweb are not going away anytime soon.

Exercise 2: Downloading sensor data and the Sensor Observation Service standard

The next exercise gives you a chance to download data from networked things. We will download sensor data from some of the networked buoys deployed by the US National Oceanic and Atmospheric Administration (NOAA), taking a look at a structured data format that is beginning to emerge for the Sensor Observation Service (SOS) standard for sensor network devices.

The Open Geospatial Consortium (OGC), an organization dedicated to promoting open standards for geospatial data, developed the SOS standard so that data from a wide variety of different sensors could be structured in a standard format. SOS, when combined with SensorML – another standard approved by the OGC for structuring sensor measurements and processes – lays the groundwork for a common data structure for networked sensor data.

The Integrated Ocean Observing System (IOOS) is an example of a large network (or, more accurately, a network of networks) that can benefit from a set of data standards for the multiplicity of sensors taking measurements on oceans and lakes. Many of the sensors across the IOOS take advantage of the OGC sensor standards to help facilitate data manipulation and translation across multiple networks. For example, NOAA's National Data Buoy Center provides access to an SOS for retrieving near-real-time data on air and water temperature, waves, wind, and more.

Navigate to sdf.ndbc.noaa.gov to view a map of more than 900 networked buoys (Figure 10.3). Here you can select the data measure and time range of interest and download the data as a CSV file. Let us try downloading sea water temperature data for a single day. Select "Water Temperature" from the dropdown menu under "Select a data type," and enter a day of your choice in the YYYY-MM-DD format. Select "CSV" as your data format and then click on the "Get Data" button.

(Continued)

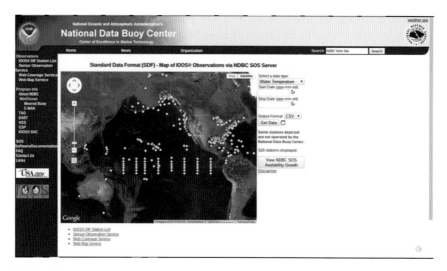

FIGURE 10.3 Map of Integrated Ocean Observing System (IOOS) data available from the National Data Buoy Center © National Oceanic and Atmospheric Administration

	station_id	sensor_id	latitude (degree)	longitude (degree)	date_time	depth (m)	sea_water_temperature (C)
2	urn:ioos:station:wmo:0y2w3	urn:ioos:sensor:wmo:0y2w3::watertemp1	44.794	-87.313	2015-06-03T18:05:00Z		8
3	urn:ioos:station:wmo:18ci3	urn:ioos:sensor:wmo:18ci3::watertemp1	41.73	-86.91	2015-06-03T13:35:00Z		13
4	urn:ioos:station:wmo:41002	urn:ioos:sensor:wmo:41002::watertemp1	32.382	-75.415	2015-06-03T00:50:00Z	1	25.3
5	urn:ioos:station:wmo:41002	urn:ioos:sensor:wmo:41002::watertemp1	32.382	-75.415	2015-06-03T01:50:00Z	1	25.4
6	urn:ioos:station:wmo:41002	urn:ioos:sensor:wmo:41002::watertemp1	32.382	-75.415	2015-06-03T02:50:00Z	1	25.3
7	urn:ioos:station:wmo:41002	urn:ioos:sensor:wmo:41002::watertemp1	32.382	-75.415	2015-06-03T03:50:00Z	1	25.1
8	urn:ioos:station:wmo:41002	urn:ioos:sensor:wmo:41002::watertemp1	32.382	-75.415	2015-06-03T04:50:00Z	1	25
9	urn:ioos:station:wmo:41002	urn:ioos:sensor:wmo:41002::watertemp1	32.382	-75.415	2015-06-03T05:50:00Z	1	24.7
10	urn:ioos:station:wmo:41002	urn:ioos:sensor:wmo:41002::watertemp1	32.382	-75.415	2015-06-03T06:50:00Z	1	24.4
11	urn:ioos:station:wmo:41002	urn:ioos:sensor:wmo:41002::watertemp1	32.382	-75.415	2015-06-03T07:50:00Z	1	24.3
12	urn:ioos:station:wmo:41002	urn:ioos:sensor:wmo:41002::watertemp1	32.382	-75.415	2015-06-03T08:50:00Z	1	24.3
13	urn:ioos:station:wmo:41002	urn:ioos:sensor:wmo:41002::watertemp1	32.382	-75.415	2015-06-03T09:50:00Z	1	24.5
14	urn:ioos:station:wmo:41002	urn:ioos:sensor:wmo:41002::watertemp1	32.382	-75.415	2015-06-03T10:50:00Z	1	24.6
15	urn:ioos:station:wmo:41002	urn:ioos:sensor:wmo:41002::watertemp1	32.382	-75.415	2015-06-03T11:50:00Z	1	24.6
16	urn:ioos:station:wmo:41002	urn:ioos:sensor:wmo:41002::watertemp1	32.382	-75.415	2015-06-03T12:50:00Z	1	24.6
17	urn:ioos:station:wmo:41002	urn:ioos:sensor:wmo:41002::watertemp1	32.382	-75.415	2015-06-03T13:50:00Z	1	24.6
18	urn:ioos:station:wmo:41002	urn:ioos:sensor:wmo:41002::watertemp1	32.382	-75.415	2015-06-03T14:50:00Z	1	24.6
19	urn:ioos:station:wmo:41002	urn:ioos:sensor:wmo:41002::watertemp1	32.382	-75.415	2015-06-03T15:50:00Z	1	24.6
20	urn:ioos:station:wmo:41002	urn:ioos:sensor:wmo:41002::watertemp1	32.382	-75.415	2015-06-03T16:50:00Z	1	24.7
21	urn:ioos:station:wmo:41002	urn:ioos:sensor:wmo:41002::watertemp1	32.382	-75.415	2015-06-03T17:50:00Z	1	24.6
22	urn:ioos:station:wmo:41004	urn:ioos:sensor:wmo:41004::watertemp1	32.5	-79.09	2015-06-03T00:50:00Z	0.6	27.1
23	urn:ioos:station:wmo:41004	urn:ioos:sensor:wmo:41004::watertemp1	32.5	-79.09	2015-06-03T01:50:00Z	0.6	27.1
24	urn:ioos:station:wmo:41004	urn:ioos:sensor:wmo:41004::watertemp1	32.5	-79.09	2015-06-03T02:50:00Z	0.6	27
25	urn:ioos:station:wmo:41004	urn:ioos:sensor:wmo:41004::watertemp1	32.5	-79.09	2015-06-03T03:50:00Z	0.6	26.9
26	urn:ioos:station:wmo:41004	urn:ioos:sensor:wmo:41004::watertemp1	32.5	-79.09	2015-06-03T04:50:00Z	0.6	26.8
27	urn:ioos:station:wmo:41004	urn:ioos:sensor:wmo:41004::watertemp1	32.5	-79.09	2015-06-03T05:50:00Z	0.6	26.4
28	urn:ioos:station:wmo:41004	urn:ioos:sensor:wmo:41004::watertemp1	32.5	-79.09	2015-06-03T06:50:00Z	0.6	26.4
29	urn:ioos:station:wmo:41004	urn:ioos:sensor:wmo:41004::watertemp1	32.5	-79.09	2015-06-03T07:50:00Z	0.6	26.3
30	urn:ioos:station:wmo:41004	urn:ioos:sensor:wmo:41004::watertemp1	32.5	-79.09	2015-06-03T08:50:00Z	0.6	26.4
31	urn:ioos:station:wmo:41004	urn:ioos:sensor:wmo:41004::watertemp1	32.5	-79.09	2015-06-03T09:50:00Z	0.6	26.4

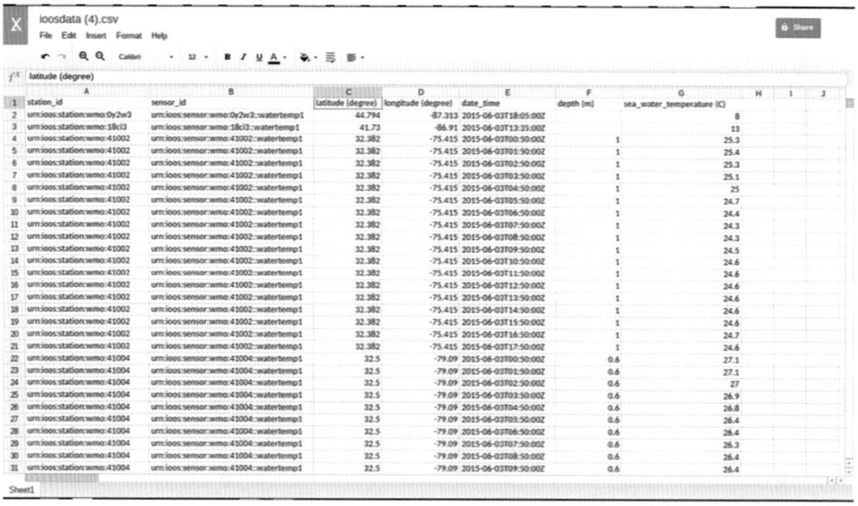

FIGURE 10.4 Large dataset of hourly sea temperature measures, including latitude and longitude of each buoy providing data

Once your dataset has downloaded, open it up in your spreadsheet software to take a look (Figure 10.4). You should now have a large dataset of hourly sea temperature measures that includes the latitude and longitude of each buoy providing data.

You can also download sensor data by clicking on "Sensor Observation Service" in the menu on the left-hand side of the NDBC page. Click on the link and then scroll down to the "GetObservation" tables. Go to the table for air temperature and find the row for the most recent observations at all stations. Click on the "CSV" link to download the file.

Since the file includes latitude and longitude for each buoy, we can make a quick map of our data in Google Fusion Tables. We will first need to join the two separate latitude and longitude columns into one, however, so that Fusion Tables will recognize the column and geocode it. This can be done easily in your spreadsheet software using the "concatenate" tool. Create a new empty column beside the two latitude and longitude columns in your file. Name the new column something like "LatLon," then enter the following formula in the second row of your new column:

```
=(C2&","&D2)
```

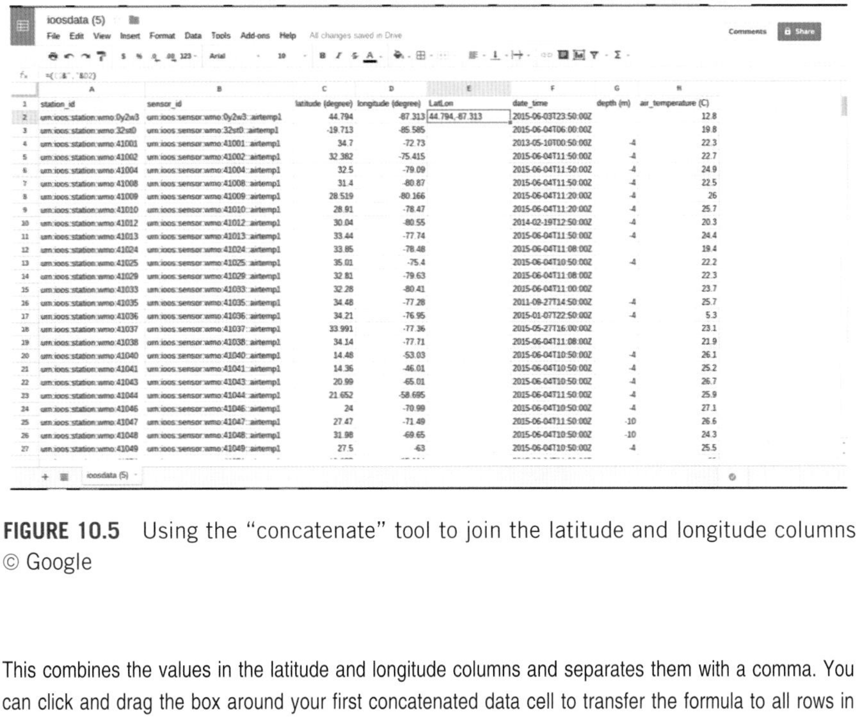

	A	B	C	D	E	F	G	H
1	station_id	sensor_id	latitude (degree)	longitude (degree)	LatLon	date_time	depth (m)	air_temperature (C)
2	urn:ioos:station:wmo:0y2w3	urn:ioos:sensor:wmo:0y2w3::airtemp1	44.794	-87.313	44.794,-87.313	2015-06-03T23:50:00Z		12.8
3	urn:ioos:station:wmo:32st0	urn:ioos:sensor:wmo:32st0::airtemp1	-19.713	-85.585		2015-06-04T06:00:00Z		19.8
4	urn:ioos:station:wmo:41001	urn:ioos:sensor:wmo:41001::airtemp1	34.7	-72.73		2013-05-10T00:50:00Z	-4	22.3
5	urn:ioos:station:wmo:41002	urn:ioos:sensor:wmo:41002::airtemp1	32.382	-75.415		2015-06-04T11:50:00Z	-4	22.7
6	urn:ioos:station:wmo:41004	urn:ioos:sensor:wmo:41004::airtemp1	32.5	-79.09		2015-06-04T11:50:00Z	-4	24.9
7	urn:ioos:station:wmo:41008	urn:ioos:sensor:wmo:41008::airtemp1	31.4	-80.87		2015-06-04T11:50:00Z	-4	22.5
8	urn:ioos:station:wmo:41009	urn:ioos:sensor:wmo:41009::airtemp1	28.519	-80.166		2015-06-04T11:20:00Z	-4	26
9	urn:ioos:station:wmo:41010	urn:ioos:sensor:wmo:41010::airtemp1	28.91	-78.47		2015-06-04T11:20:00Z	-4	25.7
10	urn:ioos:station:wmo:41012	urn:ioos:sensor:wmo:41012::airtemp1	30.04	-80.55		2014-02-19T12:50:00Z	-4	20.3
11	urn:ioos:station:wmo:41013	urn:ioos:sensor:wmo:41013::airtemp1	33.44	-77.74		2015-06-04T11:50:00Z	-4	24.4
12	urn:ioos:station:wmo:41024	urn:ioos:sensor:wmo:41024::airtemp1	33.85	-78.48		2015-06-04T11:08:00Z		19.4
13	urn:ioos:station:wmo:41025	urn:ioos:sensor:wmo:41025::airtemp1	35.01	-75.4		2015-06-04T10:50:00Z	-4	22.2
14	urn:ioos:station:wmo:41029	urn:ioos:sensor:wmo:41029::airtemp1	32.81	-79.63		2015-06-04T11:08:00Z		22.3
15	urn:ioos:station:wmo:41033	urn:ioos:sensor:wmo:41033::airtemp1	32.28	-80.41		2015-06-04T11:00:00Z		23.7
16	urn:ioos:station:wmo:41035	urn:ioos:sensor:wmo:41035::airtemp1	34.48	-77.28		2011-09-27T14:50:00Z	-4	25.7
17	urn:ioos:station:wmo:41036	urn:ioos:sensor:wmo:41036::airtemp1	34.21	-76.95		2015-01-07T22:50:00Z	-4	5.3
18	urn:ioos:station:wmo:41037	urn:ioos:sensor:wmo:41037::airtemp1	33.991	-77.36		2015-05-27T16:00:00Z		23.1
19	urn:ioos:station:wmo:41038	urn:ioos:sensor:wmo:41038::airtemp1	34.14	-77.71		2015-06-04T11:08:00Z		21.9
20	urn:ioos:station:wmo:41040	urn:ioos:sensor:wmo:41040::airtemp1	14.48	-53.03		2015-06-04T10:50:00Z	-4	26.1
21	urn:ioos:station:wmo:41041	urn:ioos:sensor:wmo:41041::airtemp1	14.36	-46.01		2015-06-04T10:50:00Z	-4	25.2
22	urn:ioos:station:wmo:41043	urn:ioos:sensor:wmo:41043::airtemp1	20.99	-65.01		2015-06-04T10:50:00Z	-4	26.7
23	urn:ioos:station:wmo:41044	urn:ioos:sensor:wmo:41044::airtemp1	21.652	-58.695		2015-06-04T11:50:00Z	-4	25.9
24	urn:ioos:station:wmo:41046	urn:ioos:sensor:wmo:41046::airtemp1	24	-70.99		2015-06-04T10:50:00Z	-4	27.1
25	urn:ioos:station:wmo:41047	urn:ioos:sensor:wmo:41047::airtemp1	27.47	-71.49		2015-06-04T11:50:00Z	-10	26.6
26	urn:ioos:station:wmo:41048	urn:ioos:sensor:wmo:41048::airtemp1	31.98	-69.65		2015-06-04T10:50:00Z	-10	24.3
27	urn:ioos:station:wmo:41049	urn:ioos:sensor:wmo:41049::airtemp1	27.5	-63		2015-06-04T10:50:00Z	-4	25.5

FIGURE 10.5 Using the "concatenate" tool to join the latitude and longitude columns © Google

This combines the values in the latitude and longitude columns and separates them with a comma. You can click and drag the box around your first concatenated data cell to transfer the formula to all rows in your dataset.

In Google Drive, create a new Fusion Table. Import your air temperature spreadsheet as a Fusion Table and click through the settings to finish setting up the file as a Fusion Table. Your file should be automatically geocoded based on your new LatLon column. Click on the "Map" tab to see the results (Figure 10.6).

(Continued)

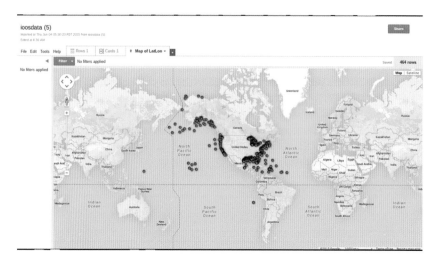

FIGURE 10.6 Map view of geocoded data © Google

Exercise 3: Capturing near-real-time sensor data with R

For this exercise, we will return to the R programming language and look at a few packages you can install to access both historical and near-real-time data from sensor networks. Specifically, we will take a look at two R packages – *weatherData* and *rNOMADS* – that you can use to access data from weather stations around the world, as well as a third package called *sos4R* that can be used to access data from any sensor network that uses a standard set by the OGC.

To begin, we will install the necessary packages from a CRAN mirror:

```
> library(weatherData)
> library(rNOMADS)
> library (sos4R)
```

Let us start by gathering some data from an airport weather station using the weatherData package. We can run the following functions to get the station ID for a particular place and find out if there is weather information available for the date we are interested in.

```
> getStationCode("Tokyo")
```

Several options are returned, including Tokyo International Airport with a code of RJTT. Now let us see if there are data available for that airport on January 1, 2000.

```
> checkDataAvailability("RJTT", "2000-01-01")
```

You can check a range of dates by entering

```
> checkDataAvailabilityForDateRange("RJTT", "2000-01-01",
  "2015-12-31")
```

Each of these functions checks the Weather Underground history files to see whether or not data are available and returns some information on the type of data columns that can be accessed. To download the minimum, maximum, and mean daily temperatures every day for one year, you can enter

```
> getWeatherForYear("RJTT", "2015")
```

If you only want the latest weather data recorded at a station, you can use

```
> getCurrentTemperature("RJTT")
```

which returns the date, time, and most recent temperature recorded (in degrees Fahrenheit).

The data you collect using the weatherData package in R can be written to a file just as we saw in the exercises in previous chapters, and with some basic plotting functions we can quickly visualize the datasets we collect. The package can also be used to access weather data from amateur stations that are part of the Weather Underground network, not just airport stations. To find the station code for a particular station, you can search the Weather Underground site by country (to find stations in the USA, for example, you would navigate to www.wunderground.com/weatherstation/ListStations.asp?selectedCountry=United+States). Some of the functions in the weatherData package require you to enter the parameter `station_type` = `"id"` in addition to the ID code since the default for station type is the three- or four-digit airport code.

Now let us turn to the rNOMADS package for R. This package provides an interface between R and NOAA's Operational Model Archive and Distribution System (NOMADS), which maintains repositories for many forecasting and climate models and provides access to real-time model data as well as archived models and datasets. Below, we will use some functions of the rNOMADS package to retrieve near-real-time data from the Distributed Oceanographic Data Systems (DODS) framework that is an open source network of shared climate data. All of the examples below are taken from the rNOMADS package reference manual, which is available online at cran.r-project.org/web/packages/rNOMADS/.

First, we can check the list of available near-real-time data:

```
> NOMADSRealTimeList("dods")
```

This should return approximately 50 different URLs linking back to currently available models. Now let us select just one of the models to see what variables are included. We will check the Global Forecast System 0.5 degree model, which has an abbreviation of gfs_0p50).

```
> urls.out <- CrawlModels(abbrev = "gfs_0p50", depth = 1)
```

Now we can use the `ParseModelPage` function to see what parameters are included:

```
> model.parameters <- ParseModelPage(urls.out[1])
```

(Continued)

157

Then type

```
> model.parameters
```

to see a rather bewildering number of possible measurements and altitude levels (for documentation on NOMADS datasets, go to nomads.ncdc.noaa.gov/). Let us try to pull out just one variable – current temperature at 2 meters' elevation – for the entire globe.

First we will need to get the most recently recorded data by retrieving a list of DODS dates and selecting only the most recent one.

```
> model.urls <- GetDODSDates("gfs_0p50")
> latest.model <- tail(model.urls$url, 1)
```

Next we will need to do the same thing for the latest DODS model runs:

```
> model.runs <- GetDODSModelRuns(latest.model)
> latest.model.run <- tail(model.runs$model.run, 1)
```

We can now write a few lines to download the most recent temperature recorded at points all over the globe.

```
> variable <- "tmp2m"
> time <- c(0, 0)
> lon <- c(0, 719)
> lat <- c(0, 360)
> model.data <- DODSGrab(latest.model,
    latest.model.run, variable, time, lon, lat)
```

You should now have thousands of temperature records stored in the model.data object. Since this is a large dataset we are better off visualizing it rather than trying to simply view the raw data. First organize your data into a grid using the ModelGrid function:

```
> model.grid <- ModelGrid(model.data, c(0.5, 0.5))
```

Now let us set up a range of colors for our map to distinguish between cooler and warmer temperatures. Don't worry too much about the code here – we will examine plots and mapping in R in more detail later. For now create an object to hold your color range:

```
> colormap <- rev(rainbow(500, start=0, end=5/6))
```

Now run the image function to plot your temperature data:

```
> image(x=model.grid$x, y=model.grid$y,
  z=model.grid$z[1,1,,],col = colormap,
  xlab="Longitude", ylab="Latitude")
```

Your output should look something like Figure 10.7, with the Prime Meridian at the zero point of your horizontal axis:

We can put an outline map of the world on our image to give it more geographic context, but we will need

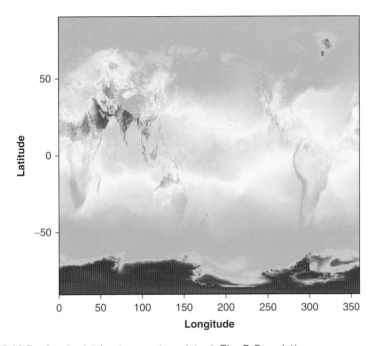

FIGURE 10.7 Graph plotting temperature data © The R Foundation

to install another package first:

```
> install.packages("GEOmap")
> library(GEOmap)
```

Now we can add an outline map to our image by entering the following:

```
> plotGEOmap(coastmap, border="black", add = TRUE, MAPcol = NA)
```

(Continued)

159

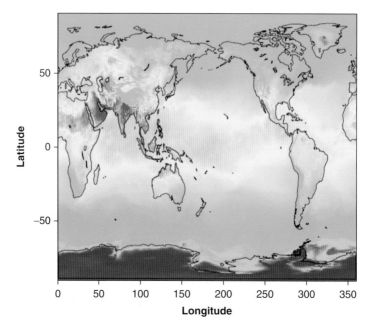

FIGURE 10.8 Graph plotting temperature data, with outline map of the world added
© The R Foundation

This gives us a nice map of the most recently recorded global temperatures (Figure 10.8).

CREATING SENSOR DATA USING ARDUINO

 Exercise 4: Creating a temperature sensor

The following two exercises focus on creating your own "thing" that can be connected to the internet in order to get a basic understanding of how the physical and digital worlds can interact. To do this, we will use the popular Arduino open source microcontroller – an inexpensive, flexible, interactive object that lets you sense and control the physical environment. Open hardware platforms such as Arduino and the Raspberry Pi (an inexpensive single-board computer) have seen enormous growth in popularity in recent years and are being used to create and implement a variety of sensor nodes and other projects. Here, we will create a simple temperature sensor that will collect temperature data from a tiny sensor and output the results to our computer screen.

For this exercise, you will need to obtain the following hardware:

- Arduino microcontroller
- Breakout breadboard

- LED
- Jumper wires
- TMP36 temperature sensor

These can be purchased separately online at retail sites such as Adafruit.com and Sparkfun.com, or you can look into purchasing a starter kit that includes the above, plus other hardware and tutorials for your own experimentation. The example below uses the Sparkfun Inventor's Kit, but does not require that you use that particular collection of hardware.

You will also need to download and install the Arduino Integrated Development Environment (IDE) in order to run the software code that will control your Arduino. To access the IDE software, navigate to www.arduino.cc/en/Main/Software and download the appropriate software for your operating system. Once you've downloaded and installed the IDE, run the program. You should see an empty screen ready for you to write or load a "sketch" (Figure 10.9).

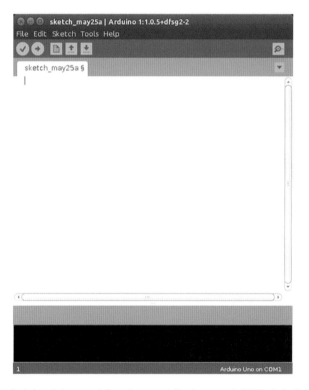

FIGURE 10.9 Arduino Integrated Development Environment (IDE) © Arduino

The Arduino IDE comes loaded with several example sketches to give you an idea as to how the code works. Let us load up a simple sketch and take a look at the basic makeup of the code. In the Arduino IDE, go to **File** > **Examples** > **01.Basics** > **Blink**. The code for blinking an LED should load (Figure 10.10).

(Continued)

FIGURE 10.10 Arduino IDE displaying the code for blinking an LED © Arduino

The typical Arduino sketch has two main routines: setup and loop. The setup routine initializes variables, loads any needed libraries, and other tasks necessary to begin running your main program, which is found inside the loop routine. In this Blink sketch example, we see that a variable name `led` is given to pin 13 on the Arduino board (pin 13 has an LED on most varieties of Arduino board), and that the pin is set to `OUTPUT` mode. This tells the Arduino that the code inside the loop routine will be sent to pin 13.

The loop routine contains the code that the Arduino will run. Just as it sounds, the loop routine runs continuously and is only interrupted when you stop the program or cut off the power supply to the board. In our simple example above, we see that our program alternates the voltage of the pin from `HIGH` to `LOW` with a 1-second interval between each transition. This code, then, should blink the LED on pin 13 continuously until we interrupt the loop.

Let us try connecting an Arduino to our computer and compile the Blink code. Your Arduino should have come with a cable that enables you to connect the board to your computer via USB. Plug in your board and install any necessary drivers. Once your Arduino is successfully connected, click on the checkmark icon or select **Sketch** -> **Verify/Compile** to make sure your code contains no errors. If the IDE returns a "Done compiling" message without any errors, your code is ready to run. Click on the "Upload" button or choose **File** -> **Upload** to install your program on the Arduino board. Once your code has finished uploading, you should see the LED on your Arduino board blink continuously.

If you have a separate LED bulb, you can plug it into the GND and 13 pins (the short leg of the LED should be inserted into the GND pin). The external LED should now blink instead of the on-board LED (Figure 10.11).

FIGURE 10.11   External LED bulb plugged into the GND

Try altering the code a bit to change the blink rate of your LED. For example, you can slow the blink rate to every 5 seconds by changing the delay time when the LED is set to LOW from `delay (1000)` to `delay (5000)`. Compile your code again to verify that it will run, then upload it to your Arduino. Your LED will now blink once every 5 seconds.

Now that you have a basic understanding of what an Arduino sketch is made up of, let us take a look at a sketch that reads the output of a temperature sensor and outputs it to the screen. We will use the simple and inexpensive TMP36 temperature sensor for this example, which comes with many Arduino starter kits. The TMP36 is an analog sensor with a voltage output linearly proportional to Celsius temperature. In this example we will connect the temperature sensor to a breadboard, give it some power, read the voltage output and convert it to temperature in Celsius, and display the temperature on our computer screen.

Disconnect your Arduino from the power supply, and then wire it and the breadboard as demonstrated in Figure 10.12. You need to provide power to one leg of the TM36, ground another, and connect the middle leg to one of the analog in pins on the Arduino.

We can now write a simple sketch that will read the voltage from the temperature sensor and convert it to degrees Celsius. We can also tell the Arduino to print out the values for both voltage and temperature

(Continued)

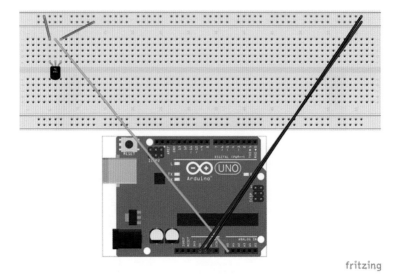

fritzing

FIGURE 10.12   Wiring the Arduino to the breadboard

with the `print` and `println` commands (the `println` command enters a carriage return after the output, so that the next output is printed on the line below). The `Serial.begin(9600)` command sets the rate for bits per second (baud) in order to transmit the output to your computer. Most computers use a baud rate of 9600 (Figure 10.13).

FIGURE 10.13   Arduino code to print out the values for both voltage and temperature
© Arduino

Compile the code to verify that you have written it correctly. Then upload the code to your Arduino. Nothing seems to happen, but that is because we need to open up the serial monitor. In the Arduino IDE, click on the magnifying glass icon in the upper right corner, or select **Tools** > **Serial Monitor**. You should see the voltage and the temperature output on the monitor every 2 seconds (Figure 10.14).

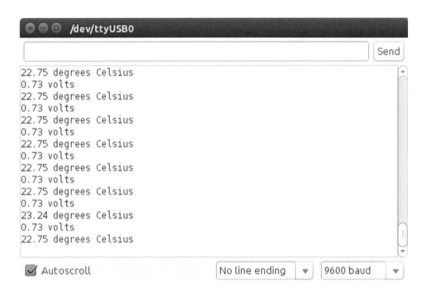

FIGURE 10.14   Voltage and temperature output readings on the monitor © Arduino

---

Exercise 5: Connecting your sensor to the web with Twitter

Now that we have the hardware and software up and running, we can return to the R programming language to send our temp sensor data with Twitter. Recall the code we wrote in Exercise 3 of Chapter 9 that used the streamR package. We used the `filterStream` command to collect a specified number of geo-coded tweets, then stored those tweets in a CSV file. The streamR package also lets you update your Twitter status, so with just a few lines of R code we can access the temperature data from our sensor connected to the Arduino and send it out in a tweet or direct message.

First, we will simplify our Arduino code just a bit so that we only get a single value output for each temperature reading (removing the voltage output and text). We will also reduce the delay time so that our temperature sensor is reading almost constantly (Figure 10.15).

Now open up a text editor (or, if you are using an IDE for R like RStudio, open up a new file) to store your R code as a script. For readability the command line prompt is included below, but you will not need it for

(Continued)

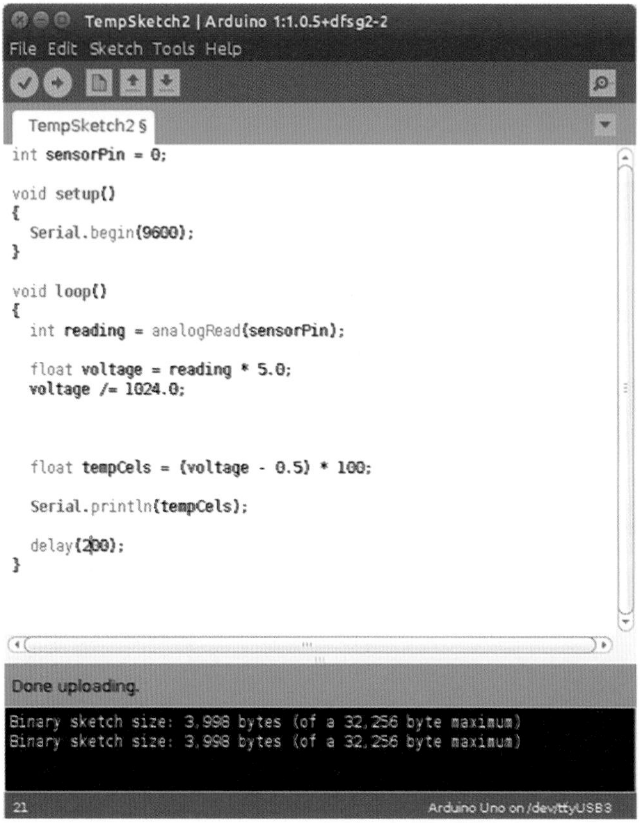

FIGURE 10.15 Arduino code to get a constant, single-value output for each temperature reading © Arduino

entering code into a text editor. First, we will access the appropriate libraries and authorize a connection to Twitter, as we did in Chapter 9:

```
> library(streamR)
> library(ROAuth)
> requestURL <- "https://api.twitter.com/oauth/request_token"
> accessURL <- "http://api.twitter.com/oauth/access_token"
> authURL <- "http://api.twitter.com/oauth/authorize"
> consumerKey <- "xxxxxyyyyyzzzzzz"
> consumerSecret <- "xxxxxxyyyyyzzzzzzz111111222222"

> my_oauth <- OAuthFactory$new(consumerKey=consumerKey,
consumerSecret=consumerSecret, requestURL=requestURL,
accessURL=accessURL, authURL=authURL)
```

```
> my_oauth$handshake(cainfo = system.file("CurlSSL",
"cacert.pem", package = "RCurl"))
```

The next step is to access the temperature data from your Arduino sensor. Return to your Arduino IDE and note the serial connection listed in the bottom right corner of your screen. You should see something like `Arduino Uno on /dev/ttyUSB1`. We can tell R to scan the file at this location to get serial output from our Arduino code, store the data returned to a new object, and then close the scan:

```
> myTemp <- file("/dev/ttyUSB1", open="r")
> latestTemp <-scan(myTemp, n=1)
> close(myTemp)
```

Here we have created an object `myTemp` that has read access to the file for our serial connection. We then create another object, `latestTemp`, that is the one line returned when the file is scanned. The final line closes the connection to the file.

We can now use the `updateStatus()` function in the streamR package to send a tweet containing our temperature sensor data (now stored in the `latestTemp` object). We can also use the `sprintf()` function in R to create a new object that is composed of the text for our Twitter update and the value stored in `latestTemp`:

```
> tempUpdate <- sprintf("The current temperature from
  my Arduino sensor is %s degrees C.", latestTemp)
```

As you can likely tell from this line, we are creating a new object `tempUpdate` and assigning it a string of text. By using the `sprintf()` function we can replace the `%s` in our text with the object that follows (`latestTemp`). We can then send our temperature data to our Twitter followers with:

```
updateStatus(tempUpdate)
```

You can also use

```
dmSend(tempUpdate, "twittername")
```

to send your temperature tweet to a specified Twitter account, where `twittername` is replaced with the actual Twitter user you want to message.

Save the file with the ".R" extension to save it as an R script. The entire code should look similar to the script in Figure 10.16 that was composed in RStudio.

This simple example demonstrates how to connect your sensor data to the geoweb using Twitter. With some additional code, you could set up your Twitter status to be updated with sensor data once a day, or only when a certain temperature threshold is met, or perhaps when a button connected to your Arduino is pressed.

(Continued)

```
TempSensor.R* ×
      Source on Save    Q            Run    Source ▾
 1  #setup Twitter handshake
 2  library(streamR)
 3  library(ROAuth)
 4  requestURL <- "https://api.twitter.com/oauth/request_token"
 5  accessURL <- "https://api.twitter.com/oauth/access_token"
 6  authURL <- "https://api.twitter.com/oauth/authorize"
 7  consumerKey <- "yourConsumerKeyHere"
 8  consumerSecret <- "yourConsumerSecretHere"
 9  my_oauth <- OAuthFactory$new(consumerKey=consumerKey, consumerSecret=consumerSecret, requestURL=request
10  my_oauth$handshake(cainfo = system.file("CurlSSL", "cacert.pem", package = "RCurl"))
11
12
13  #Get temperature data from serial connection
14  myTemp <- file("/dev/ttyUSB1", open="r")
15  latestTemp <- scan(myTemp, n=1)
16  close(myTemp)
17  print(latestTemp)
18
19  #use the updateStatus command in twitteR package to send tweet with current temp
20  tempUpdate <- sprintf("The current temp from my Arduino temp sensor is %s degrees C.", latestTemp)
21  updateStatus(tempUpdate)
22
23
```

FIGURE 10.16 R script composed in RStudio containing temperature data © The R Foundation

But perhaps you would rather not have your sensor communicate over your Twitter account, but instead would like your data to be uploaded to the web. To do this, we turn to our next exercise where we will create a channel on ThingSpeak to store and display our sensor data.

Exercise 6: Connecting your sensor to the web with ThingSpeak

Calling itself "the open data platform for the Internet of Things," ThingSpeak is an internet service that lets you create and view "channels" of connected sensors. The service offers applications and plugins that make it simple to connect different types of sensors and plot sensor data on a channel. For this exercise, we will first view a public channel on the ThingSpeak website, then we will set up a ThingSpeak account so that we can begin creating our own channel. From there we will modify our R code from the previous example so that our Arduino temperature sensor output will be sent to our ThingSpeak channel instead of our Twitter account.

At Thingspeak.com, click on the dropdown menu labeled "Channels" and select "Public Channels." This will take you to the public channels page where you can view featured channels or search by tag or username. Trying clicking on a few of the featured channels to see some examples of sensor data being displayed. In the example in Figure 10.17, we can see the data from a water-level data logging device located on the border between Kenya and Tanzania. In this example the latitude and longitude of the sensor have been included in the channel settings and located on a map of the region.

Having spent some time looking over a few of the channels, you can register with ThingSpeak to set up your own account. Return to the site's homepage and register to create an account. Once you have successfully set

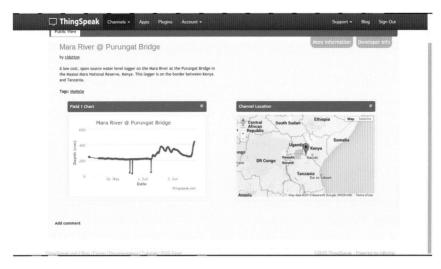

FIGURE 10.17 Water level data at Thingspeak.com © The MathWorks, Inc.

up a new account, you will be taken to the main channels page where you can click on "New Channel" and begin setting up a channel for your temperature sensor data. On this page you can name your sensor, and if you plan to make it public you can include a brief description and any descriptive tags you would like to use. Also note that you can include the latitude and longitude for your sensor, and you can check the box marked "Make Public?" if you would like to make your sensor data available to anyone (Figure 10.18).

FIGURE 10.18 Setting up a channel for your temperature sensor data © The MathWorks, Inc.

(Continued)

The "Field" boxes are where our data will go. Since we only have our temperature sensor we will just use Field 1, but note that you can have up to eight different fields for each channel you create.

Once you have set up your channel, click on the "Data Import/Export" tab at the top of the page. Your channel has been assigned an API key that will be needed in order to update your channel with sensor data. Note that you have the option to upload a CSV file to your channel, but since we want to feed our channel live temperature data we do not need this option. We will need, however, the example URL that shows how we can write data to our channel (replace YOURKEYHERE with your actual API key):

```
https://api.thingspeak.com/update?key=YOURKEYHERE&field1=0
```

We will use this line in our modified R code to send our sensor data to our new ThingSpeak channel.

Return to the R script we wrote in Exercise 5. We will remove the streamR functions for sending our data to Twitter and replace them with new functions that allow us to write data to the web. (You can put a '#' in front of your streamR functions instead of actually removing them.)

We first need to add two libraries to our script:

```
> library(RCurl)
> library(httr)
```

(If these are not available you can add them using the install.packages() function.)

These libraries give us tools for reading and writing data to the web. With just a couple lines of R code we can grab our temperature sensor data and send it directly to our ThingSpeak channel.

First, we will use the sprintf() function as before to concatenate our ThingSpeak URL with our latest sensor reading:

```
> TempUpdate <-
  sprintf("https://api.thingspeak.com/update?key=YOUR
  KEYHERE&field1=%s", latestTemp)
```

As before, the %s in the URL will be replaced with whatever value is currently in our latestTemp object. Updating our ThingSpeak channel is then as simple as:

```
> post <- POST(TempUpdate)
```

Once you have run this in R, refresh your ThingSpeak channel page. Field 1 should now include your latest temperature reading instead of "0," and your chart should reflect this change. If so, you have connected your temperature sensor to the internet of things. We can also use this approach for other sensor data as in the next exercise.

Exercise 7: Proximity sensor using an RFID reader and Arduino

As mentioned earlier in this chapter, radio frequency identification is being used across the geoweb to generate proximity data between physical things. The small size of RFID keys, along with their low cost and energy demands, has led to the proliferation of RFID tags that measure everything from individual consumer purchases to large-scale deployments across transportation networks and global supply chains. Anything containing a tiny RFID tag can be read by an RFID reader once the tag comes within a certain distance of the reader; the reader, in turn, provides the RFID tag number to the software running it which can then trigger the software to update a database, trigger other sensors, issue an alert, and more. In the example below, we will write a very basic Arduino sketch that simply triggers an LED and prints out the RFID tag ID to the serial console.

This exercise uses the following inexpensive hardware, in addition to an Arduino Uno board:

- an RDM6300 RFID reader module;
- an RFID tag (Figure 10.19).

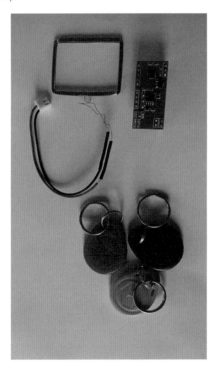

FIGURE 10.19 An RDM6300 RFID reader module and RFID tags

(Continued)

We will first connect our RFID reader module to the Arduino as shown in Figures 10.20 and 10.21. We only need three connections to set up our RFID reader: 5V, GND, and digital pin 0 for communicating the reader's output to the Arduino (Figure 10.20).

FIGURE 10.20   Connecting the RFID reader module to the Arduino (photo)

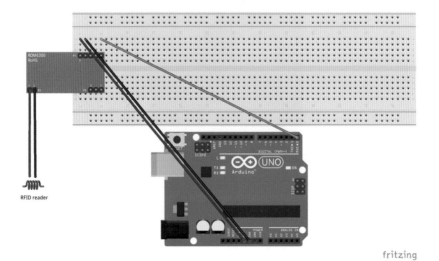

FIGURE 10.21   Connecting the RFID reader module to the Arduino (instruction manual image)

Once we have set up our hardware, we can write the sketch shown in Figure 10.22.

This sketch creates a variable called `data` for us to store the data we get from our serial connection, then begins listening to the serial connection in the `void setup()` section. The loop then simply listens to the serial connection to see if any data other than 0 come in, and if so the data are read into our data variable and printed to the serial console. The delay code slows down the printing so that we can more easily read the input.

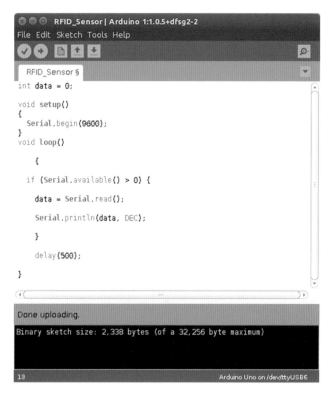

FIGURE 10.22   Arduino sketch © Arduino

Compile the sketch to make sure it contains no errors. Before uploading it to your Arduino, you will need to temporarily disconnect the wire connected to the top pin of the RFID reader (otherwise you will get an error). Upload the sketch, then reconnect the wire.

Open the serial console so you can see any output from the reader. As long as there are no RFID tags near the coil of your reader you should not see anything happening on your console. Now wave your RFID tag close to the coil to see what happens. You should start to see some output on your screen (Figure 10.23).

The RFID tags used in this example have ID numbers that begin with 2 and end with 3, so if you hold the tag over the coil you will see these numbers repeated. We can also add our LED code from Exercise 5 (Figure 10.24) and blink an LED to indicate that an RFID tag is being read. The additional code simply turns on the LED when the serial connection receives data from an RFID tag with the `digitalWrite(13, HIGH)` line of code, and turns off the LED with `digitalWrite(13, LOW)` when there are no data being received.

(Continued)

FIGURE 10.23   Output on the Arduino screen © Arduino

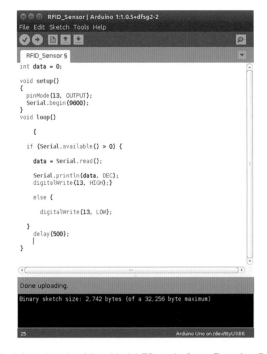

FIGURE 10.24   Arduino sketch with added LED code from Exercise 5 © Arduino

This simple sketch should give you an idea as to how you could use proximity data to trigger other commands or activities. As with our previous examples, you could use RFID data to send out a status update over Twitter or to update a channel on ThingSpeak. With multiple geolocated RFID readers, you could track the location of something and put that location on a map. Some individuals have even gone so far as to embed RFID tags in their skin so that they can control various aspects of their surrounding environment (though you may not care to go to that extreme).

Chapter summary

This chapter has examined the rapidly evolving internet of things, paying particular attention to some of the spatial aspects that make the IoT a layer of the larger geoweb. As more of the physical world around us becomes both geolocated and networked, we will begin to see formerly disparate entities able to communicate and respond to stimuli like we have never seen before. The world around us is becoming increasingly "smart," and location and proximity play a very important role in the growth of these intelligent things.

This chapter also covered some simple examples to give you a working knowledge of how to collect geolocated data from sensor networks and the IoT as well as create your own sensor node that can be added to the IoT. While basic, the exercises demonstrated some ways to move data back and forth across networks using the Arduino and R programming languages. With some additional study and creativity, these languages can be used to both capture and create a wide variety of data as you work to harness the power of "where" across the geoweb.

While some maps were included in this chapter, at this point you might be wondering how to create more sophisticated maps and do some additional spatial analysis on the geodata you collect or create. To do this, we turn to geographic information systems. In the next two chapters, we will take a look at two powerful open source GIS software programs – QGIS and GRASS. The chapters after that will examine web-based mapping applications and the use of R for visualizing spatial data. A solid understanding of GIS is essential for engaging with the geoweb, and the next few chapters will give you enough understanding of some key principles of GIS so that you can confidently employ these tools in your own work.

Further reading

Kooijman, M. (2015) *Building Wireless Sensor Networks Using Arduino*. Birmingham: Packt Publishing.

COMPANION WEBSITE

Visit https://study.sagepub.co/abernathy for:

- Links to the websites and free software packages discussed in this chapter
- Downloadable versions of all datasets presented in this chapter

11

Visualizing Data in Geographic Information Systems with QGIS

 **Overview**

This chapter includes:

- Exercise 1: Download, view and query vector data
- Exercise 2: Join tabular data to an existing shapefile
- Exercise 3: Displaying coordinate data
- Exercise 4: Introduction to vector geoprocessing
- Exercise 5: Download, view and query raster data
- Exercise 6: Creating raster data with heatmapping and spatial interpolation
- Exercise 7: Creating a map layout with the QGIS print composer

We saw in the previous chapter that the physical world is increasingly being connected to the digital world, giving rise to the "internet of things." Given our definition of the geoweb from Chapter 1 – *a distributed digital network of geolocated nodes that capture, produce, and communicate data that include an explicitly spatial component* – we can make the case that the geoweb encompasses that subset of the broader IoT where geography matters. And as we have seen in examples from sensor networks to social media, information on location and proximity is quite often a key component of the networked data being generated across the web.

As such, the visualization of data being generated across the geoweb is a necessary precursor to our being able to make sense of it. Ordering data spatially – *mapping* it – can help us see patterns and understand trends in ways that would be difficult or impossible without such visual representation. We have seen some examples of this in previous chapters, where we viewed maps of networked sensor data and created our own maps of geocoded data. In this chapter, we will expand on our ability to create and manipulate spatial data by using software designed to work with geographic information. Typically referred to as "geographic information systems," such software tools can greatly enhance our ability to make sense of the geoweb and help us formulate new questions based on the visualizations we create.

After briefly introducing some of the important concepts of GIS, this chapter will give you an opportunity to work with spatial data using a free and open source software package called QGIS. You will learn to import, query, manipulate, and visualize spatial data using some of the powerful tools found in this software package. You will also gain an understanding of the primary data models used in GIS and learn how to translate your data to and from them. By the end of the chapter, you will have enough familiarity with GIS to be able to create maps and look for spatial relationships in your own sets of geodata as you interrogate the geoweb.

DIGITAL MODELS OF THE PHYSICAL WORLD

As we saw in Chapter 2, geographic information systems emerged in the 1960s as a tool for land management. The use of computers for analyzing and visualizing geographic information caught on as computing power increased and the cost of computing decreased, and soon GIS was widely employed across a diverse array of fields where spatial data and analysis proved beneficial. Today, GIS is big business, flourishing across dozens of economic sectors, employing thousands of technicians, and serving as the backbone of the growing field of geographic information science.

Simply put, GIS is a collection of tools used to create digital models of the physical world. We use GIS to store, visualize, analyze, and manage spatial data on everything from transportation networks to the spread of infectious disease. GIS is used to make maps, for sure, but can also be used to query out subsets of data, create new data based on existing geographic relationships, and identify spatial patterns in datasets that might otherwise be overlooked. GIS can also be used to test models of spatial relationships that are merely hypothetical, such as land use planning scenarios, wildfire simulations, or patterns of population growth and migration.

One of the key strengths of GIS is the ability to analyze multiple datasets, or "layers," and look for relationships among them. A GIS analyst might examine a map of crime data, for example, and look for other spatial data – gang activity, perhaps, or lack of proper lighting – that might help policy-makers work to mitigate crime in the future. Similarly, an environmentalist might examine land use and human activity near rivers and lakes to identify causes of water pollution, while an epidemiologist might study transportation networks and patterns of human behavior when trying to understand the geographic patterns of a disease outbreak. Combining multiple data layers into one analysis allows us to explore spatial relationships between the data – including location, distance, proximity, and clustering – that might provide clues about the nature of those phenomena.

Two main data models are used in GIS to represent the physical world – vector and raster (Figure 11.1). The vector data model uses points, lines, and polygons to identify specific features in a dataset. Roads and rivers would be represented by lines, for example, while urban areas or political districts might be made up of polygons. Each feature in the vector model has one or more descriptive *attributes*, or labels. A line feature representing a road would most certainly have an attribute for the name of the road, but it could also have additional attributes describing the type of road (paved, gravel), the number of lanes, the speed limit, and more. Furthermore, the attributes of vector features in a database can be queried so that some subset of data can be extracted. We might be interested in mapping only those cities with a population greater than a million, for example, or perhaps we want to examine the locations of hemlocks in a tree database.

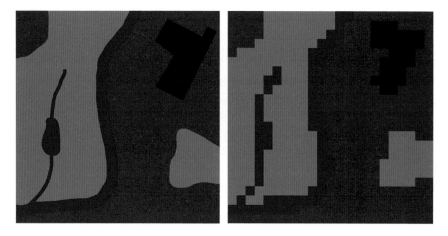

FIGURE 11.1   Vector (left) and raster (right) data models (Source: Wikimedia Commons)

The raster data model, in contrast, represents the physical world not as one of discrete features but rather as a continuous surface. Elevation, precipitation, and temperature are examples of phenomena that are more suitably modeled with raster data than vector. Raster data are made up of a grid of cells, with each cell representing some portion of the physical world and containing a specific value, such as elevation or a land use code. We can query raster data as well, asking questions about the values contained in each cell of the data. We could select only those cells above a certain elevation, for example, or only those cells representing impervious surfaces in a city.

GIS software allows us to use these two main data formats to store, manipulate, and visualize spatial data we collect from the geoweb. In the exercises below, we will use both raster and vector data to create maps, explore patterns, and query out subsets of data based on attributes. We will examine some of the key vector geoprocessing tools of GIS, including buffer and overlay, as well as querying raster data using a raster calculation tool. Finally, we will create a couple of map layouts that can be used to share the results of our analyses. To get started, let us take a tour of the first GIS software package we will use: QGIS.

QGIS is a free and open source GIS software package that has become popular in recent years. It is available on multiple desktop operating systems and is both powerful and user-friendly. It also has a large and growing user base, a wide collection of documentation and tutorials, and a dedicated team of volunteers who continue to revise and update the software on a regular basis. For these reasons, it is a good choice for those wanting to learn the basics of GIS.

To download the software, go to the QGIS website at www.qgis.org. Here you can review the features of QGIS, see screenshots of maps, read over documentation, and download the version of the software that is appropriate for your operating system. New versions of QGIS are released every few months, and there are also stable and experimental releases, so pay attention to the particular version you choose to download.

FIGURE 11.2 © QGIS

Once you have downloaded and installed the software, run it to open up a new project window (Figure 11.2). You will notice that your screen is divided into sections, with the main portion of the screen dedicated to the map "canvas." This is where your maps will appear. The smaller window, called "Layers," acts as your table of contents and is where you will manage the various data layers you bring into your project. The dropdown menus and buttons at the top of your screen give you access to some of the most popular tools for manipulating and analyzing your spatial data.

Exercise 1: Download, view and query vector data

To get familiar with the QGIS desktop, let us download and open a vector dataset. We will use a common vector format called a *shapefile*. A shapefile is actually a collection of files that together make up the necessary components of a vector data layer, including the attribute data, information on the geographic projection used, and more. Note that a shapefile can only include one of the three types of vector data – points, lines, or polygons – so if you want a map of both state boundaries (polygons) and roads (lines) you will need to download two separate shapefiles.

The US Census Bureau provides several boundary files for different geographic regions in the country. Navigate to https://www.census.gov/geo/maps-data/data/tiger-cart-boundary.html and take a look at the list of boundary shapefiles available for download. For this exercise, we will download two polygon shapefiles: State and County.

Click on the link labeled "State" and you will be taken to the download page for that set of files (Figure 11.3). Note that you can choose between different years and also different resolution levels (the level of detail in geographic features such as coastlines is greater in files with a higher resolution level, but this can mean larger file sizes and slower rendering speeds). Choose the "2013" tab and select the middle state file for download: cb_2013_us_state_5m.zip. This should start the download process for a zipped shapefile of the 50 states in the USA. Once the file has downloaded you will need to use an unzipping utility on your computer to extract the files from the zipped folder.

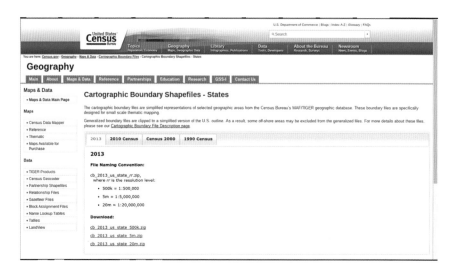

FIGURE 11.3 Cartographic Boundary Shapefiles at https://www.census.gov/geo/maps-data/data/tiger-cart-boundary.html © U.S. Census Bureau

Once you have extracted your shapefile (again, actually a collection of several files) into a folder, return to QGIS to open the shapefile. Go to **Layer** > **Add Layer** > **Add Vector Layer** (or click on the "Add Vector

Layer" button on the toolbar) and navigate to the location of your downloaded shapefile for state boundaries. Select the file cb_2013_us_state_5m.shp and open it in QGIS.

A map should appear on your canvas. Because this dataset includes US territories such as Guam, much of your map canvas will be white space. To zoom in on only the lower 48 states of the continental USA, use the magnifying glass icon with a plus on it to click and drag a rectangle around the states. The continental USA should now fill your map canvas (Figure 11.4).

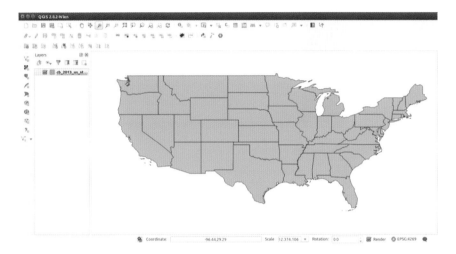

FIGURE 11.4 Map file cb_2013_us_state_5m.shp in © QGIS

You should spend some time familiarizing yourself with some of the tools included in the toolbars that appear by default (you can manage which toolbars appear on your screen by navigating to **View** > **Toolbars**). Several tools help you quickly move about your map, zoom in and out, pan, and more.

At the bottom of your screen you will see the coordinates used (in this case, we see latitude and longitude), the current scale, and the EPSG code, which refers to the coordinate reference system used to project the map on a flat surface. In this case we see that the EPSG is 4269, which is the code for the North American Datum 83 (NAD83) coordinate reference system. We can ignore this for now, but know that if you are trying to overlay datasets from multiple sources you may have to work with the coordinate systems for your data to line up.

Next, double-click on the name of your map layer in your Layers window to access the Layer Properties window for your map layer (Figure 11.5). Here you can control several aspects of your vector layer, including the coordinate reference system, the colors and symbols used, map labels, and more. Click on "Style" to access some tools for changing the color of your map.

Returning to your main map window, right-click on the name of your map layer in the Layers column. Here you have access to more tools and operations you can use to manipulate your data. Select "Open Attribute Table" to access the attributes associated with the geographic features on your map (Figure 11.6).

Each row of your attribute table represents one geographic feature on your map, and each column of the table represents an attribute of that feature. We can see that this table includes some codes, the state names and abbreviations, and two columns that look like measurements for land area and water area.

(Continued)

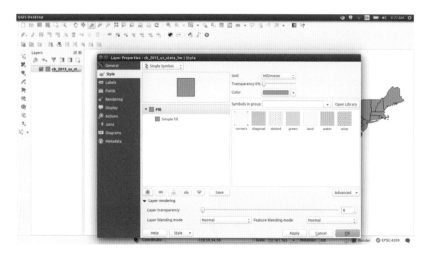

FIGURE 11.5 Layer Properties window in © QGIS

	STATEFP ▲	STATENS	AFFGEOID	GEOID	STUSPS	NAME	LSAD	ALAND	AWATER
0	04	01779777	0400000US04	04	AZ	Arizona	00	294205037082	1027846143
1	05	00068085	0400000US05	05	AR	Arkansas	00	134772954601	2958815561
2	06	01779778	0400000US06	06	CA	California	00	403482685922	20484304865
3	09	01779780	0400000US09	09	CT	Connecticut	00	12541965607	1815409624
4	13	01705317	0400000US13	13	GA	Georgia	00	148962779995	4947803555
5	15	01779782	0400000US15	15	HI	Hawaii	00	16634306900	11777540017
6	16	01779783	0400000US16	16	ID	Idaho	00	214045724209	2397731902
7	18	00448508	0400000US18	18	IN	Indiana	00	92789545929	1536677621
8	19	01779785	0400000US19	19	IA	Iowa	00	144669089481	1076358640
9	21	01779786	0400000US21	21	KY	Kentucky	00	102262346149	2393411962
10	22	01629543	0400000US22	22	LA	Louisiana	00	111900249547	23750998594
11	24	01714934	0400000US24	24	MD	Maryland	00	25143900187	6987136329
12	27	00662849	0400000US27	27	MN	Minnesota	00	206236444424	18924485103
13	28	01779790	0400000US28	28	MS	Mississippi	00	121532029877	3928362662
14	30	00767982	0400000US30	30	MT	Montana	00	376963164340	3868401373
15	32	01779793	0400000US32	32	NV	Nevada	00	284331148012	2049094356
16	34	01779795	0400000US34	34	NJ	New Jersey	00	19048566189	3542812673
17	36	01779796	0400000US36	36	NY	New York	00	122057170733	19239602457
18	39	01085497	0400000US39	39	OH	Ohio	00	105830932641	10266771053
19	40	01102857	0400000US40	40	OK	Oklahoma	00	177662456563	3374830738
20	42	01779798	0400000US42	42	PA	Pennsylvania	00	115883827546	3396206283
21	45	01779799	0400000US45	45	SC	South Carolina	00	77857755333	5074898120
22	46	01785534	0400000US46	46	SD	South Dakota	00	196348852055	3379925468
23	49	01455989	0400000US49	49	UT	Utah	00	212881323171	7003101744

FIGURE 11.6 Attribute table in © QGIS

Click on the number beside one of the rows in your table to highlight it. You will note that the corresponding feature on your map is also highlighted. For example, if I select the row for the state of Florida, I can see that the state is highlighted on my map (Figure 11.7).

We can also select features from our map using an expression. By using Structured Query Language (SQL) to ask questions of our geodata, we can pull out subsets of data and make new map layers from our selection. To select the state of California, for example, we return to the attribute table and click on the "Select

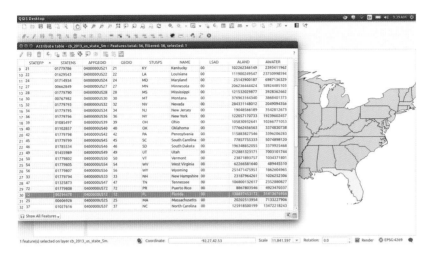

FIGURE 11.7 Interaction between attribute table and map in © QGIS

features using an expression" button to access a dialog box allowing us to build an expression. In the list of functions on the right, click on the "Fields and Values" arrow to see the fields available for query. Then double-click "NAME" to add it to the expression window. Then type the equals sign (or click on the button) and then type 'California' (single quotes), as shown in Figure 11.8. Click on the "Select" button to run the full expression "NAME" = 'California' to highlight the state on your map.

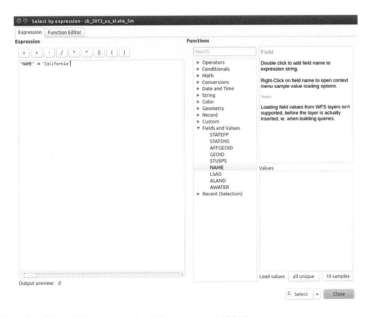

FIGURE 11.8 "Select by expression" feature in © QGIS

(Continued)

While California is still selected, return to you main map window and right-click on the name of your map layer in the Layers window. Select "Save As…" to save a new layer. Select ESRI Shapefile for your format, give it a name, and check the box marked "Save only selected features." Click "OK." You now have a new shapefile of the single state of California (Figure 11.9).

FIGURE 11.9   Creating a shapefile of the single state of California © QGIS

Now let us add the county shapefile to our map and extract just the counties in the state of California. Extract the zipped county shapefile, click on the "Add Vector Layer" button in QGIS, and add the shapefile to your map. You should now have a map layer that includes more than 3000 polygon features. Use the "Identify Features" tool (Figure 11.10) to click on one of the counties in California to access the attribute data for that feature. We can see an attribute called "STATEFP" in our results window, and if we click around the counties in California we see that each county has this same state code.

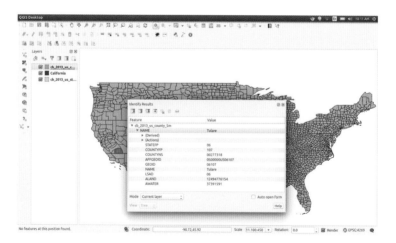

FIGURE 11.10   "Identify Features" tool in © QGIS

We can build an expression similar to before in order to select all of the counties in California. Go to the attribute table for the county map layer and enter the expression "STATEFP" = '06' in the expression builder dialog box to highlight all of the counties in the state. As before, right-click and save a new layer, preserving only the selected counties. Now uncheck the boxes for your original state and county shapefiles, leaving only the state and county layers for California that you created. Make sure that your county layer is on top of your state layer in the Layers window so that your counties are visible on the map (Figure 11.11). Zoom in on the state to get a better view of your new datasets.

FIGURE 11.11   State and county layers on the map in © QGIS

Exercise 2: Join tabular data to an existing shapefile

Being able to query out a subset of data in a shapefile and create a new map layer is a very useful skill. But often the shapefiles we load into QGIS do not have the attribute data that we are interested in visualizing. Suppose you wanted to create a map of population by county in California – there are no population data columns in the attribute table of your California county shapefile. Fortunately, you can create or acquire tabular data on population in a spreadsheet and then join it to the existing shapefile. In this exercise, we are going to download some population data for California, clean it up in a spreadsheet program, bring it into QGIS and join it to our shapefile so that we can create a graduated color map of county-level population.

We can obtain some population data for California by going to http://www.dof.ca.gov/Forecasting/ Demographics/Estimates/e-1/. Download *Table B-3 – Total Population, California & Counties*, and the State Population Estimates with Annual Percentage Change, January 1, 2015 and 2016. Once downloaded, open

(Continued)

the file in your spreadsheet software and click on the second tab of the spreadsheet (Figure 11.12). We see a list of California counties along with population data for 2015 and 2016. Unfortunately, while wide, empty rows and borders separating columns helps humans read tables such as these, they actually hinder the ability of GIS programs to read such data. Therefore, we need to do some cleaning up of the data before attempting to import them into QGIS.

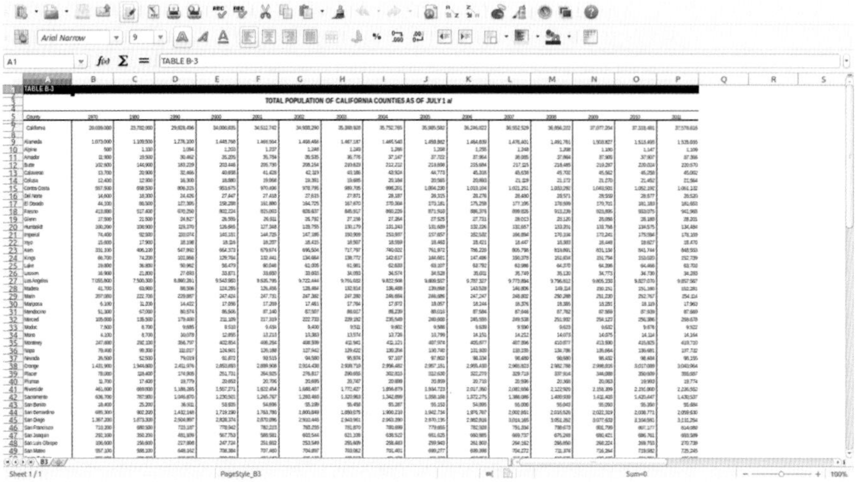

FIGURE 11.12   Spreadsheet of population data for California counties © State of California

Using the tools of your spreadsheet program, eliminate any empty rows and all data that are not part of the data we actually want (just the county names and the population data in the columns. Go ahead and take out the row containing the total population for California, as that will not be helpful when we work on making our map. Let us also remove the column containing the percent change, since for now we are just interested in mapping the variation in population by county. You should now have a simple file with only three columns: the name of the county, the population in 2015, and the population in 2016. Select the two population columns and make sure they are formatted as numbers, not as text.

Back in QGIS, go to **Layer** > **Add Layer** > **Add Delimited Text Layer** or click on the "Add Delimited Text Layer" button on your toolbar to open the dialog box. QGIS should recognize that your file is a CSV file, but you will need to select the "No Geometry" option instead of the default "Point coordinates" as our dataset is attribute only and does not contain any spatial data. Once you have selected that option, the OK button should let you bring the text file into your QGIS project.

Now that your text file is in your QGIS list of layers, you need to join the data to your existing county map so that you can create a graduated color map of county by population. Double-click your county shapefile layer and choose the "Joins" option. Click on the small green plus button at the bottom of the Layer Properties dialog box to set up a join (Figure 11.13). Here we can tell QGIS to look at the column in your text file that contains the county names and search for a match in the NAME column of your shapefile attribute table. For the Join layer dropdown menu, make sure your text file is selected, then choose the name of the column containing county names from that file as your Join field. The Target field is the name of the column in your attribute table containing the county names – in this case it is called NAME. Click "OK" to exit this dialog box, then "OK" again to exit the Layer Properties box.

FIGURE 11.13 "Add vector join" in Layer Properties dialog box © QGIS

Nothing has changed in your map, but if you reopen your attribute table you will notice that two new columns have been added to the right-hand side of the table, the 2015 and 2016 population data. We can now create a simple map that distinguishes between counties based on population size. Close your attribute table and double-click on your county shapefile to access the Layer Properties once more. Select "Style" and change the dropdown box from "Single Symbol" to "Graduated." In the Column dropdown menu, choose one of your two new population columns to map. Because these values are numeric, QGIS can create a graduated color map that distinguishes between counties of lower and higher population based on the color ramp you choose. For now, keep the defaults and press the "Classify" button to see several classes of population range created. Click "OK."

The result does not look much different than our original map, except that we note a couple of counties in southern California colored darker than the rest of the state. This is because the population of Los Angeles county is such an outlier from the rest of our data that we are unable to distinguish between populations in other counties. To make the map a little more interesting, return to the "Style" options in the Layer Properties dialog box and change the mode of classification from "Equal Interval" to "Quantile (Equal Count)." This changes the population ranges in your five classes to ensure that there are approximately the same number of counties in each. Click "Classify" and "OK" to see the changes in your map (Figure 11.14).

(Continued)

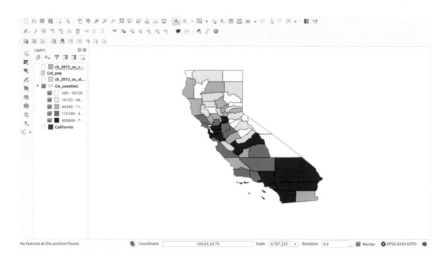

FIGURE 11.14 California map adjusted to "Quantile (Equal Count)" classification mode
© QGIS

You can try experimenting with the other options for classifying your data, increasing or decreasing the number of classes, and using different color and style options to alter the way the data are displayed in the map window. We will explore how to turn our map into a layout that can be printed or shared digitally in a later exercise, but for now you can save your analysis as a QGIS project by selecting **File** > **Save Project**.

Exercise 3: Displaying coordinate data

In previous chapters we learned how to capture geodata using GPS as well as create geocoded datasets using various tools for geocoding and geotagging. We can use GIS software to import and visualize these sorts of datasets and overlay them on a basemap to help provide additional spatial context for our data. In this exercise, you will download a geocoded dataset from the web, display the latitude and longitude coordinates using QGIS, and add a basemap beneath your coordinate points. We did this using Google Fusion Tables in an earlier chapter, but by importing your data into a GIS you can have much more control over your data and can apply additional geoprocessing tools to query out subsets of data or create entirely new data layers.

In this exercise we will use a dataset from the US Data.gov open data portal (www.data.gov). Suppose we decide that we would like to add a point layer representing all of the sites or places that are being regulated or monitored by the US Environmental Protection Agency for the state of California. On the Data. gov website, enter "EPA California" into the search box, then look for a file marked "EPA FRS Facilities Single File CSV Download for the State of California." Click on the "Zip" button to download the large file (state_combined_ca.zip), then extract the files from the zipped folder once the download has completed. Inside the folder you will see several files, including one named "CA_FACILITY_FILE.CSV." This is the file we will add to our California map in QGIS.

Return to the QGIS project you completed in Exercise 2. We can add a CSV file of latitude and longitude data just as we did with our attribute data in that exercise – by using the "Add Delimited Text Layer" tool. Click on that tool or choose **Layer** > **Add Layer** > **Add Delimited Text Layer** and select the California facility CSV file (this is a large file so it might take a little time to load). In the dialog box that appears, note that QGIS has identified the point coordinates in the data file and assigns the attribute "LONGITUDE83" as the X field and "LATITUDE83" as the Y field. QGIS also notes that the first row of the dataset includes field names (Figure 11.15).

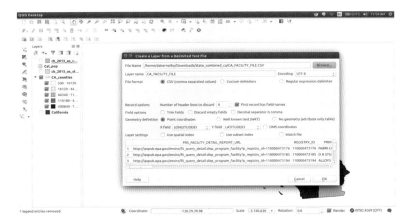

FIGURE 11.15 Creating a layer from a delimited text file in © QGIS

Click "OK" to create the layer. You will likely get a warning message since there are many records in the file without the appropriate geometry definitions. If you were conducting a real analysis you might spend time trying to identify the rows containing errors and fix them, but for the purpose of this exercise we will accept that most but not all EPA FRS facilities in California will be added to our map ("FRS" refers to the EPA's Facility Registry System for documenting places subject to environmental regulation or of environmental interest).

The next dialog box asks for a coordinate reference system (CRS). Since both your map and this EPA dataset use the NAD83 CRS, you can either just click "OK" or select "NAD83" and click "OK" (Figure 11.16).

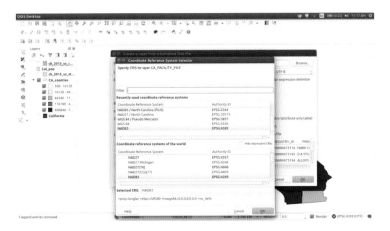

FIGURE 11.16 Coordinate reference system selector in © QGIS

(Continued)

You should see a point layer containing more than 130,000 EPA facility sites appear on top of your California map (Figure 11.17).

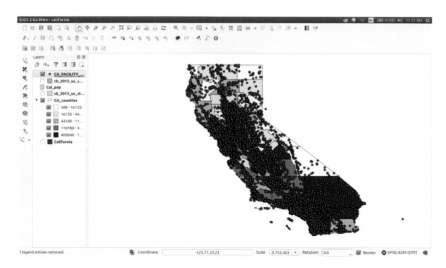

FIGURE 11.17 California map showing a point layer containing more than 130,000 EPA facility sites © QGIS

Since this dataset is somewhat overwhelming, let us pull out one particular category of EPA facilities: brownfields. Brownfields are land properties that have had some type of contaminant or pollutant that threatens or complicates future development. We can use the same data query techniques as we saw in Exercise 2 to pull out a particular facility subset of data from our larger dataset.

Open the attribute table for your facility point layer and then click on the "Select features using an expression" tool at the top of your attribute table. In the dialog box that opens we can click on the arrow by "Fields and Values" to see the many attribute column names in our table (Figure 11.18). Double-click on

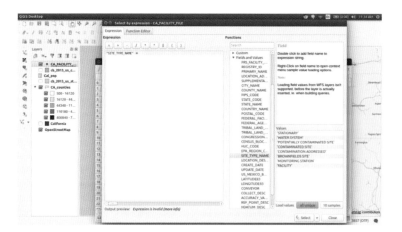

FIGURE 11.18 "Select features using an expression" tool in © QGIS

"SITE_TYPE_NAME" to begin writing your query expression. Click on the "=" button. Since we do not know what values are available under the SITE_TYPE_NAME field, click on the "all unique" button in the bottom right of the dialog box to see what values are included in this attribute column.

We can see that "BROWNFIELDS SITE" is one of the values included in this field, so double-click on that value to complete your expression in the dialog box. Click "Select," then "Close."

Now back in your main QGIS window, right-click on your facility point layer to save only the selected points. Select "Save As," make sure to check the box marked "Save only selected features," and give your new file a name. Click "OK." The file will automatically be added to your map layers. Once we turn off our original facility layer we can see a map of California brownfields (Figure 11.19).

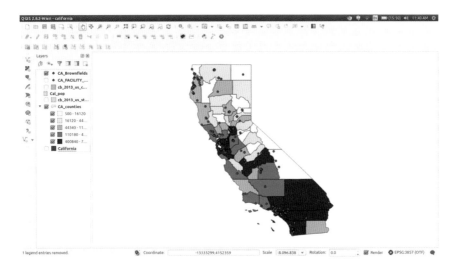

FIGURE 11.19   California map showing brownfields © QGIS

Our final steps for this exercise will help make our map display visually a little more appealing. To do this, we will add a basemap to show the western United States and we will make our county layer semi-transparent so that we can see the basemap features for California. First, let us add a basemap to our display. We can do this using a *plugin* in QGIS. Plugins are tools that do not come with the core QGIS software download but can easily be added via the internet. There are hundreds of plugins available for you to download and use for free in your QGIS projects.

In the menu bar at the top of your screen, select **Plugins** > **Manage and Install Plugins**. In the search box that appears, enter "OpenLayers Plugin." This plugin provides access to several basemaps for your projects. Install the plugin.

Once the plugin is installed, return to the top menu bar and select **Web** > **OpenLayers plugin** and then choose a basemap for your brownfields map. For example, Figure 11.20 shows a terrain basemap from the OSM/Stamen basemap options.

Our final step is to make the county layer semi-transparent. To do this, double-click your counties layer to access the Layer Properties dialog box. Under "Style," change the Transparency option from

(Continued)

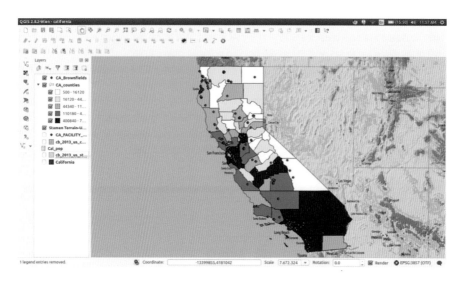

FIGURE 11.20 Terrain basemap from the OSM/Stamen basemap options © QGIS

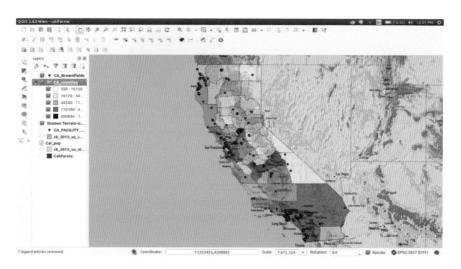

FIGURE 11.21 Making the county layer semi-transparent on the California map © QGIS

0 to 40 or 50 and click "Apply" and "OK." You should now be able to see the basemap underneath your county layer (Figure 11.21). You can experiment with the transparency percentage to make the county layer more or less transparent. Once you are satisfied with the look of your map, save your project.

Exercise 4: Introduction to vector geoprocessing

In addition to providing us with tools for visualizing and querying datasets, geographic information systems also include powerful tools for *geoprocessing*. Geoprocessing refers to the manipulation or transformation of a dataset by performing an operation on an input layer and creating a new output layer. Using some of the most common geoprocessing tools, we can perform tasks such as creating buffers of a specified distance around our vector data, overlay multiple vector layers to see where overlap occurs, and perform "cookie-cutter" operations to select subsets of data based on their proximity to other vector features.

For this exercise, you will perform two of the most common geoprocessing tasks – buffer and overlay – to answer the question: are any of the Native lands in California close to a brownfield site? To conduct this analysis, we will add a new vector polygon layer to our previous project, buffer our brownfield point layer by a specified distance, then see if our buffers overlap with the polygons representing Native lands.

Begin a new, empty project in QGIS. Add two of the vector layers you created to your empty map canvas: the polygon layer of California counties and the point layer of brownfields (Figure 11.22). Now return to the US Census Cartographic Boundary Files page and download the boundary file labeled *American Indian Areas/Alaska Native Areas/Hawaiian Home Lands*. Download the zipped folder and extract the files as you did with the US county layer.

FIGURE 11.22   New QGIS project with the polygon layer of California counties and the point layer of brownfields © QGIS

Once you have downloaded and extracted the file, add it to your QGIS project. You should see a vector polygon layer of all designated Native lands for the 50 US states. Since we are focusing on

(Continued)

California, we can perform our first geoprocessing operation to clip out only the Native land polygons that fall inside the state boundary.

Using the QGIS dropdown menus at the top of your screen, select **Vector** > **Geoprocessing Tools** > **Clip**. In the dialog box that appears, choose the Native lands vector layer as your input layer and your California counties layer as your clip layer. Provide a name for the new output layer, make sure the "Add result to canvas" box is checked, and click "OK." Close the dialog box, and uncheck the box next to your original Native lands layer in your list of layers. You should now have a new shapefile that includes only those Native lands found in California.

Our next step is to create a buffer of a specified distance around each of our brownfield sites. Suppose we are interested in knowing if there are any Native lands within 10 kilometers of a brownfield site. Our buffer distance, therefore, would be 10 km. However, our current project has a CRS that is unprojected, meaning that QGIS will only measure distance in decimal degrees. Before we can conduct our next geoprocessing step, then, we will need to make sure our data are projected in such a way that we can measure distance in meters.

Getting our data into an appropriate projection will take a couple of steps. First, click on the grey globe in the bottom right corner of your screen to open the CRS tab of your project properties. Check the box at the top labeled "Enable 'on the fly' CRS transformation" to allow QGIS to reproject your project data. Since we are working with California, let us search for California projections in the filter box. Type in "California" to filter out coordinate systems used in that state, then select "NAD83 / California Albers" as your projected coordinate system. Click "OK" and you will notice that the shape and orientation of your project layers change slightly, reflecting the new projection. You will also notice in the bottom right corner of your screen that your projection is now listed as "EPSG:3310 (OTF)."

We now have our map layers reprojected on our map canvas, but there are additional steps we need to take before we can create our buffers. While our map canvas shows the equal Albers projection, our individual layers still have their original CRS. To see this, right-click on your brownfields point layer and open the layer properties. Under the "General" tab, note that the CRS is still listed as EPSG 4326, meaning that the layer itself has not been reprojected. To do this, we will need to save the layer as a new file containing our desired coordinate system.

Close the properties dialog box and then right-click on your brownfields layer again. Select "Save As" to open up the "Save vector layer" dialog box. Enter a name for your projected brownfields layer, then change the CRS to the EPSG 3310: NAD83 / California Albers CRS. Make sure the "Add saved file to map" box is checked and click "OK." You should see a new point layer appear on your map directly on top of your existing brownfields layer. Uncheck the box next to your original brownfields layer so that only your new projected layer appears.

Next, repeat the same steps for your Native lands polygon layer, saving a new version of the file with the EPSG 3310 projection and adding it to your map. If you like, you can remove your unprojected layers by right-clicking and selecting "Remove."

Now that the data layers have been reprojected, we are ready to conduct the next geoprocessing step: creating a buffer. Using the dropdown menus, select **Vector** > **Geoprocessing Tools** > **Buffer(s)**. Make sure your newly reprojected brownfield layer is selected as your input layer, input "10000" as your buffer distance, and enter a new name for the buffer output file. You might also want to check the "Dissolve buffer results" box, as this will remove the lines of any overlapping buffers in your output file. Click "OK" to run the geoprocessing tool, then close the dialog box to view your output on the map canvas (Figure 11.23). You now have a new polygon layer representing a 10 km buffer around each of your brownfield points.

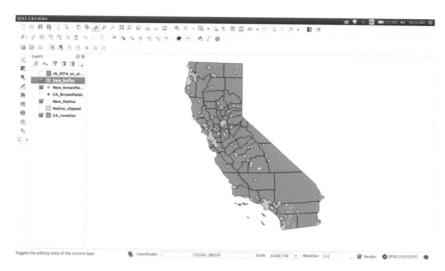

FIGURE 11.23   Creating a buffer in © QGIS

You can move your brownfield point layer on top of the buffer layer in your layer list so that you can see both layers. Zoom in to a section of your map to get a better view of your buffer output (Figure 11.24).

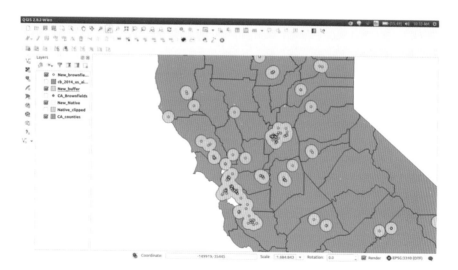

FIGURE 11.24   Zoomed-in view of buffer output © QGIS

Now that we have a new layer representing a 10 km buffer around all of the brownfields, we can run our final geoprocessing tool – overlay – to see if there are any areas where our buffer polygons and the Native land polygons overlap. To do this we will use the "Intersect" tool in QGIS. Again in your dropdown menus,

(Continued)

select **Vector** > **Geoprocessing Tools** > **Intersect**. For your two input vector layers, choose your buffer polygon layer and your reprojected Native lands polygon layer. Create a name for your output file and click "OK." You now have another new shapefile, this time representing all Native land areas that fall within your buffer zone. Zoom in to the southern part of California and you can see what your resulting layer looks like in greater detail (Figure 11.25).

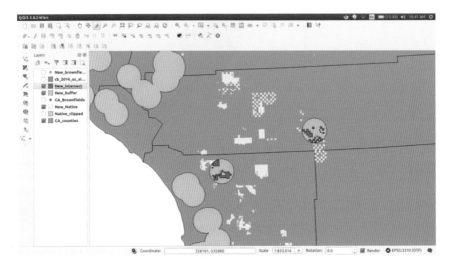

FIGURE 11.25   Zoomed-in view of southern California with buffer polygon layer and reprojected Native lands polygon layer © QGIS

As you can see, geoprocessing tools in QGIS can be very helpful in creating new vector datasets and exploring the spatial relationships between multiple datasets. By using a combination of attribute query, buffer, and overlay, we can ask questions of our spatial data, select subsets of data based on certain attributes, and create effective geographic visualizations. Next, we turn to the second important model for representing spatial data in a geographic information system: the raster model.

 **Exercise 5: Download, view and query raster data** ▬▬▬▬▬▬▬▬▬▬

As mentioned earlier in this chapter, the raster data model differs from the vector model in that it represents geographic features as a continuous surface instead of as discrete points, lines, and polygons. Whereas we might represent elevation as a set of contour lines in the vector model, the raster model represents elevation by assigning elevation values to every cell in a grid representing some portion of the Earth's surface.

Phenomena that vary continuously over space – such as elevation, temperature, and precipitation – are often modeled with the raster data model.

For this exercise, we will download and display a digital elevation model (DEM) stored as raster data. We will perform a simple operation on the raster to create a shaded relief layer in order to better visualize the terrain. And, similar to our data query using the vector model, we will extract a subset of data from our raster using the "raster calculator" tool.

As with vector shapefiles, there are many online sources of raster data for download. When obtaining raster data it is important to pay attention to the grid size of the dataset; a raster with a larger cell size means that you have fewer data values for a given portion of the Earth's surface than a raster with a smaller cell size. Rasters with smaller cell sizes can provide a more detailed model but can also be large and somewhat cumbersome to work with. For this example, we will download a DEM for an individual county in North Carolina with a cell size of 20 feet by 20 feet. This is a high-resolution DEM created as part of a statewide flood mapping program using a technology called "light detection and ranging" (LIDAR).

To obtain the DEM, visit the companion website: https://study.sagepub.com/abernathy and navigate your way to the Chapter 11 resources. There you will find a zipped file called "Lidar2007_Buncombe.zip". Download this file to a folder on your computer. This is a large file, so it may take some time to download. From here you can select an individual county to see what datasets are available. Select Buncombe County from the drop-down menu and click "Search." The first options for download are contour maps in the shapefile vector data format. Scroll down the page until you get to the LIDAR data products. Click on "Elevation Grid @ 20 Foot Cell Size" to begin downloading the zipped DEM. This is a large file, so it may take some time to download.

Once you have downloaded the data, unzip it to a folder on your computer. You should now have a folder named "Lidar2007_Buncombe." Open QGIS and begin a new mapping project. Click on the "Add Raster Layer" button or go to the dropdown menu at the top of your screen and select **Layer** > **Add Layer** > **Add Raster Layer**. Navigate to your unzipped folder, click on the "Elevation_Grid" folder, then the "elevation" folder, and finally the file named "w001001.adf." Click "Open." The raster elevation layer will appear on your map canvas (Figure 11.26).

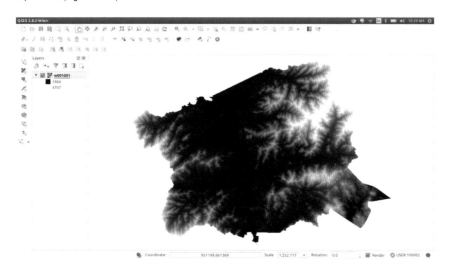

FIGURE 11.26 Raster elevation layer on © QGIS map canvas

(Continued)

The model represents lower elevations as dark and higher elevations as light. You can use the "Identify Features" tool to click around the map and see that cells representing higher elevation do indeed have higher values than cells representing lower elevation. We can make this even clearer by creating a shaded relief operation that gives our data a more three-dimensional feel.

Returning to the dropdown menus at the top of your screen, select **Raster > Analysis > DEM (Terrain Models)**. In the dialog box that appears, enter a name for your output file and make sure that "Hillshade" is selected as your Mode option. Leave all the other parameters as the defaults, click the box next to "Load into canvas when finished," and click "OK." After a few moments you will have a new hillshade layer (Figure 11.27).

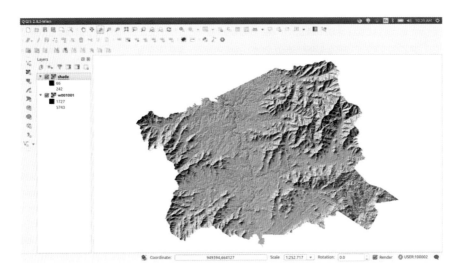

FIGURE 11.27   Hillshade layer on © QGIS map canvas

It is important to note that this hillshade layer is for visualization purposes only and cannot be used for further analysis. If you want to change the color of your hillshade from grayscale to color, for example, you can change the properties of your original DEM and place it on top of your hillshade layer instead of changing the properties of the hillshade itself. Reorder your layers so that your original DEM is back on top, then open up the layer properties for the layer. In the Style menu, change the render type from singleband gray to single-band pseudocolor. Under "Generate new color map" select "Spectral," check the box next to "Invert," and click "Classify." This will generate five colors representing progressively higher elevation ranges on your DEM.

Next, go to the "Transparency" tab in the Layer Properties window, and change the transparency of your DEM from 0% to 50%. Click "OK." You now have a semi-transparent DEM classified by elevation draped over a shaded relief layer (Figure 11.28).

We can also create new data layers by querying out subsets of data, much as we did with vector data in the previous exercise. To perform operations on raster data we can use a tool called the raster calculator. If we are interested in mapping a specific elevation range, for example, we can use the raster calculator to query out all of the cells in our grid that fall within that range. To create a new layer representing only the areas on our map that fall within the 3000–4000 foot range, for example, we can open the raster calculator by selecting **Raster > Raster Calculator** to open the dialog box.

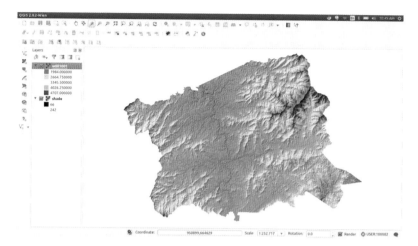

FIGURE 11.28   Semi-transparent DEM classified by elevation draped over a shaded relief layer on © QGIS map canvas

Be sure to perform your raster calculations on the original DEM, not your hillshade. Provide a name for your output layer, then enter the following expression in the expression window:

```
"w001001@1" >= 3000 AND "w001001@1" <= 4000
```

Run the calculation. QGIS will then evaluate each cell in your raster to see if the criteria in your expression are met. If true, the cell will receive one value, and if not it will receive a different value. The resulting output should look something like Figure 11.29.

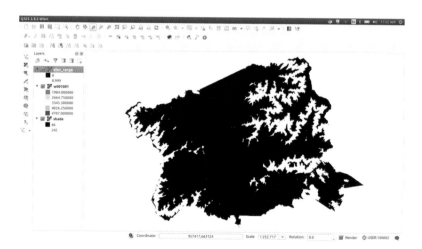

FIGURE 11.29   Mapping a specific elevation range on © QGIS map canvas using the raster calculator

(Continued)

To create a better visualization that emphasizes only the elevation range of interest, go to the "Style" tab in the Layer Properties for your newly created raster. Change the render type to singleband pseudocolor, change your mode from "Continuous" to "Equal Interval," and change the number of classes to 2. Click "Classify." This will assign one color to the cells inside your elevation range and another color to those outside it.

Now go to the "Transparency" tab in the Layer Properties. Change the global transparency to 50% (Figure 11.30). In the Custom transparency options, designate the value 0 as 100% transparent. This way we can highlight only those cells meeting our elevation range criteria on top of our original hillshade.

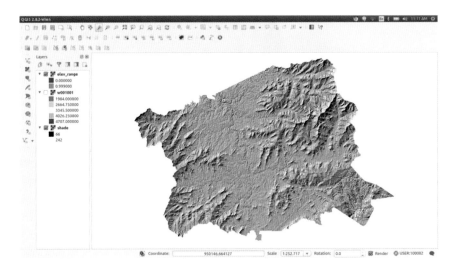

FIGURE 11.30 © QGIS map canvas with 50% global transparency

Exercise 6: Creating raster data with heatmapping and spatial interpolation

In addition to downloading existing raster datasets, we can generate our own raster data by performing operations on existing vector point datasets. If we have a large collection of points identifying the location of crime incidents, for example, we can analyze the point density to locate those areas where crime is more common – crime "hotspots." Likewise if we have a geographically dispersed collection of point data we can use mathematical interpolation to predict values for those places where we do not have point data.

Suppose you are moving to southern California and are interested in the crime rate. We can easily make a map of crime hotspots to know which places might be less safe than others. To access crime data, navigate to data.sandiegodata.org and enter "crime" into the search window. Then click on "San Diego Region Crime Incidents 2007-2013" to read about the data. You will notice that the data are available in shapefile format, so download the incidents-shapefiles.zip file and unzip it into a folder on your computer. You should have individual folders for the crime data for each year.

Start a new QGIS project and open the shapefile for crime incidents in 2013. There are 9904 points included in this dataset, making it difficult to interpret any sort of pattern (Figure 11.31). To help make sense of this dataset, we will use a plugin that allows us to create a heatmap based on the density of our points. We can then analyze our heatmap further to identify those places where crime is more prevalent.

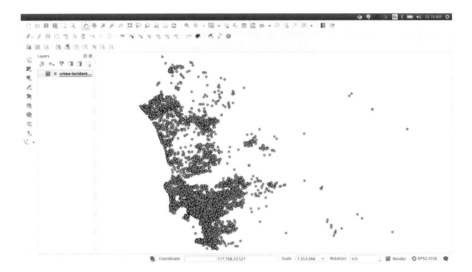

FIGURE 11.31   Heatmap identifying places where crime is most prevalent © QGIS

To access the heatmap tool, go to **Plugins** > **Manage and Install Plugins** in the dropdown menu of QGIS. Type "heatmap" into the search box to access the Heatmap plugin. Install the plugin and return to your QGIS project.

Under the "Raster" dropdown menu, select **Raster** > **Heatmap** > **Heatmap**. Use the 2013 crime point data as your input layer, create a name for the output, and keep the defaults for output format and radius. Click "OK" to run the tool and create a new density raster (Figure 11.32).

Here we can begin to see some patterns in our data, with darker shades representing lower density and lighter shades representing higher density, but the layer is still difficult to interpret and not as useful as we would like. Let us make some adjustments to our new data layer and add a base layer to help with our interpretation of the crime data.

First, add a basemap by going to your QGIS menu and selecting **Web** > **OpenLayers plugin** > **OSM/Stamen** > **Stamen Terrain-USA/OSM** to add a base layer to your project. Then, go to the Style menu in the Layer Properties for your heatmap and change the render type from gray to pseudocolor. Choose a color map for your raster and click "Classify." In the transparency menu of your Layer Properties, change the level of transparency to 30%. Then click "OK" to view the changes on your map (Figure 11.33).

(Continued)

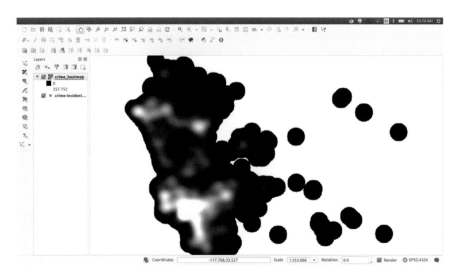

FIGURE 11.32 New density raster on heatmap © QGIS

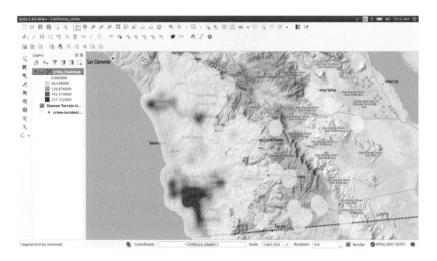

FIGURE 11.33 Pseudocolor heatmap with added basemap © QGIS

Not surprisingly, crime density is greater in the same areas where population density is greater, so our heatmap largely reflects the general distribution of the population in southern California. To drill down a little deeper, let us select one particular type of crime from our point data, create a heatmap for that crime, and then search for those places that are well above the mean.

Open the attribute table for your crime incident vector shapefile. Click on the "Select features using an expression" tool to open the dialog box. Enter the following expression:

```
"desc" = 'RESIDENTIAL BURGLARY'
```

202

Click "Select" to highlight the points representing burglary on your map and close the dialog box. Then save your selected points by right-clicking your point layer, selecting "Save As," and checking the box for "Save only selected features." Add the new layer to your map and turn off your original point layer and your heatmap (Figure 11.34).

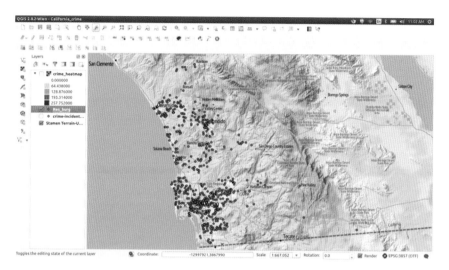

FIGURE 11.34 "Residential burglary" layer on basemap © QGIS

Now run the heatmap plugin tool on your new burglary layer, changing the color scheme and transparency as before (Figure 11.35).

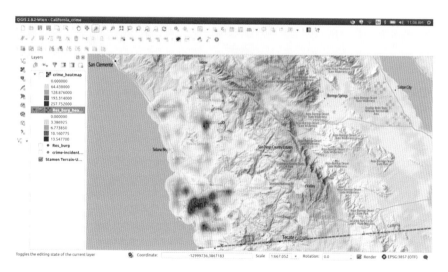

FIGURE 11.35 "Residential burglary" layer on basemap using heatmap plugin tool © QGIS

(Continued)

Open the Layer Properties window for your new heatmap and click on the "Metadata" tab. In the Properties box, you will notice that the mean density is approximately 2.5, and that the standard deviation is approximately 3.47. We can use the raster calculator tool to identify those parts of our heatmap raster that have a higher density of residential burglary than one and two standard deviations above the mean.

Close the Layer Properties box and open the raster calculator. To identify those areas where burglary is at least one standard deviation above the mean, enter the following expression:

```
"Res_burg_heatmap@1" > 6
```

Provide a name for your output file and run the tool. We enter "6" in our expression since our mean of 2.5 plus one standard deviation of 3.47 is approximately 6. The resulting output (Figure 11.36) shows those areas meeting our expression criteria colored white.

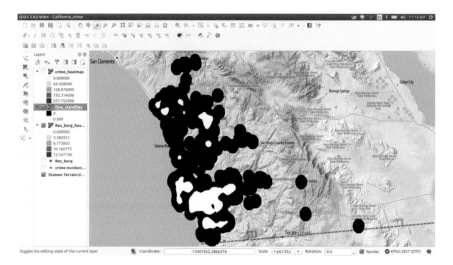

FIGURE 11.36 Using the raster calculator tool to identify those parts of our heatmap raster that have a residential burglary density more than one standard deviation above the mean © QGIS

Now let us run the raster calculator tool again, this time selecting those areas where burglary crime density is at least two standard deviations above the mean. Change the expression from 6 to 9.5 to represent an additional standard deviation, and run the tool again (Figure 11.37). As you would expect, there is now a smaller area of our density raster that meets our expression.

Run the raster calculator tool one more time to see if there are any areas that have a density more than three standard deviations above the mean. Now we can manipulate the symbology of our layers to create a hotspot map of residential burglary in southern California.

For each of your three new raster layers, go to the "Transparency" tab, enter 25% for the global transparency, and enter "0" as an additional no data value. Click on the green "+" symbol to add it to the transparent pixel list, and make sure that the transparency level is 100. For the style properties of each layer, change the

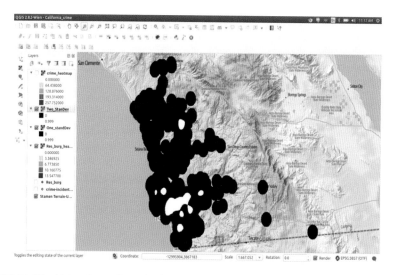

FIGURE 11.37 Using the raster calculator tool to identify those parts of our heatmap raster that have a residential burglary density more than two standard deviations above the mean © QGIS

color from gray to pseudocolor, the mode to equal interval, the number of classes to 2, and a min of 0 and max of 1. Click "Classify." A color is assigned to your 0 values but will not appear on the map since you designated those pixels as transparent. If you desire, you can change the color of the other value. In the example in Figure 11.38, the three-standard-deviation layer is assigned red, the two-standard-deviation layer orange, and the one-standard-deviation layer yellow.

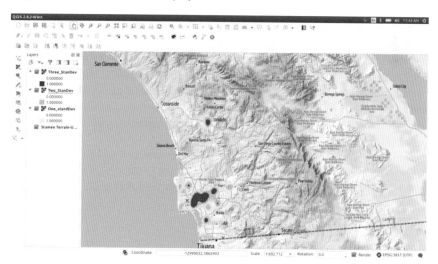

FIGURE 11.38 Heatmap with three-standard-deviation layer in red, two-standard-deviation layer in orange, and one-standard-deviation layer in yellow © QGIS

(Continued)

Point density layers or "heatmaps" can be useful when you are trying to interpret patterns in a large point dataset. Spatial interpolation, on the other hand, can be used to predict values for areas where there are no known values but where values are available nearby. You can estimate the rainfall from a given precipitation event for an area if you have data from a set of nearby rain gauges, for example. In the exercise below, we will create an interpolated raster from a point vector dataset.

To create a raster of interpolated data from a set of known point data, we must first have a point layer containing the values we want to use for the interpolation. In this example, we will use weather data accessed from the US National Centers for Environmental Information. On the web, navigate to www.ncdc.noaa.gov/cdo-web/ to access tools for acquiring climate data, then click on "Browse Datasets" to see the data available for download. Click the "+" beside "Annual Summaries" and then select the "Search Tool" to begin your search. Select "Monthly Summaries" for your observation dataset, choose a date range to select the months and years you are interested in, keep "Stations" in the "Search For" box, and enter a city as your search term. For the example below, we will use the city of Asheville, North Carolina, as the city for our search. Click on "Search" to continue.

You are now directed to a map interface that includes a list of the stations in your search area. Click "ADD" next to each one to add the data for all of the stations to your cart for download. Once you have selected all of the stations, click on the "Cart" icon at the top right of your map to continue the download process. Choose CSV as your preferred output format, make sure your date range is correct, then scroll to the bottom of the page and select "Continue." On the next page, be sure to check the box next to "Geographic location" so that your data download will include latitude and longitude. Then check the boxes next to the data you would like to include – in this case we will select precipitation. On the final page you will be prompted to enter an email address and then submit your order.

Your data should arrive via email in a short amount of time. Once you have received notification that your order is complete, download the CSV and open it in a spreadsheet program to take a look. You will see latitude and longitude data for each station, one date row for each month of your selected data range, and several columns of data (most of which will be filled with –9999, meaning that no data are available). The TPCP column is the one that we are interested in, as it contains the monthly total precipitation (to the nearest tenth of a millimeter) for each station for each month of our date range. Save the CSV file and open QGIS.

In QGIS, use the "Add Delimited Text Layer" tool to import your CSV. Make sure that QGIS recognizes that your file contains latitude and longitude data and that your column headers are correct, then click "OK." QGIS will then ask for a coordinate reference system for your point layer – since we are working with unprojected data we can just enter WGS 84. Click "OK" and you should see a point layer with the weather stations you selected appear on the map canvas.

Let us query out one month of precipitation data from our layer to use in our interpolation analysis. Open the attribute table of your layer and pick a month you would like to use. Use the "Select by expression" tool to query out a subset of data as we have done before to query out a particular month. For example, you might enter:

```
"Date" = 20150401
```

To query out the data for April 2015. Once you have created your selection, save it as a new layer in your QGIS project.

The interpolation tool for QGIS is a plugin, so you will need to go to **Plugins -> Manage and Install Plugins** and search for the interpolation plugin. Once you have installed the plugin, it should be available in the "Raster" dropdown menu in QGIS. Run the tool to open the interpolation dialog box. Input your new vector layer as the input, and select "TPCP" as your interpolation attribute. Click on "Add" to add the layer to list of vector layers. For your output options, you can keep the defaults. You will notice that there are two interpolation methods available; for this example we will be using inverse distance weighting (IDW), which is a common statistical approach to interpolation (you can access the QGIS help guide to learn more about how IDW works). Create a name for your output file and click "OK."

You should now have a raster of interpolated precipitation values for the region you are analyzing (Figure 11.39).

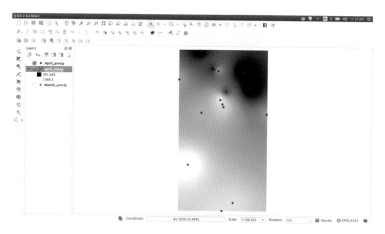

FIGURE 11.39 Raster of interpolated precipitation values © QGIS

Let us change the color of the raster and add a basemap. Go to the Layer Properties for your new raster and select the "Style" tab. Change the render type from singleband gray to singleband pseudocolor. Choose the spectral color map and click "Classify," then click "OK." Now our raster has greens and blues in areas of more precipitation and reds and oranges in areas with less precipitation (Figure 11.40).

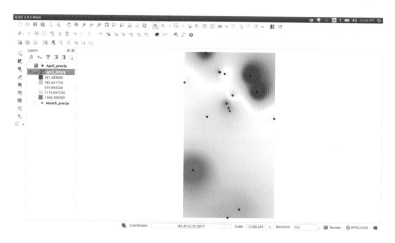

FIGURE 11.40 Spectral color map © QGIS

(Continued)

Finally, we can add a basemap to provide additional geographic context to our raster and weather station layers by accessing the OpenLayers plugin from the Web dropdown menu. Make your precipitation raster 30% transparent so that the underlying terrain is visible (Figure 11.41).

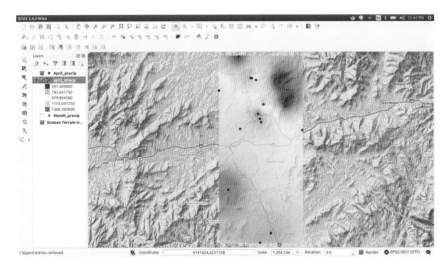

FIGURE 11.41   Spectral color map with added basemap © QGIS

Exercise 7: Creating a map layout with the QGIS print composer

The final exercise of this chapter focuses on creating map layouts in QGIS so that you can save and share maps with others who might not have access to GIS software, either as printed maps or as digital images. To create layouts that include important map elements such as a legend, a scale bar, and a north arrow we can use the QGIS print composer tools.

Let us make a simple map layout of our precipitation interpolation from Exercise 6. In the QGIS dropdown menus, select **Project** > **New Print Composer** and give your new layout a title. The Print Composer window appears with a blank map canvas. From here it is simple to drag and drop the map items we would like to add to our layout.

On the left-hand side of the Print Composer window, you will see a set of tools that let you add various map elements to your layout. Select the "Add New Map" button and then click and drag a rectangle on your layout (Figure 11.42). Using the same technique, add a scale bar and a legend to your layout (Figure 11.43).

To add a north arrow, click on the "Add image" button and draw a small rectangle on your layout where you would like your arrow to appear. Then in the "Item properties" tab on the right-hand side of your screen, click the small arrow next to "Search directories." Several images will appear, including a few options for your north arrow. Select one to add it to your map.

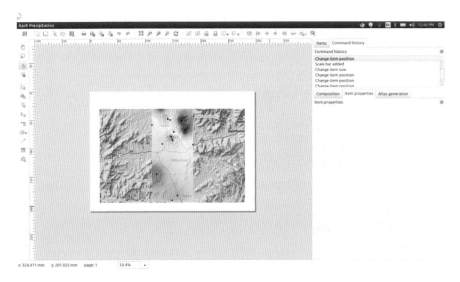

FIGURE 11.42   Spectral color map in © QGIS print composer

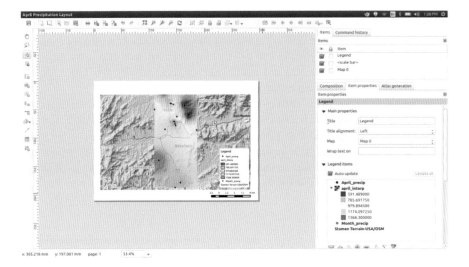

FIGURE 11.43   Spectral color map in © QGIS print composer with scale bar and legend

Finally, add a title to your map at the top of the layout. Click on the "Add new label" button and draw a rectangle at the top of your layout where you would like your text to appear. Back in "Item properties," you can type your text in the Label window. Click on the "Font" button to change the font and size of your text (Figure 11.44).

You now have a simple map layout of your interpolation data. From here you can print your layout or save it as a graphic image for use in publications or on the web. There are several more tools in the QGIS Print Composer that you can use to make professional-looking maps, but this exercise has at least given you an overview of how to create a layout of your work.

(Continued)

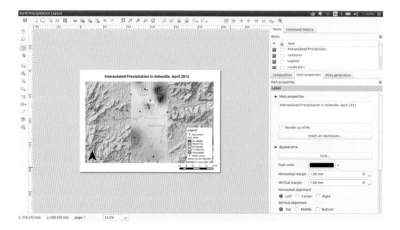

FIGURE 11.44 Spectral color map in © QGIS print composer with title

 **Chapter summary**

This chapter has introduced you to QGIS, a free and open source GIS package for viewing and manipulating spatial data. QGIS provides powerful tools for visualizing vector and raster data layers, performing geoprocessing operations such as buffer and overlay, and creating and querying raster data. It also has layout composition tools that can help you create presentation-quality maps.

In the next chapter, we turn to another popular free and open source GIS package: the Geographic Resources Analysis Support System (GRASS). While it has tools for vector and raster analysis much like those we saw in QGIS, GRASS has some additional powerful tools for analysis and visualization. In addition, much of the GRASS functionality can be accessed in QGIS by using a plugin, so the two GIS packages can be used together to conduct more sophisticated analyses. As such, in the following chapter we will explore both the stand-alone GRASS software and the plugin for use in QGIS.

 **Further reading**

Sherman, G. and Mitchell, T. (2012) *The Geospatial Desktop*. Williams Lake, BC: Locate Press.
Menke, K., Smith Jr, R., Pirelli, L. and Van Hoesen, J. (2015) *Mastering QGIS*. Birmingham: Packt Publishing.

COMPANION WEBSITE

Visit https://study.sagepub.co/abernathy for:

- Links to the websites and free software packages discussed in this chapter
- Downloadable versions of all datasets presented in this chapter

12

Working with Geodata in GRASS

Overview

This chapter includes:

- Exercise 1: Download and install GRASS and begin a new project
- Exercise 2: Working with vector data
- Exercise 3: Working with raster data
- Exercise 4: 3D raster visualization
- Exercise 5: Temporal data analysis
- Exercise 6: Using GRASS tools in QGIS to work with an existing mapset
- Exercise 7: Importing data to create a new mapset
- Exercise 8: Data conversion

In this chapter you will continue working with vector and raster spatial data in another powerful GIS software package: the Geographic Resources Analysis Support System, commonly known as GRASS. GRASS GIS, like QGIS, is a free and open source collection of software tools designed for the visualization, management, and analysis of geospatial data and comes with some very powerful analytic modules. Originally developed by a research branch of the US Army Corps of Engineers, GRASS has been embraced by the open source community and is now an official project of the Open Source Geospatial Foundation. While some consider GRASS to have a steeper learning curve than QGIS, GRASS has an active developer community and a wide variety of tutorials and forums that, when coupled with the comprehensive collection of available tools, make it another good choice for those starting out with GIS.

In the first exercise below, you will download and install GRASS, download some sample data from the GRASS website, and create a new GRASS location and mapset. The following two exercises will focus on vector and raster data manipulation and visualization, allowing you to see how GRASS is both similar to and differs from QGIS in its approach to data analysis. Next, you will examine some of the GRASS tools for 3D visualization and temporal data analysis. Finally, we will return to QGIS and install the GRASS plugin, showing how the two software suites can be used together to provide you with a comprehensive GIS toolkit for working with geodata.

Exercise 1: Download and install GRASS and begin a new project

To download and install GRASS, navigate to the GRASS GIS website at grass.osgeo.org. Here you will find useful information for newcomers to GRASS, along with abundant documentation and tutorials, a gallery of screenshots, and more. Click on the "Download" tab to proceed with your software download. Your browser should notice what operating system you are using and highlight the appropriate package for download; there are files and documentation for Mac, Windows, and Linux. There is also a software bundle called OSGeo4W (http://trac.osgeo.org/osgeo4w/) for Windows that allows you to install GRASS, QGIS, and many other open source GIS software packages with one installer.

While on the GRASS website, you should also go ahead and download some of the sample data provided. Under the "Download" tab, click on "Sample data" to see the available datasets. For the exercises below, we will be using the GRASS 7 data subset of the NC location, which has a smaller file size (50 MB) than the complete NC location dataset. Download the version of the dataset that is appropriate for your operating system and unzip it. Create a new folder on your computer called 'grassdata' and place your unzipped folder inside it.

Once you have downloaded and installed GRASS, run it to see the GRASS startup screen (Figure 12.1). Before you can begin working with data in GRASS, you must first select a database directory, select a GRASS location, and select a GRASS mapset to use. The database directory is where you will store all of

FIGURE 12.1 The GRASS GIS startup page © GRASS Development Team

your GRASS projects (in our case this will be the 'grassdata' folder we just created). The location is the region of analysis for your project and is defined by a map projection, a coordinate system, and the geographical extent of your area of interest. Each location has one or more mapsets, which could be created for different users or different subregions of the location.

To create a new GRASS project using the North Carolina sample data, browse to your 'grassdata' folder and select it as your GRASS GIS database directory. Your downloaded folder of sample data should now appear in your list of available GRASS locations. Click it once to see the available mapsets, which should be "PERMANENT" and "user1." The PERMANENT mapset is set up as a mapset that can only be modified by the owner of the mapset, which is useful for projects where more than one person is involved in the project. Select "user1" for your mapset (you can rename it to something more personal if you like) and then click on "Start GRASS session" at the bottom of the dialog box.

Once GRASS has initialized, you should see two separate windows appear – the Layer Manager and the Map Display. You may notice that a GRASS command line window also appears. GRASS can also be run at the command line or in the command console located in the Layer Manager. The Layer Manager window (Figure 12.2) lets you manage your data layers, select tools for analysis and geoprocessing, and run commands in the command console. The Map Display window is where the results of your operations in the Layer Manager will appear.

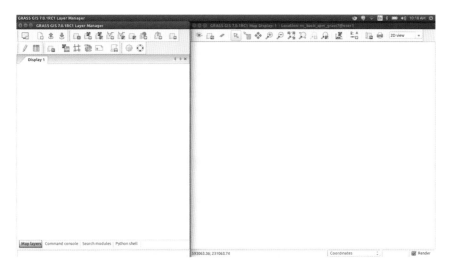

FIGURE 12.2   Layer Manager window in GRASS © GRASS Development Team

If you set up your database, location, and mapset correctly, you should now be able to open data from the North Carolina sample data folder. In your Layer Manager, click on the "Add vector map layer" button (you will notice that it looks quite similar to the same button in QGIS) and then click on the small arrow to the right of the box under "Name of vector map" to see all of the available vector data layers in the NC sample data. Note that all of the available vector layers are in the PERMANENT mapset, even though you are working in a different mapset. Any data layers you create, however, will be saved in your current mapset. Try adding the vector layer named "boundary_state" to add an NC boundary layer to your Map Display (Figure 12.3).

(Continued)

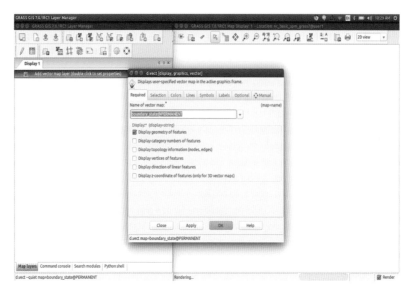

FIGURE 12.3 Adding the "boundary_state" vector layer to the GRASS Map Display © GRASS Development Team

Next, try adding a raster layer to your project. Click on the "Add raster map layer" button in your Layer Manager and then click on the dropdown menu as before to see the list of available rasters in the NC sample data. Add the raster "elevation" to your project. Note that the elevation raster is not for the entire state of North Carolina but rather a small rectangle in the interior of the state. You can use the "zoom in" tool in your Map Display to get a better look at the raster layer (Figure 12.4).

FIGURE 12.4 Adding the "elevation" raster layer to the GRASS Map Display © GRASS Development Team

Spend a few moments familiarizing yourself with the tools for moving around your data layers found in the Map Display window. Again, you will notice that some of these tools look familiar from your experience with the QGIS user interface, while others look quite different. Also, be sure to notice the button in your Layer Manager that looks like a life buoy, as this will take you to the GRASS reference manual. As you begin working with vector and raster modules in the exercises below, you will also notice that individual tools typically include a tab for the specific section of the reference manual that will help you with that particular tool. The reference manual is comprehensive and extremely useful, so be sure to consult it frequently.

Exercise 2: Working with vector data

Now that you have set up your GRASS project and have added vector and raster data to your Map Display, let us examine some of the many tools included in GRASS for data analysis, geoprocessing, and visualization. GRASS gives you several ways to access what may seem like a bewildering number of tools. With your Layer Manager window active, look at the dropdown menu options at the top of the screen. Here you will see tools organized into several categories: File, Settings, Raster, Vector, Imagery, 3D raster, Database, Temporal, and Help. You can also access a similar categorization of tools by clicking on the "Search modules" tab at the bottom of the Layer Manager window.

Let us try adding another vector layer to our map and then buffering it. Click on the "Add vector layer" button and add the vector layer named "schools" to your Map Display. Then, either using the dropdown menu in your Layer Manager or the "Search modules" tab, choose the "Buffer vectors" module to open the dialog box (Figure 12.5). Here you will see that GRASS organizes the various inputs and optional parameters with tabs and highlights which parameters are required in order for the tool to run successfully.

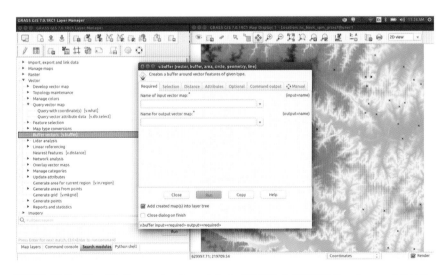

FIGURE 12.5 The "Buffer vectors" module in GRASS © GRASS Development Team

(Continued)

In the "Required" tab, choose the schools vector layer as your input and create a name for your output. Leave the "Selection" tab as is, since we are wanting to buffer all of the schools. In the "Distance" tab, note that you can input different buffer values for the major axis and minor axis, but for now we will keep these the same and enter a value of 500 for both. The rest of the options we can ignore. You might want to click on the "Manual" tab to see notes and examples on running the buffer tool. Click on the "Command output" tab and then click "Run" to see the output as GRASS runs the buffer tool (Figure 12.6).

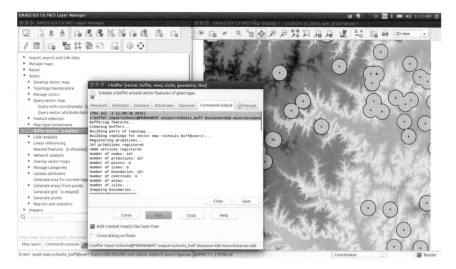

FIGURE 12.6   The output of the GRASS buffer tool © GRASS Development Team

Scroll to the top of the output window and you will notice the following line (where output equals the name of the output file you provided):

```
v.buffer input=schools@PERMANENT
output=schools_buff distance=500 minordistance=500
```

This is the command that was given to GRASS when you ran the "Buffer vectors" (v.buffer) tool. To see how you could run this directly without going through the dialog box, click on the Command console at the bottom of your Layer Manager and place your cursor in the small white box just above the tab. We will change our output file name and increase our buffer distance to 1000. Enter the following line in the command window and then hit Enter:

```
v.buffer input=schools@PERMANENT output=schools_buff1
distance=1000 minordistance=1000
```

You should see a new vector layer with a buffer distance of 1000 added to your map. The command line can be useful in GRASS for running tools quickly and for writing shell scripts for more complicated analyses.

We can also use GRASS tools to query out subsets of vector data and create new vector layers. Suppose, for example, that you are interested in creating a map of all of the elementary schools in the "schools" dataset provided in the NC sample data. To do this we can use the v.extract module in GRASS.

Add the "schools" vector layer in the PERMANENT mapset to your Map Display (Figure 12.7). Double-click on the layer to open the display options and click on the "Symbols" tab. Change the symbol to a large circle and change the symbol size to 8 so that the schools are more visible on your map.

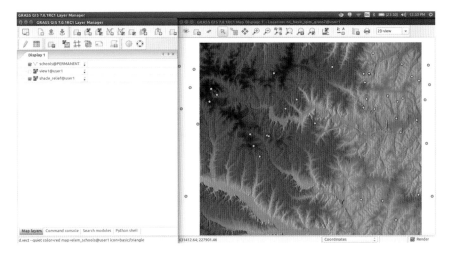

FIGURE 12.7 Adding the "schools" vector layer to the GRASS Map Display © GRASS Development Team

Now take a look at the attribute table. You will see that one of the attribute columns in the table is labeled "GLEVEL" and categorizes each school as elementary, middle or high with the abbreviations "E," "M," or "H." We can select by attributes and immediately create a new layer with the v.extract module. In the dropdown menus in the Layer Manager (or using the "Search modules" tab), go to **Vector** > **Feature selection** > **Select by attributes [v.extract]**. Use the "schools@PERMANENT" vector layer as your input, create a name for your output file, then click on the "Selection" tab. In the "WHERE conditions" box, enter the following query to select all of the points categorized as elementary schools:

```
GLEVEL='E'
```

Run the module and close the dialog box. You now have a new vector layer representing all of the elementary schools extracted from your larger schools dataset (Figure 12.8). Change the symbology of your new layer so that the elementary schools are clearly visible on your map.

(Continued)

FIGURE 12.8 Adding a new vector layer to the GRASS Map Display representing all of the elementary schools extracted from your larger schools dataset © GRASS Development Team

Exercise 3: Working with raster data

Now let us take a look at a couple of the raster analysis tools in GRASS. Return to the "Map layers" tab in your Layer Manager and uncheck the boxes next to all of your layers except for the elevation raster. As we did in QGIS, we can easily create a shaded relief map. Using either the dropdown menu or the "Search

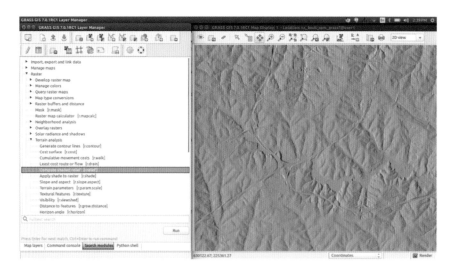

FIGURE 12.9 Shaded relief map of the elevation raster in GRASS © GRASS Development Team

modules" tab, go to **Raster** > **Terrain Analysis** > **Compute shaded relief [r.relief]**. Select your elevation raster as your input (you might notice that there is already a shaded relief map included in the dataset, but we will make our own anyway) and give a name to your output raster. Keep all of the options as their defaults and click "Run" to create a shaded relief map of the elevation raster (Figure 12.9).

Now return to your terrain analysis tools and run the "Apply shade to raster [r.shade]" tool. This tool lets you drape your original elevation raster on top of your new shaded relief raster. Input your new shade raster from your user1 mapset, the elevation layer from your PERMANENT mapset, and provide a name for the output file. You now have a shaded relief map with a color map based on your original elevation raster layer (Figure 12.10).

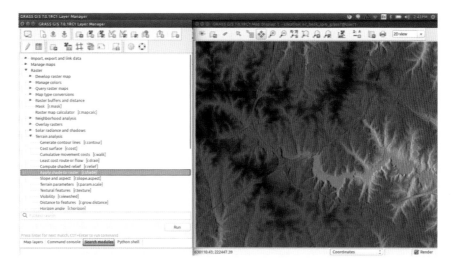

FIGURE 12.10 Shaded relief map with a color map based on the original elevation raster layer © GRASS Development Team

Another common tool that can be applied to a raster elevation layer is the slope and aspect tool. This tool enables you to calculate the slope and direction faced for each cell in an elevation raster. Again in your terrain analysis tools in GRASS, choose the "Slope and aspect [r.slope.aspect]" tool and enter the name of the elevation raster from your PERMANENT mapset. In the "Outputs" tab of the dialog box, enter a name for your slope output and for your aspect output, leaving the rest of the options blank. In the "Settings" tab you can choose to calculate slope in either percent or degrees. Click on the "Command output" tab and then click "Run" to watch the output as GRASS creates your new raster layers. The resulting output may be difficult to understand without further analysis, but we can use the raster calculator tool in GRASS to query out subsets of data from our new rasters.

Right-click on your slope raster in the Layer Manager, and then select "Histogram." The histogram shows that the majority of the cells in your slope raster are between 0 and 10 percent slope, fewer in the 10–20 percent range, and very few above 20 percent (Figure 12.11).

Let us query out the cells in the 10–20 percent range and drape them over our shaded relief raster. In the Layer Manager, click on the "Raster Map Calculator" tool to open the GRASS raster calculator. In the expression box, type the following:

```
slope@user1 >= 10 & slope@user1 <= 20
```

(Continued)

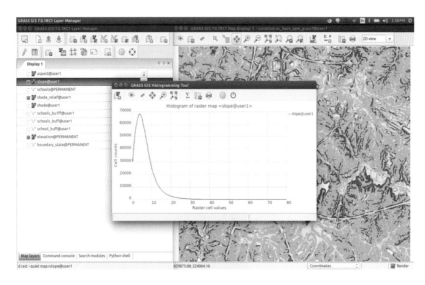

FIGURE 12.11   The "Histogram" tool © GRASS Development Team

Provide a name for your output raster and run the tool. You now have a raster with only two colors – one representing all the areas on your slope raster where your expression is true, and all of the areas where it is false. Back in your Layer Manager, right-click on your newly calculated raster and select "Properties." In the d.rast dialog box, go to the "Selection" tab and enter a "1" in the box for values to be displayed and click "OK." Now only the areas that met the criteria of your expression are displayed on the map. To change the color of the slope layer, right-click it again in Layer Manager and select "set color table." In the r.colors dialog box that appears, click on the "Define" tab and choose a color table from the dropdown menu beside "Name of color table." Run the tool to see the results (Figure 12.12).

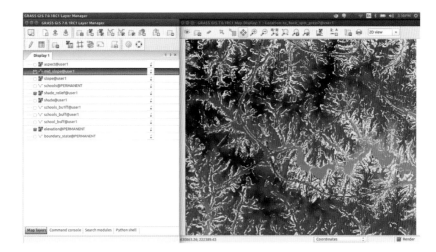

FIGURE 12.12   Color slope raster © GRASS Development Team

Using our same set of raster terrain analysis tools, we can use GRASS to create a visibility map, or viewshed, from a chosen observer point on the map. The tool, called Visibility [r.viewshed], runs an algorithm on the raster to determine which cells would be visible from the selected observer point and creates an output raster of those cells.

To run the tool, click on "Visibility" in the collection of raster terrain analysis tools. Enter the elevation raster from your PERMANENT mapset as the input elevation, create a name for the output raster, and select a coordinate for the observer point. You can click on the arrow beside the coordinate box to click on a location on the map, or you can enter a known coordinate pair. Under the "Settings" tab, keep the default observer height at 1.75 meters to approximate the height of an average human, or increase it to gain some height above the surface of the terrain. Keep the remaining parameters at their defaults, then click on the "Command output" tab and then run the module. This might take some time, so let the module run until the Command output window notifies you that the operation is finished. Depending on the location of your observer point, you should now see a visibility raster showing the visible cells (Figure 12.13).

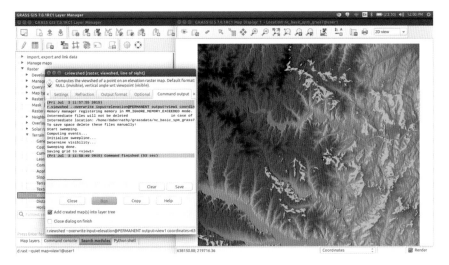

FIGURE 12.13   Visibility raster © GRASS Development Team

You can experiment with running r.viewshed at different locations, with different observer heights, and with some of the optional parameters selected, such as curvature of the Earth and atmospheric refraction. As always, the reference manual is very useful as you work through a new tool, as it typically provides a detailed description of the tool and provides helpful notes and examples. Also, note that GRASS constructs the command line syntax at the bottom of the dialog box for most tools in case you wish to run modules directly from the command line. In our viewshed example above, for example, GRASS constructed the following line at the bottom of the r.viewshed dialog box:

```
r.viewshed input=elevation@PERMANENT output=view1
coordinates=638460.924033,220997.864299
```

(Continued)

If we change the observer height to 10 meters, for example, and choose to account for the curvature of the Earth, our command line output would then read:

```
r.viewshed -c input=elevation@PERMANENT output=view1
coordinates=638460.924033,220997.864299
observer_elevation=10
```

For frequently used modules it can be faster to write commands than to wade through a series of tabs in a dialog box.

Exercise 4: 3D raster visualization

GRASS includes several tools for the visualization and analysis of raster data in three dimensions. To view an elevation raster in 3D, begin a new GRASS project and add the "elevation@PERMANENT" raster layer to your Map Display. In the upper right corner of your toolbar, toggle from 2D to 3D. A new "3D view" tab appears in your Layer Manager and you now see several controls for moving around the 3D raster (Figure 12.14). This can take some time to get used to, so try changing some of the controls to see how they change the perspective of your raster. If you lose sight of the raster from your Map Display,

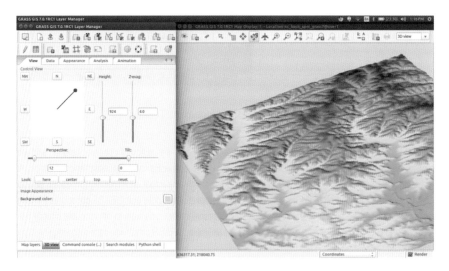

FIGURE 12.14   3D elevation raster © GRASS Development Team

click the "reset" button in your Layer Manager to return to the original perspective. Note that you can exaggerate the variation in elevation by changing the z-values.

We can also add a vector data layer to our 3D map and have it draped across the elevation surface. Try adding the "schools@PERMANENT" point vector layer and the "streams@PERMANENT" line vector layer to your display. In the "Data" tab of the 3D view tools in your Layer Manager, you now have a vector dropdown menu that allows you to change the symbology of your layers and opt to display them on the elevation surface (Figure 12.15).

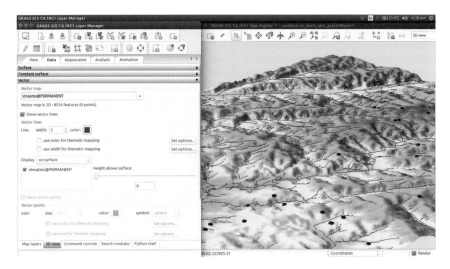

FIGURE 12.15 Vector data layer on the 3D elevation raster © GRASS Development Team

To save a 3D map as an image, click on the "Save display to file" button in your Map Display toolbar. You can then select an image size and save the map display as a TIF file.

Another useful 3D tool in GRASS is the Profile Analysis Tool. This tool lets you draw a transect line across an elevation raster and create an elevation profile of that line. To run the tool, however, you need to return to the 2D view in your Map Display window. Once in 2D view, click on the "Analyze map" button and select "Profile surface map." Select your elevation raster to profile, then select the "Draw transect in map" tool in the Profile Analysis Tool toolbar. Hover over your elevation raster and note that your cursor is now symbolized as a pencil, indicating that the transect tool has been enabled. Click once on your map to begin your transect line, then click on one or more additional locations on your map to create an elevation profile. You can also click the "Plot statistics" button to get additional information about your transect (Figure 12.16).

(Continued)

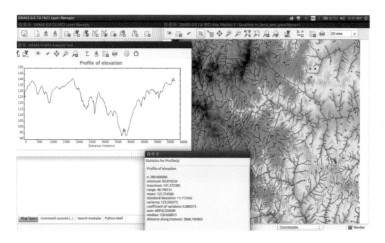

FIGURE 12.16   Profile Analysis Tool © GRASS Development Team

 **Exercise 5: Temporal data analysis**

Time series analysis is another important component of GIS. Being able to monitor changes in geodata over time can provide insights and help us understand spatial phenomena in ways that might otherwise be impossible. In this exercise, you will download another dataset to use as you examine some of the GRASS tools for working with spatiotemporal data. You will need to be running GRASS 7 or higher in order to access the temporal data analysis tools.

The datasets used in this exercise have been made available by North Carolina State University as part of a GRASS workshop that was conducted at a conference on open source GIS software. To begin, navigate to the Github site created for the workshop at ncsu-osgeorel.github.io/grass-temporal-workshop. From there, scroll down to the data download section and download the nc_spm_temporal_workshop zipped folder. This is a large file so it will take some time to download. Once the download is complete, unzip the file into your grassdata folder.

Start a new GRASS session and choose "NC_spm_temporal_workshop" as your GRASS location. Select "climate_2000_2012" as your mapset and then click "Start GRASS session." In the Layer Manager, click the "Add raster" button and take a look at the available rasters. You will notice that there are monthly temperature and precipitation rasters from January 2000 to December 2012. Select the first temperature raster in the set, 2000_01_tempmean, and add it to your project. You can add a legend to the map in your Map Display by clicking the "Add map elements" button and selecting "Show/hide legend" (Figure 12.17).

Next, we can use the t.create tool to create a new space-time dataset, which is a sort of container for the rasters we would like to include in our analysis. At the top of your Layer Manager window, choose **Temporal > Manage datasets > Create [t.create]**. Create a new space-time dataset called "spacetime," keep "mean" as the semantic type, and give the dataset a title and description. Click "Run" to create the dataset.

Now we can add multiple temperature rasters to our dataset by registering them. Back under the "Temporal" dropdown menu, select **Manage maps in datasets > Register maps in datasets [t.register]**. Add the name of your newly created space-time dataset as the input, then click the dropdown arrow next to "Name of the input maps." From here you can select a few months of either temperature or precipitation

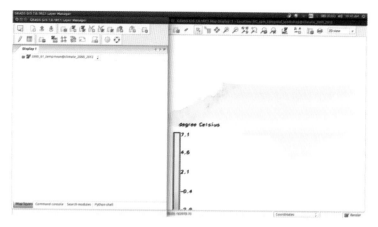

FIGURE 12.17 Map of "2000_01_tempmean" raster with legend © GRASS Development Team

rasters (but not both). Try entering at least six months or so of data for one of the variables. (This is another example of where having some familiarity with the command line can be very valuable, as you could use the g.list module to query "temp" or "precip" from the list of rasters and then paste the results into the map input window, rather than having to select them one at a time).

Now click on the "Time Date" tab in the t.register dialog box. Check the box next to "Create an interval" to mark the start and end time of your animation. Select "months" as your time stamp unit and enter "1" for your time increment. Click on the "Output" tab to watch GRASS run the t.register command and click "Run." GRASS will register your raster maps and update your space-time dataset.

In your Layer Manager window, go to the top menu and select **Temporal** > **GUI Tools** > **Animation tool [g.gui.animation]**. In the top row of tools that appear in the animation dialog box, select "Add, edit or remove animation," then click "Add." In the "Add new animation" dialog box, click on "Add space-time dataset layer" and change the input data type to "Space time raster dataset" (Figure 12.18).

FIGURE 12.18 Adding the "space-time" dataset layer © GRASS Development Team

(Continued)

Click on the dropdown arrow to select the raster dataset you created and then click "OK." Click "OK" twice more to close the animation dialog boxes (Figure 12.19). The rasters registered in your space-time dataset are now rendered and you can run through the series of maps by clicking on the "Play forward" button in the animation dialog box. You can use the additional animation tools provided to adjust the time interval between rasters, loop the animation repeatedly, change the background color, and more. You can also export the animation as an image sequence, animated GIF, or AVI video file.

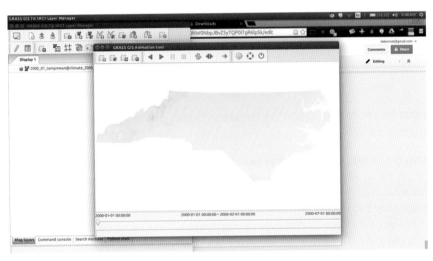

FIGURE 12.19 GRASS Animation tool © GRASS Development Team

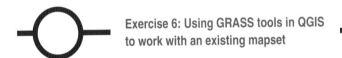

Exercise 6: Using GRASS tools in QGIS to work with an existing mapset

In the remaining exercises of this chapter, we will take a look at the GRASS plugin tool for QGIS. With this tool, you can combine the power of GRASS tools with the QGIS interface (which many find more intuitive and easier to use). For this exercise we will open our existing mapset in QGIS to see how we can interact with our GRASS data.

To begin, run QGIS and start a new project. You may already have the GRASS plugin installed, depending on the version of QGIS you are running. To check, go to the top dropdown menu and select "Plugins." If you see GRASS listed as one of your installed plugins you are ready to go; if not, go to "Manage and Install Plugins" and search for the GRASS plugin to install. You should also have some additional buttons for interacting with GRASS data on your QGIS interface.

Click on the "Open Mapset" button to search for available GRASS locations and mapsets. QGIS should recognize your existing "grassdata" folder and the location we set up back in Exercise 1. If not, make sure that "Gisdbase" is set to your grassdata folder, "Location" is set to the location we downloaded from the GRASS website (e.g., "nc_basic_spm_grass7"), and "Mapset" is set to "user1." Click "OK" to close the dialog box.

Now you can add vector and raster layers from your mapset by using the GRASS buttons provided with the plugin. Click on "Add GRASS raster layer" and select the shaded relief raster you created earlier. The raster is added to your list of layers and displayed on your map canvas inside a large red rectangle, which denotes the full extent of your GRASS location (Figure 12.20).

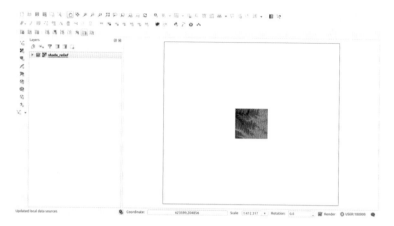

FIGURE 12.20 GRASS raster layer within full extent of GRASS location © GRASS Development Team

You can use the QGIS tools for zooming and panning to move about your map. Try zooming into your shaded relief raster to get a better view. Then click on "Open GRASS tools" to access the GRASS modules dialog box (Figure 12.21).

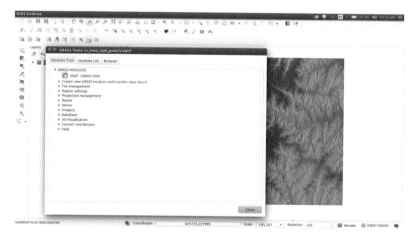

FIGURE 12.21 The GRASS modules dialog box © GRASS Development Team

(Continued)

Note that the modules are listed both in a tree directory structure and as a list. The list view provides the grass module name, a brief description of the tool, and some visual cues as to what the tool does. There is also a filter window available that allows you to narrow the list of modules based on a search term. Click on the "Modules List" tab and enter "random" as your filter search term. The modules list is now narrowed to only those tools that contain some sort of randomization element.

Select the "r.random" module to create a new vector layer of random points within the geographic extent of our current surface raster. Select the shaded relief raster as your input, pick a number of points to allocate, and create a name for the point vector output layer. Click on the "Output" tab and click "Run" to watch GRASS run the module and generate a new point vector layer. Click on "View output" to see the new layer added to your map canvas (Figure 12.22).

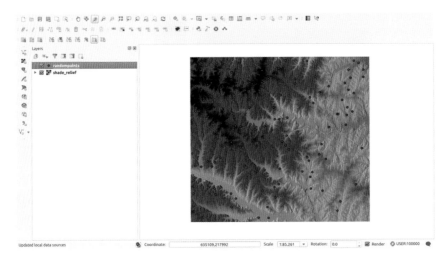

FIGURE 12.22   New point vector layer added to map canvas © GRASS Development Team

Next, try running the GRASS buffer module on your random point layer. In the modules list of the GRASS tools dialog box, enter "buffer" in the filter window to see the available buffer tools: r.buffer and v.buffer. Since we would like to buffer a point vector layer, select v.buffer. Enter your point layer as the input vector map, select a buffer distance of 500, and create a name for your output buffer layer. Run the module and then select "View output" to see your new layer. Reorder the layers so that your points are visible on top of the buffer (Figure 12.23).

Next, let us take a look at some of the GRASS raster surface tools that you can access from within QGIS. Uncheck or remove the current layers, and click on "Add GRASS raster layer" to select a new raster. In the dialog box that appears, change the mapset from "user1" to "PERMANENT" to see the original raster datasets that came with the North Carolina sample data. Choose "elevation" to add the digital elevation model to your map canvas (Figure 12.24).

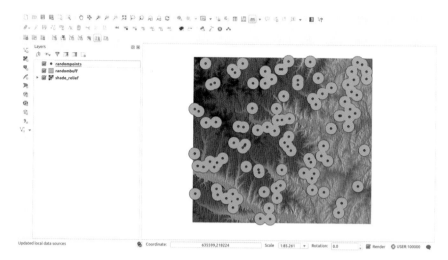

FIGURE 12.23 The point vector layer on top of an output buffer layer © GRASS Development Team

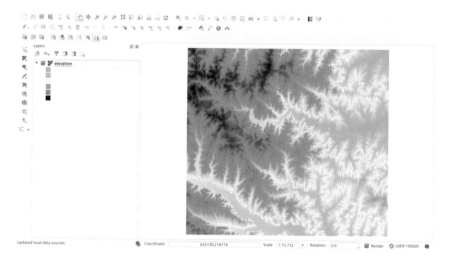

FIGURE 12.24 Digital elevation raster added to map canvas © GRASS Development Team

Open the GRASS tools dialog box once again, and enter "shade" as the filter term in the "Modules List" tab. The r.shaded.relief tool appears. Enter your elevation raster as the input map, create a name for the output raster, and click "Run" to create a shaded relief raster. Once the module has completed running, click on "View output" to view the new raster on your map canvas (Figure 12.25).

(Continued)

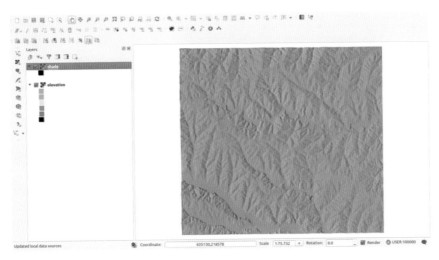

FIGURE 12.25 Shaded relief raster added to map canvas © GRASS Development Team

To create new rasters of slope and aspect, we can use the r.slope and r.aspect GRASS tools. Filter your modules by "slope" to find the r.slope tool module and enter the required parameters to create a new slope layer. Repeat the same steps for the r.aspect module. Add both rasters to your map canvas (Figure 12.26).

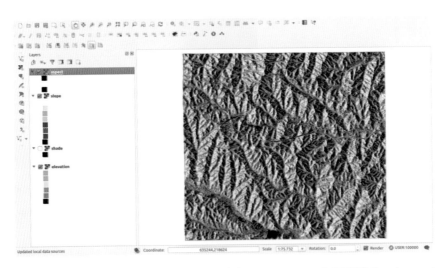

FIGURE 12.26 Slope and aspect rasters added to map canvas © GRASS Development Team

Suppose you wanted to highlight the areas on your map that met all of the following criteria: elevation values above the mean elevation of 110.37, slope values above the mean slope of 3.86, and aspect values that represent east-facing slopes (reminder: you can find the mean values for each raster layer in the "Metadata" tab of the Layer Properties window). To conduct this analysis, we can use the GRASS raster calculator tools.

In the filter window of the "Modules List" tab in your GRASS tools dialog box, enter "calc." Select the module r.mapcalculator to open the dialog box. We can assign each of the rasters needed in our analysis to a layer designated by a letter of the alphabet. Enter your elevation raster as raster "A." your slope layer as raster "B," and your aspect layer as raster "C" (Figure 12.27).

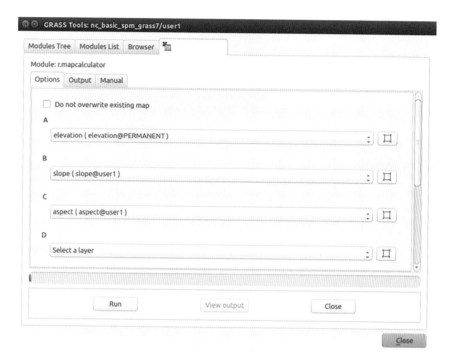

FIGURE 12.27   The r.mapcalculator module © GRASS Development Team

Click on the boxes next to your three layers to choose the region of analysis. Now scroll down until you see the "Formula" window. To construct a formula that meets the criteria of our desired analysis, enter:

```
A > 110.37 & B > 3.86 & (C > 75 & C < 115)
```

This formula will create a new binary raster, where the "true" values are only those cells that have an elevation higher than 110.37, a slope steeper than 3.86, and an aspect between 75 and 115 degrees (our rough definition of "east-facing"). Create a name for the output raster and run the module. Once the module has finished, we can manipulate the colors of our new raster and drape them over our gray-shaded relief map to show those areas meeting all of our criteria (Figure 12.28).

(Continued)

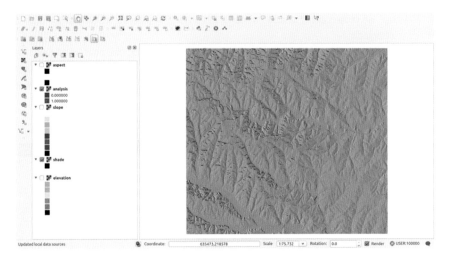

FIGURE 12.28 Binary raster layer in red on top of gray-shaded relief map © GRASS Development Team

---

  Exercise 7: Importing data to create a new mapset

The exercises in the chapter thus far have been working with an existing GRASS location and mapset downloaded from the main GRASS website. But what if you are working with your own geodata in QGIS and decide that you need one or more of the GRASS modules for your analysis? In the following exercise, you will use an existing geodata layer from QGIS to create a new fitted location. You will then import an additional layer into that location so that you begin applying GRASS tools to the layers from within QGIS.

For this exercise, suppose you are working with the Buncombe County LIDAR raster in QGIS that you used for Exercise 5 in Chapter 11. You have the raster loaded in QGIS and have created a shaded relief layer using the QGIS terrain modeling tools (Figure 12.29), but now decide that you would like to use some of the hydrology tools from GRASS to conduct a watershed analysis.

You will notice that the GRASS tools button is grayed out on your toolbar, since you do not currently have an open mapset. To begin working with the QGIS data in GRASS, you will first need to import the elevation raster into GRASS and use its existing geographic information to create a new location.

Click on the "New Mapset" button in the GRASS buttons provided with the plugin for QGIS. In the dialog box that appears, select your existing "grassdata" database for your new mapset and click "Next." For location, select "Create a new location," give it the name "Buncombe," and click "Next." The next dialog box asks for coordinate system information, which we can see from our QGIS screen (bottom right) is EPSG 100002. Enter this number into the filter window to pull up the user-defined coordinate system we are using in QGIS, click once on the coordinate system to select it, then click "Next." The next dialog box sets your default region, and includes a world map where you should see a tiny red box in the eastern US

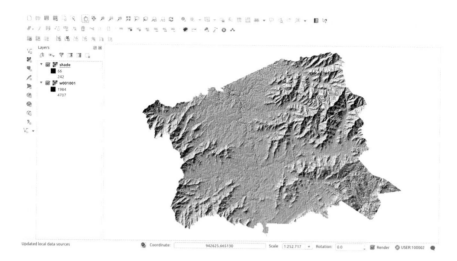

FIGURE 12.29 Shaded relief layer created using the QGIS terrain modeling tools
© GRASS Development Team

that marks your designated location. Click "Next." Enter a name for your new mapset, and click "Next" again. Click "Finish" to create the new location and mapset.

Now that the location and mapset have been created, the GRASS tools button is activated and we can begin importing data layers. Click on the GRASS tools, go to the "Modules Tree" tab, and click the dropdown arrow next to "File management." From there, drill down to **Import into GRASS > Import raster into GRASS > Import raster into GRASS from QGIS view > import loaded raster [r.in.gdal. qgis]**. This tool lets you import any raster into GRASS that is currently loaded in QGIS. Load your elevation raster (named "w001001" unless you renamed it) as your input layer, create a name for your output raster, and click "Run." As long as the coordinate reference system information matches that of your newly created GRASS location, the raster is imported and is now available for further analysis using the GRASS plugin in QGIS. You will need to run the r.in.gdal.qgis tool again on any additional rasters you have loaded in QGIS, such as the shaded relief layer you created. Alternatively, you can import rasters into your new location that are not currently loaded in QGIS using the r.in.gdal tool. Vector import is handled in a similar way, with any currently loaded vector layers imported using the v.in.ogr.qgis module and any vectors not in QGIS imported with v.in.ogr. (See the end of the chapter for more on the GDAL and OGR data translation tools.)

We can also create a new GRASS location from within the GRASS tools. To create a new location that is exactly fitted to the LIDAR raster you are using, go to the "Modules Tree" in the GRASS tools and select **Create new GRASS location and transfer data into it > Create new GRASS location from raster data > Import loaded raster and create a fitted location [r.in.gdal.qgis.loc]**. Once again, we enter our raster elevation layer loaded into QGIS as our input layer, then create a name for both the output raster and a new GRASS location. This module then creates a new GRASS location and mapset based on the coordinate reference information from the input raster. Click on the "Open Mapset" button to navigate to your new mapset and add the imported raster. This time you will notice the red box around your raster, since you created a GRASS location fitted to the extent of your imported raster (Figure 12.30).

(Continued)

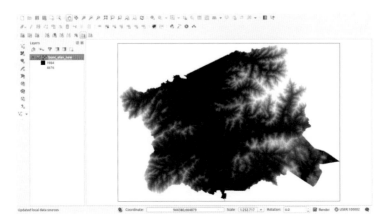

FIGURE 12.30 Elevation raster added to new GRASS location and mapset © GRASS Development Team

Now that we have imported a raster into GRASS and can see that we have a fitted location, we can run analysis modules from the GRASS tools dialog box. In the "Modules List," tab, enter "water" to filter the modules list, then select the Watershed Analysis [r.watershed] module. This module is a fairly complex one, so it is a good idea to click on the "Manual" tab to read more about the inputs and parameters used in the module. To quickly create new rasters representing stream segments and watersheds, go to the "Options" tab of the watershed module, enter your newly imported raster as the elevation input, and choose "10000" as the minimum size for each basin. Create names for the stream segments and watershed basin output rasters, then click "Run." The GRASS module will run through the necessary steps to create your output rasters. Once finished, click on "View output" to add the two new rasters to your map canvas. Make your watershed layer semi-transparent and drape it over a shaded relief layer to see the delineated watersheds (Figure 12.31).

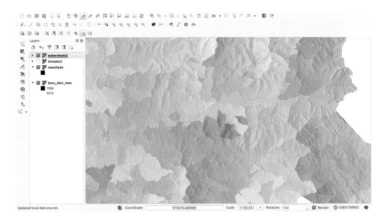

FIGURE 12.31 Watershed basin output raster on top of a shaded relief layer © GRASS Development Team

If you add your newly created streams raster to the map, however, it is not very visible. To make our stream layer more useful, we can conduct one last GRASS operation in QGIS: convert raster data to vector.

Exercise 8: Data conversion

Being able to convert datasets from one format to another is often quite useful in geographic analysis. In our example above, we have a raster dataset representing the stream data we created with the r.watershed tool, but the raster is not useful for visualization since the small cells get lost in our other data layers. If we convert the raster lines to a set of vector lines, however, we can further manipulate the symbology to better accentuate our stream layer.

In your GRASS tools, click on the "Modules List" tab and enter "convert" as your filter search term. You will notice that there are many tools for data conversion; in our case we want to convert raster lines to vector lines so we select the "Convert raster to vector lines tool [r.to.vect.line]." In the dialog box, enter your streams raster as the input map, create a name for your vector output, and click "Run." Click "View output" to add the new vector layer to your map canvas.

Double-click your new streams vector layer to access Layer Properties and change the symbology of your lines to the "River" symbol provided. Change the width of your river lines to "0.5," then click "Apply" to see the resulting vector symbology on your map (Figure 12.32).

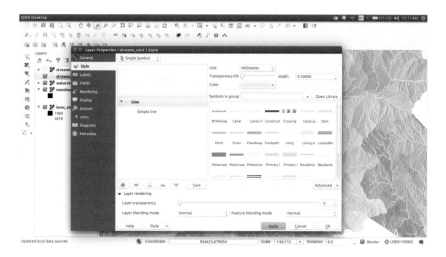

FIGURE 12.32 Adjusting the vector symbology of the stream segment raster in Layer Properties © GRASS Development Team

Chapter summary

This chapter introduced you to another powerful desktop software program for geographic information analysis and display: GRASS. This free and open source geographic information system contains more than 350 modules for the manipulation and visualization of geodata, making it a powerful suite of tools to include

(Continued)

235

in the toolkit for anyone wishing to work with geodata. The chapter also provided some examples of how you can use QGIS and GRASS together for data analysis and visualization using the GRASS plugin developed for QGIS. Combining the strength of these two software packages increases your versatility and flexibility when working with geodata, and each has an active developer community and strong user base which can provide tips, answer questions, and share examples of useful data analysis.

In the next chapter, we turn to yet another tool for geodata visualization: the R programming language. While not considered to be a stand-alone desktop GIS software suite like QGIS and GRASS, R nevertheless has several useful tools for manipulating and visualizing geospatial information. And just as new plugins are being developed for QGIS and new modules are being created for GRASS, there are packages being created for R that provide additional functionality for working with geodata. We saw how R could be used to capture geodata in an earlier chapter, and now we return to R to see how it can be used to create maps and conduct basic geoprocessing operations.

GDAL/OGR

An important set of tools for converting between various types of raster and vector data formats is the Geospatial Data Abstraction Library (GDAL/OGR). GDAL provides the capability for reading and writing in a variety of raster data formats, while the OGR Simple Features Library provides the same capability for vector data. Both GRASS and QGIS use GDAL/OGR for reading and writing raster and vector data, and there are also several useful command line utilities, such as ogr2ogr, that allow for easy data translation in a terminal. For more on GDAL/OGR, visit www.gdal.org.

Further reading

Neteler, M. and Mitasova, H. (2007) *Open Source GIS: A GRASS Approach.* New York: Springer.

COMPANION WEBSITE

Visit https://study.sagepub.co/abernathy for:

- Links to the websites and free software packages discussed in this chapter
- Downloadable versions of all datasets presented in this chapter

13

Working with Geodata in R

 Overview

This chapter includes:

- Exercise 1: Download and install RStudio
- Exercise 2: Import and map vector data
- Exercise 3: Geocoding and web mapping using the ggmap package
- Exercise 4: Mapping with the GISTools package
- Exercise 5: Mapping Twitter data with R
- Exercise 6: Using R with GRASS
- Exercise 7: Creating an interactive web map in R with Shiny

In the previous two chapters we worked with geodata in two of the most popular open source geographic information system software packages, QGIS and GRASS. Back in Chapters 9 and 10, we worked with the R programming language to collect data from Twitter and from sensor networks. In this chapter, we return to the R programming language to see some ways in which it can be used as a geographic information system itself for the analysis and visualization of geodata.

You will recall that R is a very flexible programming language, with thousands of additional tools, called *packages*, available for download from the CRAN package repository for everything from animal activity statistics to XML parsing. Some of the packages created for R have been designed for working with geodata, allowing the user to carry out many of the tasks – data conversion, analysis, visualization – that are typically reserved for dedicated geographic information system packages like GRASS and QGIS. The speed and flexibility of R, combined with its growing popularity as a tool for data science, make it an important addition to your geoweb toolkit.

The previous exercises we conducted in R all took place at the R command line, where we downloaded and installed packages and ran individual R command lines. In this chapter, we will continue working with the R command line, but we will also work with a free and open source software package called RStudio. RStudio is an integrated development environment (IDE) for R that provides many useful features, including dedicated tabs for packages and plots, an editor for R scripts, a workspace window to view the objects in your current project, a searchable command history, and more. In the exercises below, we will use RStudio to download and install several packages from the CRAN repository that are useful for the analysis and visualization of geodata. Later in the chapter we will also explore a web application framework for R, called Shiny, that allows us to create interactive web applications with R data. We will also take a look at using R in GRASS. By the end of the chapter you should feel comfortable using R to work with geodata and understand how its power and flexibility make it a useful geographic information system for analysis and mapping.

Exercise 1: Download and install RStudio

Before we begin exploring the various R packages for working with geodata, let us download and install the RStudio IDE and take a quick tour of the user interface. In a web browser, navigate to www.rstudio.org and click on the download button. Download the RStudio Desktop software package appropriate for your operating system and install the program on your computer. Once you have successfully installed the program, run it and take a look at the tools and windows that appear in the user interface (Figure 13.1). The bottom

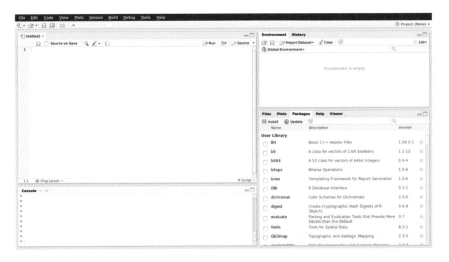

FIGURE 13.1   RStudio user interface © The R Foundation

left window is the familiar R console, where you can write code at the command line just as we did in our prior exercises using R. Above that window is a script editor, where you can write multiple lines of code and save them as a script file. On the top right, you see the "Environment" tabs where any objects you create in the workspace will be shown, as well as a "History" tab that will store any commands we run in our current workspace. Finally, the window in the bottom right portion of the screen has several tabs for viewing files, plots, and a list of packages installed in the current workspace.

Try creating a new object to see how RStudio provides additional functionality to the command line console. In the console, type the following to create a new object named *x* and assign it a value of 100:

```
> x <- 100
```

You should now see the object and its assigned value listed in your "Environment" tab, and if you switch over to the "History" tab you will see the line of code you wrote in the console. Next, try loading the *maps* package from the list of installed packages by clicking the checkbox beside the package name. You will see the command for loading a package library appear in the console window. Uncheck the box next to the "maps" package to unload the library. Now, in the console window type the following:

```
> library(maps)
```

The checkbox next to "maps" in the Packages window is once again selected and the package library is loaded.

To install a package that is not listed in your workspace you can either use the `install.packages()` command that we saw in earlier chapters or you can click on the "Install" button in the Packages tab. Click on the button and type in "maptools" in the dialog box that appears, then click "Install" (Figure 13.2). You can follow the progress of the package download and installation in the console window.

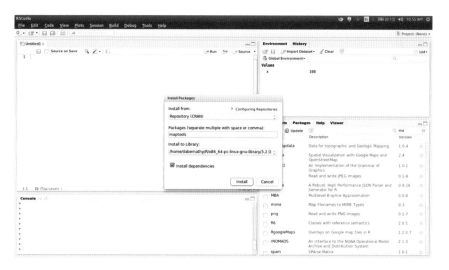

FIGURE 13.2   Installing the maptools package © The R Foundation

(Continued)

Once the package is installed, it will appear in the list of packages available for loading. Click the box next to the maptools package to load the library. (*Note.* Most R packages available for download from the CRAN repository have detailed documentation. You can navigate to cran.r-project.org to see the list of available packages in the repository, then click on the name of the package to get more information about it. On the page for the maptools package, for example, you can find a link for the reference manual named maptools.pdf.)

Next, let us load a sample dataset and make a simple plot to see the plot window in action. In the command console, type "airmiles" to load a sample time series dataset from 1937 to 1960. To make a graph of the data, simply type `plot(airmiles)` in the command console and the graph appears in the "Plots" tab (Figure 13.3).

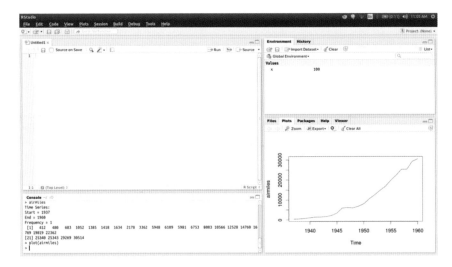

FIGURE 13.3   Graph of the "airmiles" dataset appearing in the "Plots tab" © The R Foundation

Finally, let us download a dataset from the internet and load it in Rstudio. Navigate to https://www.census. gov/quickfacts/dashboard/PST045215/00 to see a web interface for accessing data from the U.S. Census Bureau. The United States is selected by default, so click on the "Download" button to access several ways to download or share the data (you may need to click the "More" button to access the download tools). Choose "CSV" to download a comma-separated file.

In RStudio, select "Import Dataset" in the "Environment" tab and choose "From Local File." Select the CSV file you just downloaded.

RStudio accesses the file and provides a preview of the data before actually importing it (Figure 13.4).

Click "Import" and the data are loaded into R. A new tab is added for the dataset, and the data are listed under "Data" in the "Environment" tab. You can also import downloaded text files into RStudio using the "Import Dataset" tool. In the next exercise, we will download and import a vector shapefile into R using the maptools package we installed above.

FIGURE 13.4 RStudio preview of the soon-to-be imported data © The R Foundation

Exercise 2: Import and map vector data

For this exercise we will download and import a world map into R. To access the data, navigate to www.naturalearthdata.com/downloads and select the cultural datasets from the medium scale data collection. Select "Download countries" from the "Admin 0 – Countries" section of the cultural vectors list. Unzip the downloaded file and save it in a folder on your computer.

Back in RStudio, make sure that the maptools package is installed and loaded. Loading this library should also load the sp library, which is a collection of classes and methods for spatial data. If this package is not loaded in your R workspace, load the library by checking the box in the "Packages" tab or by typing `library(sp)` in the command console. The maptools library should also load the rgeos library – if not, install that package and load it as well.

We can use the `ReadShapeSpatial()` command in the maptools package to import our downloaded shapefile into R. In the command console, enter the following code to import the shapefile and assign it to an object named `world`:

```
> world <-
readShapeSpatial("Downloads/ne_50m_admin_0_countries/ne
_50m_admin_0_countries.shp")
```

Be sure to include the appropriate path to the folder where you unzipped the files. To view the data (Figure 13.5), simply enter:

```
> plot(world)
```

(Continued)

241

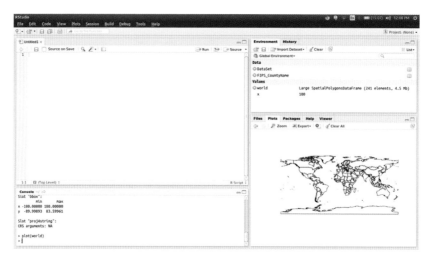

FIGURE 13.5 World map shapefile downloaded into R © The R Foundation

To see a list of the attribute names associated with the shapefile (Figure 13.6), enter the following:

```
> names(world)
```

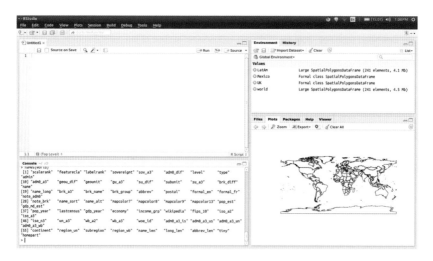

FIGURE 13.6 List of attribute names associated with the shapefile © The R Foundation

To see a summary of the attribute data, enter:

```
> summary(world)
```

Because there are a lot of attribute data and we are not writing R scripts, close the scripting window so that you can expand the size of the console window (Figure 13.7).

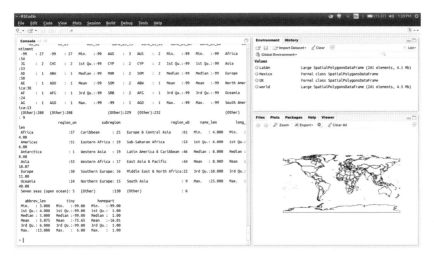

FIGURE 13.7   Expanded console window © The R Foundation

To plot an individual country outline based on its name in the attribute data and plot it (Figure 13.8), we can write the following:

```
> Australia <- world[world$admin == "Australia", ]
> plot(Australia)
```

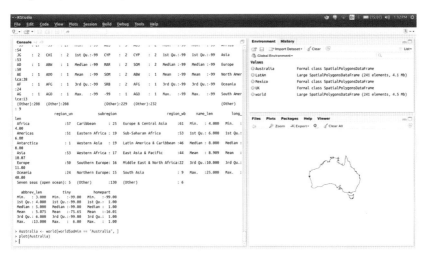

FIGURE 13.8   Plotting an individual country outline from the attribute data © The R Foundation

(Continued)

To change the color of the map (Figure 13.9), we can add one additional parameter to our plot:

```
> plot(Australia, col="blue")
```

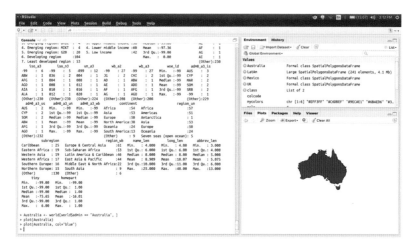

FIGURE 13.9   Changing the color of the map © The R Foundation

We can quickly add some additional map elements to our map and then zoom in for a better view. With the following lines, we can add map axes, a title, and a north arrow (Figure 13.10):

```
> title(Australia)
```

```
> SpatialPolygonsRescale(layout.north.arrow(1),
offset=c(160,-50), scale=10, plot.grid=F)
```

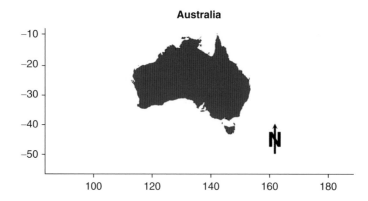

FIGURE 13.10   Map with added axes, title and north arrow © The R Foundation

You can save your plots as an image or PDF file by using the "Export" tool in the Plots window.

Exercise 3: Geocoding and web mapping using the ggmap package

While web mapping will primarily be covered in the next chapter, it is worth exploring some of the simple web mapping capabilities of R. Several R packages contain functions for geocoding, accessing online map tiles, and visualizing geodata, and the packages often include sample data that can be used to test the various functions. In this exercise, we will explore the useful *ggmap* package and see how it can be used to combine spatial datasets and web-based map tiles to create effective visualizations.

To begin, install the ggmap package and load the library:

```
> install.packages("ggmap")
> library(ggmap)
```

The ggmap package imports the additional packages you need for working with web maps, including the RgoogleMaps package which serves as an interface to Google Maps and provides access to Google's geocoding services. We can quickly geocode a place with the `geocode` function, which will return the latitude and longitude of the place entered. To geocode Barcelona, for example, we simply type:

```
> geocode("Barcelona")
```

to see that the longitude of the city is 2.173404 and the latitude is 41.38506. We can also geocode places of interest, just as we did back in the chapter on geocoding.

```
> geocode("the White House")
```

And we can geocode multiple places at once by using the concatenate function in R:

```
> geocode(c("the White House", "Lincoln Memorial",
"Washington Monument"))
```

We can save a geocode request as an object in R and plot the resulting latitude and longitude in R :

```
> wh <- geocode("the White House")
> plot(wh)
```

The output, however, is not all that exciting (Figure 13.11).

To make our geocoded output more useful and visually appealing, we can use the `qmap` function. To geocode the White House and use its latitude and longitude as the center of a map tile from Google Maps (Figure 13.12), we can write:

```
> qmap("the White House")
```

(Continued)

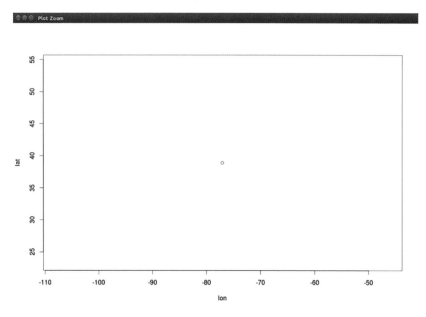

FIGURE 13.11 Basic plot of geocode request © The R Foundation

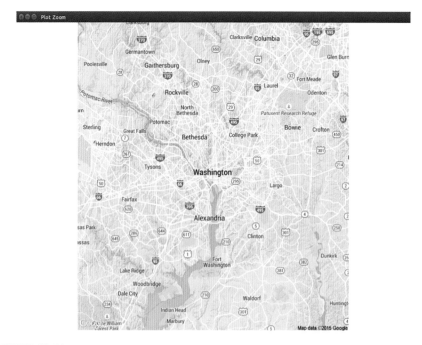

FIGURE 13.12 A Google Maps tile imported using the `qmap` function © The R Foundation

To include a point on the map at the location of the White House (Figure 13.13), we can add the `geom_point` function to specify the location, color, and size of the point.

```
> wh <- geocode("the White House")

> qmap("the White House") + geom_point(aes(x = lon, y = lat),
data = wh, colour = "red", size = 5)
```

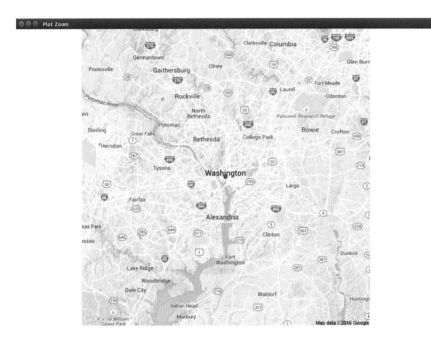

FIGURE 13.13   Location point added to Google Maps tile using the `geom_point` function © The R Foundation

We can also change the zoom level of our map in order to get a better view of Washington, DC (Figure 13.14), by setting the zoom level:

```
> qmap("the White House", zoom = 14) + geom_point(aes(x
= lon, y = lat), data = wh, colour = "red", size = 5)
```

We can change our basemap from the default terrain map to a satellite image (Figure 13.15) by including the `maptype` argument in our line of code:

```
> qmap("the White House", zoom = 14, maptype =
"satellite") + geom_point(aes(x = lon, y = lat), data =
wh, colour = "red", size = 5)
```

(Continued)

247

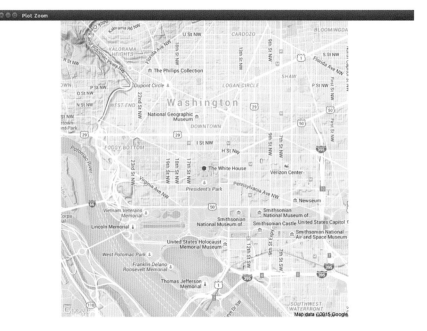

FIGURE 13.14   Zoomed-in view of the basemap © The R Foundation

FIGURE 13.15   Satellite image of the basemap © The R Foundation

It is also possible to change the basemap from Google to OpenStreetMap, Stamen, or cloud-made maps by adding the `source` argument to our code. To create a watercolor Stamen map (Figure 13.16) we can type:

```
> qmap("the White House", zoom = 14, source = "stamen",
maptype = "watercolor") + geom_point(aes(x = lon, y = lat),
data = wh, colour = "red", size = 5)
```

FIGURE 13.16   Watercolor Stamen version of the basemap © The R Foundation

The ggmap package comes with some sample data that we can use to further explore some of the package's mapping tools. A set of geocoded crime data for Houston, Texas, from January 2010 to August 2010, called "crime," is included in the package. We can get some information about the data by examining the names of the attributes and getting a summary of the data.

```
> names(crime)
> summary(crime)
```

We can see in the data summary that crime is broken down into seven categories: aggravated assault, auto theft, burglary, murder, rape, robbery, and theft (Figure 13.17). We also see that latitude and longitude attributes are included. To view a map of Houston in the Plots window, use the `qmap` function:

```
> qmap("Houston")
```

(Continued)

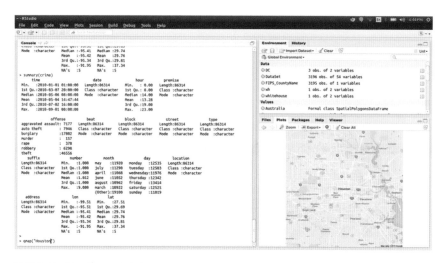

FIGURE 13.17 Geocoded data with map view in the Plots window © The R Foundation

Since there are more than 86,000 recorded crime incidents in the dataset, let us first create a subset of data for one particular category of crime. To create a subset of auto thefts, we can create a new object and assign it a category of crime:

```
> auto_theft <- subset(crime, offense == "auto theft")
```

Run a summary function on the new object to see that there are 7946 recorded auto thefts. We can add these points to our map, further distinguishing between them by symbolizing them in different colors according to the month in which the incidents occurred. First, create a new object for the map you want to use for the base layer (Figure 13.18):

```
> HoustonMap <- qmap("Houston", zoom = 14, source =
"google", maptype = "terrain")

> HoustonMap
```

Next, add together your subset of auto theft locations and the new basemap (Figure 13.19):

```
> HoustonMap + geom_point(aes(x = lon, y = lat,
colour = month, size = 2), data = auto_theft)
```

You will see a warning message in your console saying that there were rows with no values for the latitude and longitude attribute columns and therefore no points could be plotted for those rows. This is because the coordinates of those rows fall outside the bounding box of the Houston map you created. You can change the zoom level of your map to adjust to the area of Houston you are interested in seeing, but here again the

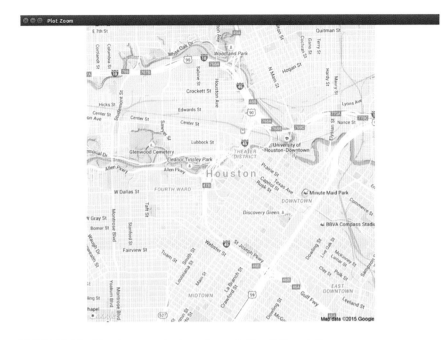

FIGURE 13.18 Houston map for base layer © The R Foundation

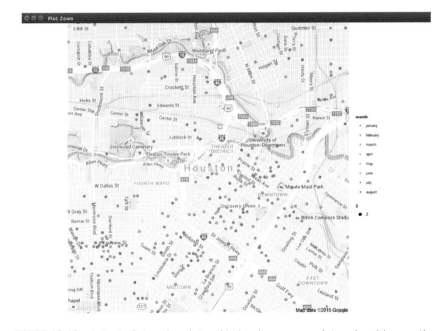

FIGURE 13.19 Auto theft location data added to basemap, points colored by month
© The R Foundation

(Continued)

large number of crime points can overwhelm the map and make it difficult to gain any useful information from the spatial patterns. To see an example of this, let us create a new map that includes the broader Houston area, and then create a map of auto thefts symbolized by day of the week.

```
> HoustonMap2 <- qmap("Houston", zoom = 10, source
= "google", maptype = "terrain")

> HoustonMap2 + geom_point(aes(x = lon, y = lat,
colour = day, size = 2), data = auto_theft)
```

When you enter these two lines in the RStudio console window you will notice that far fewer rows were omitted from the analysis, but the resulting map is somewhat of a mess (Figure 13.20).

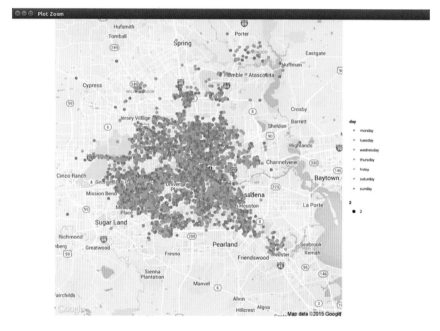

FIGURE 13.20   Map of auto theft location data that includes the broader Houston area
© The R Foundation

One way to simplify Figure 13.20 is to plot auto theft crime density rather than individual crime locations so that we can identify areas where auto theft is more prevalent (Figure 13.21). To do this, we run the stat_density2d function in ggmap:

```
> HoustonMap2 + stat_density2d(aes(x = lon, y = lat,
fill = ..level.., alpha = ..level..), size =2,
bins = 4, data = auto_theft, geom = "polygon")
```

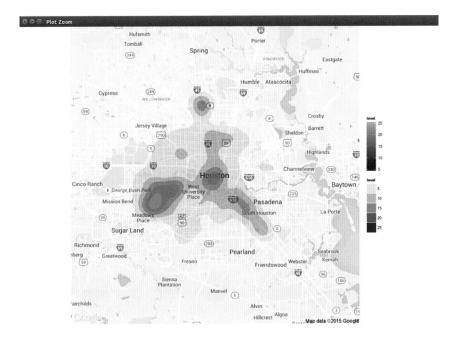

FIGURE 13.21 Plot of auto theft crime density using the `stat_density2d` function in ggmap © The R Foundation

We can also use ggmap to extend our previous work with shapefiles using the maptools package. In Exercise 2 we extracted a vector polygon from a world countries shapefile and simply placed it on a white background. But we can also turn a shapefile into a data frame that can then be overlaid on top of a basemap to make it more attractive, similar to what we did using QGIS when we made a map of EPA sites in California in Chapter 11.

Since we have been working with data from Houston, let us work on extracting the boundary polygon for the state of Texas and place it on a basemap. Using the `readShapeSpatial` function from the maptools package, we can read in the vector layer of US states that we used in Chapter 11, then examine a summary of the data:

```
> US <-
readShapeSpatial("Downloads/cb_2013_us_state_5m/cb_2013
_us_state_5m.shp")

> summary(US)
```

Scroll to the top of the summary data and you will note that no projection information is associated with the data:

```
Is projected: NA
proj4string: [NA]
```

(Continued)

This is because we did not assign any information about the projection of our shapefile when we created the US object. We can rectify this by including projection information when we assign the vector shapefile to our US object:

```
> US
<- readShapeSpatial("Downloads/cb_2013_us_state_5m/cb_2013
_us_state_5m.shp", proj4string = CRS("+proj=longlat
+datum=WGS84"))

> summary(US)
```

At the top of the summary data we now see that the projection information has changed:

```
Is projected: FALSE
proj4string : [+proj=longlat +datum=WGS84 + ellps=WGS84
+towgs84=0,0,0]
```

This is what we want to see. The map is not projected since we are using the geographic coordinates based on latitude and longitude instead of attempting to project the globe onto a flat surface, but we now have our US data in the WGS 84 datum, which we can use to align our data with a basemap.

The next step is to create a new object for the polygon representing Texas:

```
> Texas <- US[US$NAME == "Texas", ]
```

There is one additional step before we can use ggmap to plot our data. We need to "fortify" our Texas data so that R can read it as a data frame. We can create a new object called TX and convert our map to a data frame:

```
> TX <- fortify(Texas)
```

Now we should be able to plot our Texas data on top of a basemap (Figure 13.22) using a ggmap command:

```
> qmap("Texas", zoom = 6, maptype = "satellite") +
geom_polygon(aes(x = long, y = lat, group = group),
data = TX, colour = "white", fill = "black", alpha = .4,
size = .3)
```

The group parameter is needed for R to appropriately render polygons, and the alpha and size parameters define the level of transparency and the width of the boundary line, respectively.

The final two functions we will examine in the ggmap package are the functions for reverse geocoding and transportation routing using the Google Maps API. Reverse geocoding, or identifying a place or street address from latitude–longitude coordinate data, can be done in ggmap by using the revgeocode function, while mapping routes can be accomplished with the route function. Let us look at an example of each.

The revgeocode function requires that the location input be numeric. Note the difference between this:

FIGURE 13.22 Texas data plotted on basemap © The R Foundation

```
> wh <- geocode("the White House")

> wh

      lon      lat
1  -77.03653  38.89768
```

And this:

```
> wh <- as.numeric(geocode("the White House"))

> wh
[1] -77.03653  38.89768
```

If we run the `revgeocode` function on the first object we get an error, but if we run it on the second we see the following:

```
> revgeocode(wh)

[1] "1600 Pennsylvania Avenue NW, Washington, DC 20500, USA
```

(Continued)

The `route` function also taps into the Google Maps API in order to access routing information from place to place. Suppose we are interested in driving from Houston to the White House. We can create new objects for our starting and ending points, then request a route for driving:

```
> from <- "Houston, Texas"

> to <- "the White House"

> route(to, from, mode = "driving", structure = "route")
```

The resulting output breaks down the route into several legs, giving us information on distance and time. We can store this information in another new object and then use `qmap` to map out the route (Figure 13.23):

```
> my_route <- route(to, from, mode = "driving",
structure = "route")

> qmap("United States", zoom = 15) + geom_path(aes(x =
lon, y = lat), colour = "red", size = 1.5,
data = my_route, lineend = "round")
```

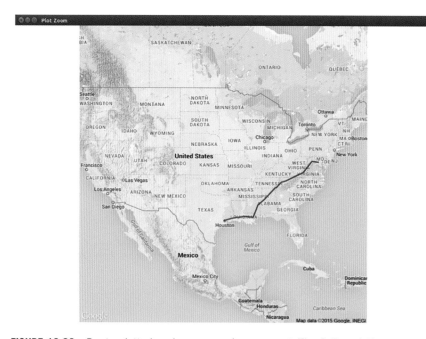

FIGURE 13.23 Route plotted on basemap using `qmap` © The R Foundation

There are several other useful functions built into the ggmap package. As with most packages for R, you can get a good overview of the available functions and some examples of how they can be used by going to the PDF manual associated with the ggmap package (cran.r-project.org/web/packages/ggmap/ggmap.pdf).

Exercise 4: Mapping with the GISTools package

Another useful R package for working with geodata is *GISTools*. As with any other R package available from the CRAN repository, we can install and load it.

```
> install.packages("GISTools")
```

```
> library(GISTools)
```

The GISTools package includes some sample datasets, including tornado touchdown data for the United States, county-level data for the state of Georgia, and several map layers for the town of New Haven, Connecticut. To examine a sample dataset, we can load it, view it in our list of datasets, and then choose a layer to plot:

```
> data(georgia)
```

```
> ls()
```

We can see that there are at least three datasets in our list that pertain to Georgia: "georgia," "georgia2," and "georgia.polys." Plot the "georgia" dataset by entering:

```
> plot(georgia)
```

A map of counties in Georgia appears in the RStudio plot window (Figure 13.24).
We can explore the attributes associated with these spatial data by entering:

```
> names(georgia)
```

```
> summary(georgia)
```

We can see that there is some sociodemographic information included in the dataset, such as the total population by county in 1990 and the percentage of the population of each county designated as rural. For the `PctRural` attribute, we can see in the summary data that the mean value is 70.18 and the maximum value is 100, which gives us some clues as to how rural the state is. To learn more, we can quickly plot a histogram of the `PctRural` attribute (Figure 13.25):

```
> hist(georgia$PctRural)
```

(Continued)

FIGURE 13.24   Map of counties in Georgia in RStudio plot window © The R Foundation

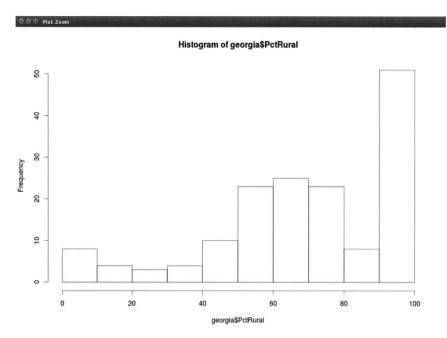

FIGURE 13.25   Histogram of the `PctRural` attribute from the Georgia dataset © The R Foundation

We can just as easily create a choropleth map of the same attribute. A choropleth map is one where the areas or polygons are shaded in proportion to the variation of the attribute being mapped, like the graduated color map we created of population by county for the state of California in Chapter 11. To create a choropleth map with the GISTools package, we simply enter:

```
> choropleth(georgia,georgia$PctRural)
```

And a graduated color map is automatically generated in the Plots window (Figure 13.26).

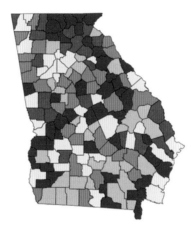

FIGURE 13.26   Choropleth map of the `PctRural` attribute © The R Foundation

R defaults to a red color scheme broken down into five categories. We can change the number of categories and the color scheme used by creating a new object that contains our preferred options. To create a map with nine classes instead of five, for example, we can create our own shading scheme (Figure 13.27):

```
> rural.shades <- auto.shading(georgia$PctRural, n=9)

> choropleth(georgia, georgia$PctRural, shading = rural.shades)
```

We can also change the colors used in the choropleth map with the *RColorBrewer* package in R, which is automatically loaded with the GISTools package. You can see all of the available graduated color schemes (Figure 13.28) by entering:

```
> display.brewer.all()
```

(Continued)

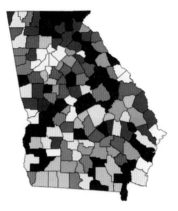

FIGURE 13.27 Choropleth map with adjusted shading scheme to show more categories © The R Foundation

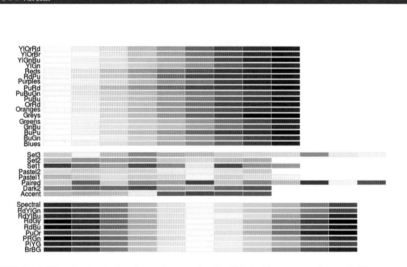

FIGURE 13.28 Graduated color schemes in the RColorBrewer package © The R Foundation

To change the color scheme from reds to six categories from yellow to red (Figure 13.29), we can enter:

```
> rural.shades <- auto.shading(georgia$PctRural,
cols=brewer.pal(6, "YlOrRd"))

> choropleth(georgia, georgia$PctRural, shading = rural.shades)
```

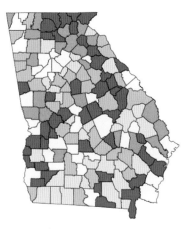

FIGURE 13.29 Choropleth map with a yellow to red color scheme © The R Foundation

We can easily add a legend to the map by using the `choro.legend` function, designating a latitude and longitude coordinate for the legend's location and using the same color scheme used for the map (Figure 13.30):

```
> choro.legend(-81, 35, rural.shades)
```

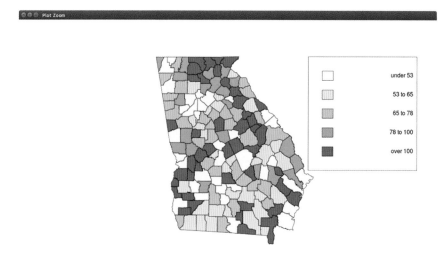

FIGURE 13.30 Choropleth map with added legend © The R Foundation

(Continued)

We can also query attribute data by creating new objects. For example, say we would like to create a map showing all of the counties whose rural population is higher than the mean rural population. We can quickly retrieve the mean for the `PctRural` attribute by entering:

```
> summary(georgia$PctRural)
```

This shows us that the mean is 70.18:

```
 Min. 1st Qu.  Median    Mean 3rd Qu.    Max.
 2.50   54.70   72.30   70.18  100.00  100.00
```

To select the counties with values above the mean, we can enter:

```
> rural.counties <- georgia$PctRural > 70.18
```

We can then plot the counties in Georgia again to create a fresh outline map (Figure 13.24):

```
> plot(georgia)
```

To highlight the counties with values above the mean, we can try:

```
> plot(georgia$[rural.counties],)
```

But that only creates a new outline map with just those counties appearing. To keep the outline map as the base and add the new plot to it, we can tell R to add the second plot to the first. We can also change the color of our second plot to highlight the counties with values above the mean, and add a title to describe our map (Figure 13.31).

```
> plot(georgia)

> plot(georgia[rural.counties,], col = "red", add = TRUE)

> title("Counties in Georgia with rural populations
above the mean")
```

The GISTools package also includes some useful geoprocessing functions. For example, we can perform a points-in-polygons analysis to calculate the number of point features contained within a polygon using the `poly.counts` function. Suppose you were asked to calculate how many tornado touchdowns were recorded for the state of Florida. An outline map of the United States is included in the vulgaris dataset that comes with the GISTools package, so we can quickly create a plot of the US and add the layer of tornadoes (Figure 13.32):

```
> data(vulgaris)
> plot(us_states)
> plot(torn, col="red", add = TRUE)
```

Counties in Georgia with rural populations above the mean

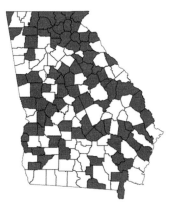

FIGURE 13.31   A plot of counties with values above the mean in red over the outline map
© The R Foundation

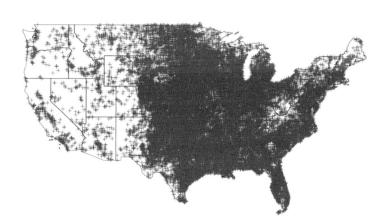

FIGURE 13.32   Layer of tornado touchdowns on top of an outline map of the United States
© The R Foundation

Next, let us extract the state of Florida and create a tornado map focusing in on the state (Figure 13.33).

```
> FL <- us_states[us_states$STATE_NAME == "Florida", ]

> plot (FL)

> plot(torn, col = "red", add = TRUE)
```

(Continued)

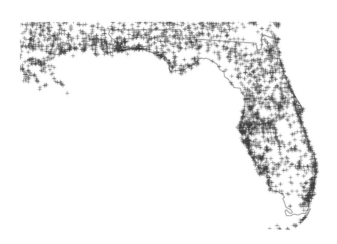

FIGURE 13.33   Tornado map focusing in on the state of Florida © The R Foundation

To count the number of tornadoes within the polygon representing the boundary of Florida, we can enter:

```
> FL.torn <- poly.counts(torn, FL)

> summary(FL.torn)
```

And we see that there were a total of 2340 tornado touchdowns in the state of Florida.

Another geoprocessing tool included in the GISTools package is a tool for creating buffers. Let us plot a map of some of the New Haven data included in the package and create a buffer around each point in the crime point layer. First, we can load the dataset and examine the layers included:

```
> data(newhaven)

> ls()
```

Let us first add the polygon layer representing blocks and the line layer representing roads (Figure 13.34):

```
> plot(blocks)

> plot(roads, col ="gray", add = TRUE)
```

FIGURE 13.34 New Haven map with polygon layer representing blocks and line layer representing roads © The R Foundation

Next, examine the crime data, named *breach*, included in the New Haven dataset.

```
> summary(breach)

Object of class SpatialPoints
Coordinates:
             min        max
Long 536895.7 569227.2
Lat   163291.0 186172.3
Is projected: TRUE
proj4string :
[+proj=lcc +datum=NAD27 +lon_0=-72d45 +lat_1=41d52
+lat_2=41d12 +lat_0=40d50
+x_0=182880.3657607315 +y_0=0 +units=us-ft +no_defs
+ellps=clrk66
+nadgrids=@conus,@alaska,@ntv2_0.gsb,@ntv1_can.dat]
Number of points: 180
```

We see that the layer is projected (which is required in order to run the buffer function) and that the distance units are in feet. Let us add the point layer to our map and then create a new object representing a 1000-foot buffer around each point by using the `gBuffer` function (Figure 13.35):

```
> plot(breach, add = TRUE)

> breach.buff <- gBuffer(breach, width = 1000)

> plot(breach.buff, col = "red", add = TRUE)
```

(Continued)

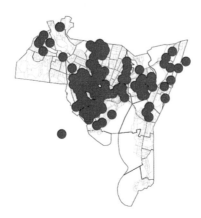

FIGURE 13.35 New Haven map with added point layer and 1000-foot buffer © The R Foundation

If we prefer to make our buffers somewhat transparent, so that the roads and crime points are visible beneath them, we can designate a desired color using values for the RGB and include a fourth value to indicate the level of transparency desired. So to make our red buffer transparent, we can alter the color of our buffer plot (Figure 13.36):

```
> plot(breach.buff, col = rgb(1, 0, 0, .4), add = TRUE)
```

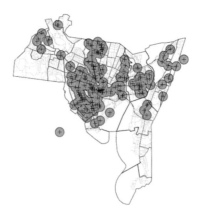

FIGURE 13.36 New Haven map with color adjusted to make red buffer transparent © The R Foundation

Exercise 5: Mapping Twitter data with R

In Chapter 9 you used tools for collecting geolocated Twitter data, including the twitteR and streamR packages in R. We can combine those tools with the mapping packages in R covered in this chapter to write a short script in RStudio that will both collect and map a selection of tweets based on given search and location parameters.

Recall that when you first open RStudio, there is a "Source" window in the top left quarter of your screen that can be used for writing R scripts. An R script lets you string together multiple R functions and run them as a program rather than writing them line by line in the command console. This is particularly useful when working with Twitter data, since we have to establish the OAuth handshake with the Twitter API before we can access any data.

In this exercise, we will construct a script that uses the streamR code we wrote in Chapter 9 with the ggmap tools we used earlier in this chapter to connect to the Twitter API, collect a set of tweets and save them in a CSV file, and then read the coordinate data from that file and plot the tweets on a map.

To begin our script, we can first load the libraries we will need:

```
library(streamR)
library(ROAuth)
library(ggmap)
```

Next, we establish the connection to Twitter via the OAuth handshake, just as we did in Exercise 3 of Chapter 9, except that we are adding the lines into a script instead of typing them in one at a time.

```
requestURL <- "https://api.twitter.com/oauth/request_token"

accessURL <- "http://api.twitter.com/oauth/access_token"

authURL <- "http://api.twitter.com/oauth/authorize"

consumerKey <- "xxxxxyyyyyzzzzzz"

consumerSecret <- "xxxxxxyyyyyzzzzzzzz111111222222"

    my_oauth <-
    OAuthFactory$new(consumerKey=consumerKey,
    consumerSecret=consumerSecret,
    requestURL=requestURL, accessURL=accessURL,
    authURL=authURL)

    my_oauth$handshake(cainfo = system.file("CurlSSL",
    "cacert.pem", package = "RCurl"))
```

(Continued)

267

The next line of code collects tweets using the `filterStream` function of streamR. In this example, we are searching for tweets coming from the Seattle area by constructing a bounding box with the coordinates of the southwest and northeast corners of our desired search area:

```
filterStream(file="SEA.json", locations=c(-123,47,
-122,48), tweets=25, oauth=my_oauth)
```

We then parse the tweets, save them in a CSV file, and read that file into R:

```
SEA.df <- parseTweets("SEA.json")

write.csv(SEA.df, "SEA.csv")

Seattle <- read.csv("SEA.csv", header=TRUE)
```

Finally, we can use the `qmap` function of ggmap to create a basemap and plot the coordinates of our tweets:

```
seamap <- qmap("Seattle", zoom = 9, source = "google",
maptype = "terrain")

seamap + geom_point(aes(x = place_lon, y = place_lat,
size = 2), data = Seattle)
```

Once the code is entered, we can click on the "Source" button at the top of the window to run it. Run the script and enter the authorization PIN that is provided by Twitter. The script will then begin collecting tweets (this might take a few minutes) and will generate a map of all of the tweets collected that have latitude and longitude coordinates that fall inside the bounding box (Figure 13.37).

To look at the Twitter data in R, we can get a list of the names of the data columns and examine the text of the tweets by entering the following in the console window:

```
> names(Seattle)

> Seattle$text
```

We can also open up the entire CSV file in a spreadsheet program to view the collected tweets. To narrow our search further based on a search term, we can add a text search to the `filterStream` function. To search the term "news" in the Seattle area, we could adjust the line of code in our R script to:

```
filterStream(file="SEA.json", locations=c(-123,47,
-122,48), track = "news", tweets=25, oauth=my_oauth)
```

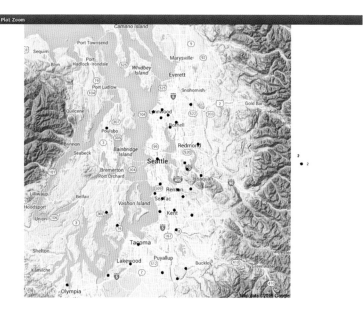

FIGURE 13.37 Map of tweets collected within the coordinates of the bounding box
© The R Foundation

Exercise 6: Using R with GRASS

In Chapter 12, we became familiar with GRASS as a suite of tools for working with geodata and explored some of the ways in which it can be used to analyze and visualize data. We did not, however, spend time exploring how GRASS and R can be used together to analyze geodata. In this exercise, we will see how to run R from the GRASS shell environment and use it to create a barplot from one of the datasets in the North Carolina sample data we downloaded previously.

To use R in GRASS, we will launch GRASS from a terminal and specify the path for the mapset and location to be used for our project. In a terminal window, launch GRASS and enter the path to the sample data we downloaded in the previous chapter:

```
grass70 $HOME/grassdata/nc_basic_spm_grass7/user1
```

This will launch the graphical user interface for GRASS that we are familiar with, but the terminal window remains open as well. From here we can enter GRASS commands as well as enter the R environment. To remind ourselves what datasets are included in the North Carolina sample mapset, we can quickly list out the raster and vector data with the g.list command in GRASS:

```
> g.list rast

> g.list vect
```

(Continued)

We can specify the region for our project with one of the layers in our mapset. Let us use the "streets" layer as our region and then start up the R environment:

```
> g.region vect=streets

> R
```

Now that you are in R, load the library for interfacing with GRASS called "spgrass7." (If this library is not installed, you can install it with `install.packages("grass7")`. If it is installed, the package should load and you will see a confirmation and your current GRASS location:

```
> library(spgrass7)
Loading required package: sp
Loading required package:XML
GRASSS GIS interface loaded with GRASS version: GRASS
7.0.1RC1 and location: nc_basic_spm_grass7
```

Now we can load one of our GRASS layers into R. Let us load the "census" vector layer from our list of vector datasets:

```
> census <- readVECT("census")
```

This interfaces with the v.ogr.out tool in GRASS to bring the layer into R. We can plot the layer (Figure 13.38) by typing:

```
> plot(census, col="gray")
```

We can view the names of the attributes for the polygon features in our map and get a summary of the data:

```
> names(census)

> summary(census)
```

Next, let us load the "points of interest" layer and add it to our map (Figure 13.39):

```
> POI <- readVECT("points_of_interest")

> plot(POI, col = "red", add = TRUE)
```

Review the attribute names and statistics using the same R commands as with the previous layer. Note that there is an attribute named `class` that organizes the points of interest into several categories, like "dam"

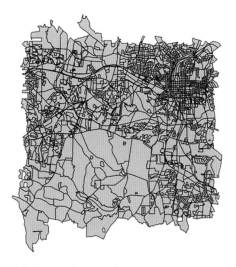

FIGURE 13.38 The GRASS "census" vector layer loaded into R © The R Foundation

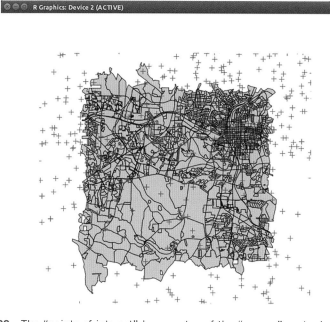

FIGUE 13.39 The "points of interest" layer on top of the "census" vector layer © The R Foundation

(Continued)

or "school." We can use R to create a barplot of the `class` attribute to show the distribution of points of interest across the categories (Figure 13.40):

```
> count <- table(POI$class)
> barplot(count, main = "Points of Interest by Class")
```

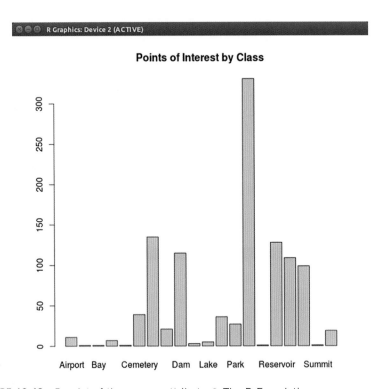

FIGURE 13.40 Barplot of the `class` attribute © The R Foundation

There are too many categories to fit all of the labels on the plot. We can examine the categories in our data with:

```
> unique(POI$class)
```

This gives us all 20 of the categories in the `class` attribute. We can switch our labels to perpendicular on our barplot (Figure 13.41) by adding one parameter to the `barplot` command:

```
> barplot(count, main = "Points of Interest by Class",
las = 2)
```

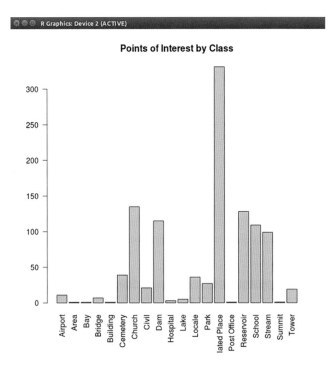

FIGURE 13.41   Barplot with all 20 `class` categories with labels switched to perpendicular
© The R Foundation

Creating charts of your GRASS data in R is just one example of how the R/GRASS integration can be useful. You could also go on to use R to run a wide variety of statistical analyses, from simple regression models to geostatistical analyses using additional R packages such as geoR or rGeostats. You can also use R for batch processing of GRASS data to automate your workflow and quickly conduct analyses on multiple datasets.

Exercise 7: Creating an interactive web map in R with Shiny

The last exercise of this chapter returns to web mapping as we explore the use of *Shiny*, a web application framework for R. Shiny provides tools for creating web pages that allow the user to interact with R data. To see an example of how Shiny works, let us install the Shiny package and load the library in R using RStudio.

(Continued)

Once you have Rstudio up and running, download the package and install it:

```
> install.packages("shiny")

>library(shiny)
```

A Shiny application has two script components – a user interface (UI) script and a server script. To get a feel for what these look like, load one of the sample applications included with the library.

```
> runExample("01_hello")
```

The RStudio console then informs you that it is listening to your computer's IP address, and a new page should appear in your default web browser. The page includes an interactive window with a slider and a histogram on the left, and two tabs for the UI and server scripts on the right (Figure 13.42).

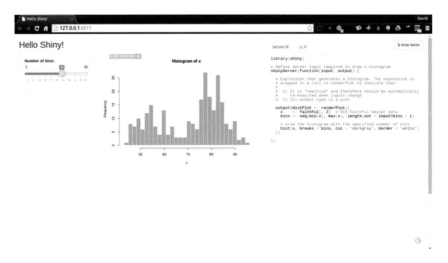

FIGURE 13.42 Shiny application interactive window © The R Foundation

Try moving the slider to change the number of bins in your histogram. The graph adjusts accordingly and the code to redraw the histogram is briefly highlighted in the server.R script. Take a look at the R code in the two scripts to get a general sense of how a Shiny application works. Note that the ui.R script creates the user interface for the application, including the title, the slider bar and the histogram plot. The server.R script contains the code to render the plot and to react to changes from the user.

In RStudio, click on the red stop sign icon at the top of the console window to stop the Shiny application. Now let us create our own version of the Shiny application above and save it in a new directory. First we will copy the existing code from the "01_hello" application into a new application, then we will adjust the code to create a different histogram using another dataset. In RStudio, click **File** > **New Project** and then select

New Directory > Shiny Web Application. You are then asked to provide a name for a new directory name and a path for its location. Create a new directory named "Shiny" and make it a subdirectory of your existing working directory, then click "Create Project." RStudio loads the ui.R and server.R scripts used in the "01_ hello" application (Figure 13.43).

FIGURE 13.43 Creating a new version of the Shiny application in RStudio © The R Foundation

In the server.R script, change the histogram color from gray to purple. Click on "Run App" at the top of the script window to launch the app in a new window (Figure 13.44).

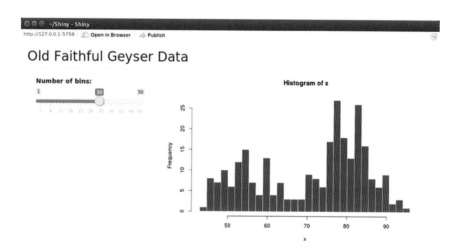

FIGURE 13.44 Purple histogram in new RStudio application © The R Foundation

(Continued)

Let us build our own simple Shiny application that will plot a map of world countries. We can use the "wrld_simpl" map that is included in the maptools package we used previously. In this example, we will load the maptools library, create a simple layout with a sidebar and main panel, and plot an outline map of countries.

In RStudio, create a new Shiny project and remove the sample code that is included in both ui.R and server.R. Let us begin by writing the code for our UI script. First we call the shiny library and write the required function to create the interface:

```
library(shiny)
shinyUI(fluidpage(
```

Next we can add our title panel:

```
titlePanel("Countries of the World"),
```

Next we create the sidebar layout and include a sidebar panel for a brief description of the map as well as a main panel where we will plot the actual map:

```
sidebarLayout(

sidebarPanel("This is the wrld_simpl map that is
included with the maptools package in R"),

mainPanel(plotOutput("mymap")
```

And then we close out all of our functions with parentheses:

```
))))
```

Next we turn to the server.R script. This runs when you start a Shiny application, so we need to load the maptools library. We can also load the data for wrld_simpl to make sure R can read it:

```
library(maptools)
data(wrld_simpl)
```

We then define the server functionality with shinyServer():

```
shinyServer(function(input, output) {
```

Next, we tell the server that the output is an object named "mymap" (the same as the "mymap" we created above in the UI script), call the renderPlot function, and plot the map:

```
output$mymap <- renderPlot({
plot(wrld_simpl)})
}
)
```

And that is all there is to it. Click on "Run App" in the script window of either script. RStudio will first prompt you to save the changes you have made to your Shiny scripts, and then launch the application in a new window (Figure 13.45).

Countries of the World

This map is the wrld_simpl map
that is included with the maptools
package in R

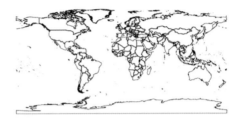

FIGURE 13.45 The "wrld_simpl" map from the maptools library uploaded into R © The R Foundation

We can switch the order of our panels by specifying the location of our sidebar panel in the `side-barLayout` code:

```
sidebarLayout(position = "right",
```

We have successfully created our first Shiny application, but Shiny is designed for interactivity and this application does not let us make any changes via the UI. Let us make our application more interesting by giving the user a chance to toggle between two different maps.

First, let us change the name of our application's title in the ui.R script:

```
titlePanel("My Shiny Mapping App"),
```

Next, we can create a selection box in our sidebar with the `selectInput()` widget, and add a list of choices to choose from:

```
sidebarLayout(position = "right",
sidebarPanel(
selectInput("maptype", label="Choose which map to display",
   choices=list("Countries of the world", "Counties of Georgia"),
   selected="Countries of the world"),
```

This code displays a dropdown menu that allows the user to choose between the two different maps. It defaults to the world map, and it stores the user input into an object we have named "maptype." (There are

(Continued)

277

many different types of input widgets you can use in Shiny; see the widget gallery at shiny.rstudio.com/gallery/widget-gallery.html for code examples for the various widgets available.)

We can create a row beneath the input box that will print out the text output of the user selection.

```
hr(),
fluidRow(column(12, verbatimTextOutput("value")))
```

These two lines create a horizontal row using Shiny's html tags, then establish a row 12 characters wide and print the value from the user's selection.

Now return to the server.R script. We need to load the GISTools library so that we can access the Georgia map we used earlier in this chapter.

```
library(GISTools)
```

FIGURE 13.46 Toggling between "Countries of the World" and "Counties in Georgia" maps
©The R Foundation

278

We also have to change our plotting code, since we want the map to reflect the user input and not just a single map. Instead of just plotting the "wrld_simpl" map, we use `switch()` to create an object that changes based on the input from the dropdown box we created in our other script:

```
output$mymap <- renderPlot({
   data <- switch(input$maptype,
   "Countries of the World" = wrld_simpl,
   "Counties in Georgia" = georgia)
plot(data)})
```

Now the map rendered depends on the user's selection. We add one more line of code so that we also print the selection beneath the dropdown box:

```
output$value <- renderPrint({ input$maptype })
```

And we're done. Now when the script is run, the user can toggle between the two different maps (Figure 13.46).

Hopefully this simple mapping application demonstrates the potential for using Shiny for developing more robust mapping applications. To see examples of mapping tools that have been developed with Shiny, visit the application gallery at shiny.rstudio.com/gallery. The Shiny home page also provides access to more complete tutorials, as well as reference articles and a full reference list of Shiny functions.

 Chapter summary

In this chapter we returned to the powerful R programming language to explore several packages for interacting with geodata. We saw how R can be used as a GIS for the manipulation and visualization of spatial datasets, and we also saw how R can be used to access online geocoding and mapping tools. The flexibility of R was made clear as we used it as an interface to our GRASS datasets, as a tool for mapping geolocated Twitter data, and as an environment for developing interactive web applications through the Shiny package.

We will continue to explore interactive web mapping in the next chapter. While desktop software applications like QGIS, GRASS and R provide us with a tremendous amount of functionality, geodata are increasingly being mapped with applications that live on the internet. Our next set of exercises, then, focuses on web mapping applications like Google Maps and Leaflet that provide us with tools for manipulating and visualizing geodata from your browser.

 **Further reading**

Bivand, R.S., Pebesma, E. and Gómez-Rubio, V. (2013) *Applied Spatial Data Analysis with R (Use R!)*.
   New York: Springer.
Brunsdon, C. and Comber, L. (2015) *An Introduction to R for Spatial Analysis and Mapping*. London:
   Sage.

COMPANION WEBSITE

Visit https://study.sagepub.co/abernathy for:

- Links to the websites and free software packages discussed in this chapter
- Downloadable versions of all datasets presented in this chapter

14

Web Mapping

 Overview

This chapter includes:

- Exercise 1: Creating a Google My Map
- Exercise 2: Mapping with the Google Maps Embed API
- Exercise 3: Creating a simple map with the Google Maps JavaScript API
- Exercise 4: Using OpenStreetMap
- Exercise 5: Using Mapbox
- Exercise 6: Using CartoDB
- Exercise 7: Using OpenLayers
- Exercise 8: Using Leaflet
- Exercise 9: Using R with Leaflet

While desktop GIS software has become increasingly popular in the last several years (and, thanks to open source, accessible and affordable), it still tends to be relegated to a subset of individuals with specific outcomes in mind and with a certain level of expertise with the software. Using maps on the web, on the other hand, is a near-ubiquitous practice among those with access to the internet. Turn-by-turn GPS navigation, viewing one's backyard in online aerial imagery, and scouring digital maps for the nearest sushi restaurant have all become commonplace activities. And, as we saw in Chapter 4, consumers of online maps are increasingly becoming producers – creating their own maps, contributing geographic information, and personalizing digital cartography by having their daily activities and personal interests added to the maps they use each day.

Web mapping goes much deeper than our daily requests for driving directions, however. There are several different internet mapping applications out there, many of which require coding experience in JavaScript or a solid understanding of Structured Query Language. As web mapping continues to mature, new services and programming interfaces are emerging seemingly daily, making it hard to keep up with developments. The exercises below provide an overview of some of the popular web mapping applications being used today. The list is by no means exhaustive, but should provide you with a solid grounding in some of the basics of web mapping.

In this chapter, we will take a look at several different platforms for viewing, editing, and creating maps on the internet. We will begin by creating a collection of points, lines, and polygons on top of a map using Google My Maps. We will then delve further into the Google Maps API to see how we can connect a database in Google Fusion Tables to a Google Map. We will also return to OpenStreetMap to learn how to edit map features in a web browser. And we will examine some of the newer and increasingly popular web mapping services, including CartoDB, Mapbox, OpenLayers, and Leaflet. By the end of the chapter, you should have a solid understanding of the basics of web mapping and feel comfortable in applying one or more of these tools to your own work.

 Exercise 1: Creating a Google My Map

You are likely quite comfortable calling up Google Maps in a browser on your computer, tablet, or phone. Let us take just a moment, though, to go over some of the features of the web interface that appears when you navigate to maps.google.com in a web browser. The most noticeable feature of Google Maps is the map itself, which takes up most of the browser's real estate (Figure 14.1). Controls are confined to the corners of the map – a search bar in the upper left, controls for moving around the map in the bottom right, and an option to toggle between a map view and a satellite image in the bottom left. What appears in the upper right corner depends on whether or not you have a Google account and are signed in. If you are signed in, some of the features on the map will reflect your search and location history.

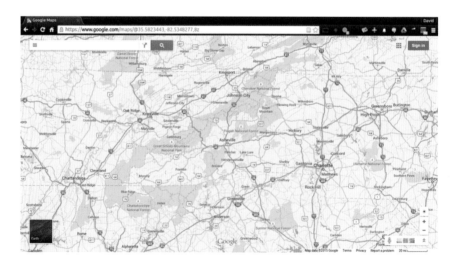

FIGURE 14.1   Google Maps interface © Google

Clicking and dragging the little yellow "pegman" in the bottom right will highlight some roads and features in blue, and dropping the pegman on one of these will transform the map into Google's Streetview imagery. There are also geotagged photos associated with the map view in the bottom right that, when, clicked, will zoom the map to the photo's location. In Earth view, additional controls for rotating and "tilting" the map provide a 3D perspective on the terrain in the map window (Figure 14.2).

FIGURE 14.2   Google Maps Earth view with additional controls for rotating and "tilting" the map © Google

The three stacked lines at top left in the search window, when clicked, provide several additional map features and tools. Some of the tools, such as current traffic conditions and transit information, are only available in certain locations. Options for printing, sharing, and embedding a map in another web page are also available in this dropdown menu. Finally, if you are logged into a Google account, the dropdown menu will also include a feature called My Maps. (The Google exercises in this chapter require you to have a free Google account. If you need to get one, go to accounts.google.com/signup to create your account.)

Once you have an account and are signed in, click on the dropdown menu and select "My Maps." A list of any maps you have created will appear, along with a button you can click to create a new map. Once you click "Create" the map window changes and some new tools appear, including tools for importing data and drawing new features. Click on "Untitled Map" to edit the title and provide a description for the map you want to make. Then click the "Base map" dropdown menu to select from several maps to use as your base layer. Next, zoom into an area on the map where you would like to add some features. In the example below, we will add point, line, and polygon features to a map of Chicago and include some attribute information for each.

Enter "Chicago" in the map search window and then zoom in to the Navy Pier. To add a point, or marker, at that location, click on the marker icon just below the search bar. Your cursor changes to a small cross. Click again on the location you would like to mark. A window appears where you can add a name, description, and a photo or video (Figure 14.3).

(Continued)

283

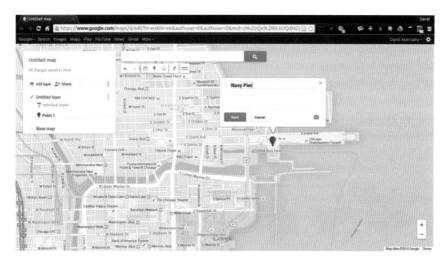

FIGURE 14.3 Adding and naming a marker on the map © Google

Let us enter the name of the marker as "Navy Pier" and enter a brief description. Then click on the camera icon and then select "YouTube search." Type "Chicago Navy Pier" into the search box and hit the search button. Choose one of the videos from the list and click on the "Select" button. The YouTube video is now embedded in your marker (Figure 14.4).

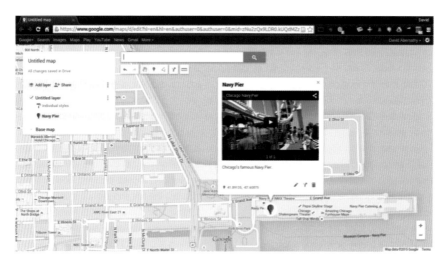

FIGURE 14.4 A YouTube video embedded in the map marker © Google © YouTube, LLC

We can add line features in the same way by choosing the "Draw a line" tool below the map search bar. As you draw a line, you can change direction with a single mouse click, and finish the line with a double-click. As with the marker above, the options to include text and photos or videos appears once the line feature is completed. A polygon feature can be created with the same tool – simply draw a polygon and double-click back at your starting point to close in the feature (Figure 14.5).

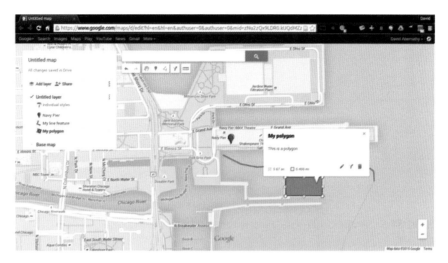

FIGURE 14.5   A polygon drawn on the map © Google

It is also possible to import geodata from a CSV or KML file (recall from Chapter 6 that Keyhole Markup Language is a common file format for storing geographic information in Google Maps and Google Earth). Underneath your map's title, click on "Add layer." In the new untitled layer that appears, select "Import" to pull up a window that allows you to drag a file into the window or select a file for upload. To add the traffic count data from Chapter 7, for example, we can select the "Average_Daily_Traffic_Counts.csv" file from Google Drive or upload it from the computer. A prompt appears to choose columns to position placemarks, and in this example the latitude and longitude from the CSV file are already selected. We can then click "Continue" and choose a column that we would like to use for display when placemarks are clicked, such as "Total Passing Vehicle Volume." Click "Finish" to complete the data import and the traffic count markers are added to the map (Figure 14.6).

The traffic count placemarks are the same color as the marker for the Navy Pier, so let us change the color to blue. Hover the cursor over the "All Items" list in the map legend and click on the small paint bucket that appears. From here we can change the color of our marker to blue and change the symbol to a star. Zooming back into the area around the Navy Pier and clicking on one of the traffic markers gives us the attribute data for that location that are included in the CSV file we uploaded (Figure 14.7).

Clicking the three vertical dots next to the name of the imported layer gives us the option to open the data table associated with our point layer (Figure 14.8). Once open, we can click the dropdown menu button next to the attribute names at the top of each column to sort the data. Click on the "Total Passing Vehicle Volume" dropdown menu and select "Sort Z -> A" to list the traffic locations from highest to lowest recorded vehicle volume. Click on the row at the top of the sorted data table to zoom to the location with the highest traffic count.

Once the map is finished, we can choose to share it. Click on the "Share" icon underneath your map's title and provide a name and description of the map if you have not done so already. The "Sharing Settings"

(Continued)

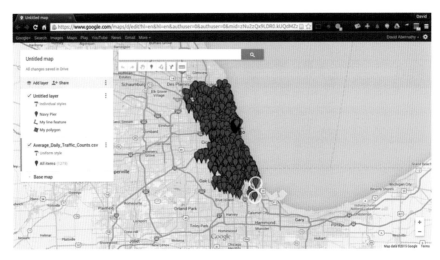

FIGURE 14.6 Traffic count data imported from a CSV file © Google

FIGURE 14.7 Attribute data for the traffic markers (now blue stars)
© Google

window then appears. We can choose to share a link to the map via email or with an application like Twitter. We can also invite people to view or edit the map. To make the map widely accessible online, we can change the privacy settings so that the map is publicly available on the web. Once the map is publicly available, we can also choose to embed the map in a separate web page.

To do that, change the privacy settings to public and close the window. Then click on the three vertical dots next to the "Share" icon below the map's title and select "Embed on my site." A pop-up window with some

FIGURE 14.8 Data table associated with the point layer © Google

HTML code appears. To test that this code works on a local HTML page, open up a text editor and paste the code into a simple document (Figure 14.9). Save the file with the ".html" extension. Close the file, then navigate to the folder where you saved the file and double-click it. The file will appear in a web browser. If you have an existing website, adding the embed code to it will allow you to include the map in your site.

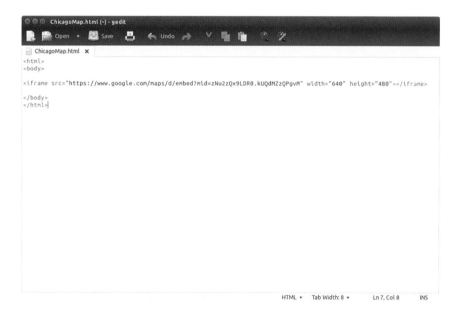

FIGURE 14.9 HTML code for embedding a map in a web page

Exercise 2: Mapping with the Google Maps Embed API

While Google My Maps provides basic functionality for creating web maps, additional tools and features can only be accessed by using the Google Maps application programming interfaces. Creating maps with the Google Maps APIs requires a familiarity with HTML and JavaScript as well as a registered key to the Maps JavaScript library. In this exercise, we will walk through the steps needed to create a simple map view with the Google Maps Embed API. Here again, you will need to be logged into a Google account in order to create a new map project. Portions of the next two exercises are modifications based on work created and shared by Google and used according to terms described in the Creative Commons 3.0 Attribution License.

First, navigate to console.developers.google.com/project and click on "Create Project." Provide a name for your project and agree to the terms of service. A project dashboard will appear once your project has been created, and you can toggle between "Google APIs" and "Enabled APIs." You do not yet have any enabled APIs, so you will need to select an API to get started. Under the Google Maps API list, select the "Google Maps Embed API" (click on "more" at the bottom of the list if you do not see it). Click on "Enable API." You should soon see a notice letting you know that the API is enabled but that you do not yet have credentials. Now click on "Go to Credentials." On the Credentials page you can select which API you will be using (in this case, the Google Maps Embed API) and where you will be calling the API from (in this case, choose "Web browser"). Now click on the button labeled "What credentials do I need?" and proceed to the step for creating an API key. Enter a name for your key and click "Create API key." You now have a long string of numbers and letters to use as your API key – be sure to select it and copy it so that you can paste it into your HTML code.

We can include the key in a frame element inside a simple HTML file, which looks very similar to the file we created for our Chicago map in Exercise 1. We can include a place request in the URL with our API key, which will then be geocoded and used as the center of our map. To create a map centered on Barcelona (Figure 14.10), for example, you would enter the following:

```
<html>
<body>
<iframe width="600" height="450" frameborder="0"
style="border:0"
src="https://www.google.com/maps/embed/v1/place?key= YOU
RKEYHERE&q=Barcelona" allowfullscreen>
<iframe>
</body>
</html>
```

In addition to the "place" mode above that centers a map on a particular location, the Embed API includes three additional map modes that can be called with the request URL: Direction, Search, and View. The Direction mode allows you to map a path between two separate locations (Figure 14.11):

```
https://www.google.com/maps/embed/v1/directions?key=YOURKEY
HERE&origin=Houston+TX&destination=Washington+DC
```

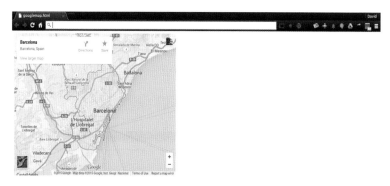

FIGURE 14.10   API key with "Barcelona" place request © Google

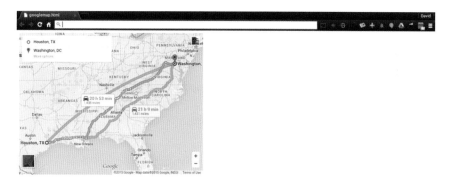

FIGURE 14.11   Mapping a path between two locations using the Direction mode © Google

Search mode (Figure 14.12) allows us to include results of a search query across a given area:

```
https://www.google.com/maps/embed/v1/search?key=YOURKEY
HERE&q=bookstores+in+San+Francisco
```

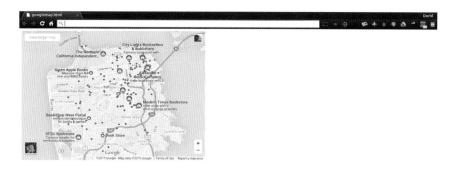

FIGURE 14.12   Search mode in the Embed API © Google

(Continued)

View mode allows us to access a map with no additional markers or directions that is centered on specified coordinates. We can also add parameters to control the zoom level and the type of map that appears. To view a satellite image of the Royal Observatory in Greenwich, England (Figure 14.13), we can enter:

```
https://www.google.com/maps/embed/v1/view?key=YOURKEY
HERE&center=51.48,0&zoom=14&maptype=satellite
```

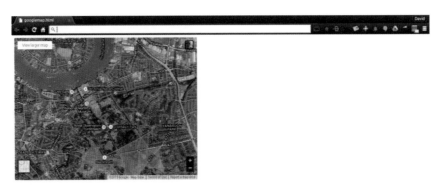

FIGURE 14.13 Satellite image of the Royal Observatory in Greenwich, England © Google

Finally, we can also use the Google Maps Embed API to access imagery from Google's Street View, a large and growing collection of georeferenced panoramic photos. To zoom in on an image of the Lincoln Memorial, for example, we can enter a pair of coordinates and specify the direction and angle of our view (Figure 14.14):

```
https://www.google.com/maps/embed/v1/streetview?key=YOURKEY
HERE&location=38.8893,-77.0501&heading=270&pitch=20
```

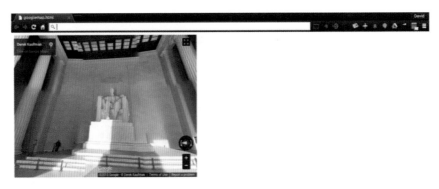

FIGURE 14.14 Google Street View image of the Lincoln Memorial with adjustable direction and angle © Google

Exercise 3: Creating a simple map with the Google Maps JavaScript API

A full introduction to HTML and JavaScript is clearly beyond the scope of this book, but we can take a look at some of the basic elements of the Google Maps JavaScript API by examining one of the examples provided by Google on their site for developers. In this exercise, we will view a simple map, examine the JavaScript and HTML needed to create the map, and then copy and paste the code into our own HTML document to create our own map centered on a different location. We will then see how we can add a couple of lines of code to import points from one of our existing Google Fusion Tables and view them on the map.

Before continuing, however, we first need to return to the Google API dashboard and enable another API. Under Google Maps APIs, click on Google Maps JavaScript API and enable it. You will not need to generate a new API key for this API, as the one you created for the Google Maps Embed API will also work for this API.

To see the code samples provided by Google, navigate to developers.google.com/maps/documentation/javascript/ and click on "Samples." Links to dozens of examples are provided, including sample code for creating controls, adding markers, and viewing additional map layers and images. To get an idea of the code behind a map, we will start with the first example provided: the "Simple map" example listed under "Basics." Clicking on the link brings up the sample map, and the JavaScript code written to create it appears just beneath the map. By default we only see the JavaScript portion of the code, but we can toggle between that window and another window that includes the necessary HTML plus the Javascript code. Take a look at the JavaScript code:

```
var map;
function initMap() {
  map = new
google.maps.Map(document.getElementById('map'), {
        center: {lat: -34.397, lng: 150.644},
        zoom: 8
  });
}
```

While again this is not a text on learning JavaScript, the code sample above demonstrates that it only takes a few lines to create a Google Map to embed in an HTML page. Essentially this code is defining a new variable called map as an instance of the JavaScript Map object. We then see the geographic coordinates for the center of the map and the zoom level desired.

Click on the "JAVASCRIPT + HTML" tab to see the JavaScript code embedded in the HTML code. After the title, metadata, and style elements in the code, we see that the JavaScript is embedded inside a `<script>` HTML element.

```
<!DOCTYPE html>
<html>
   <head>
```

(Continued)

```
<title>Simple Map</title>
<meta name="viewport" content="initial-scale=1.0">
<meta charset="utf-8">
<style>
  html, body {
    height: 100%;
    margin: 0;
    padding: 0;
  }
  #map {
    height: 100%;
  }
</style>
</head>
<body>
  <div id="map"></div>
  <script>
    var map;
    function initMap() {
      map = new
google.maps.Map(document.getElementById('map'), {
        center: {lat: -34.397, lng: 150.644},
        zoom: 8
      });
    }
  </script>
  <script
src="https://maps.googleapis.com/maps/api/js?key=YOUR_
API_KEY&callback=initMap"
    async defer></script>
</body>
</html>
```

Copy and paste this code into a new empty text document and save it as "mygooglemap.html."

Then find the saved file and double-click it to open it in a browser window. A map of southeast Australia, around Sydney, appears in the browser window. Note that by default Google includes some basic tools: controls for zooming and moving about the map, the Street View pegman, and an option to toggle between map and satellite view.

Let us change our code slightly to focus on a different part of the world and add a single line of descriptive text. Open your file in a text editor and change the latitude to 41.83 and the longitude to –87.68. Now add the following two lines of code directly beneath the <body> tag in your HTML section:

```
<br>
This is my Google Map!
```

The `<br>` tag simply creates a break return to create a bit of white space above the text in the next line. Save the file and refresh the browser window to see a new map centered on Chicago (Figure 14.15).

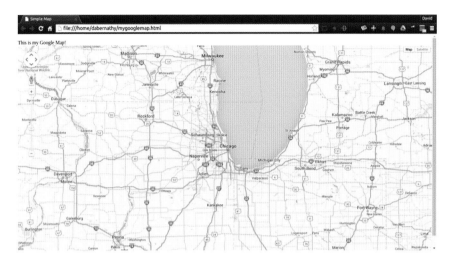

FIGURE 14.15 Chicago map created using JavaScript code © Google

Now that we have the basic framework for a Google Map, we can try adding new code snippets to add new functionality to the map. We could choose to center the map based on the location of the end user with the HTML5 Geolocation API, for example, or change the look and layout of the map controls. For this example, we will take a look at the JavaScript code for adding Google Fusion Tables to a map and import our layer of Chicago traffic count data.

Back in the text editor, let us add a new variable to our code for the new Fusion Table layer we want to add. In addition to our existing map variable, we will add one called `layer`:

```
var map, layer;
```

Now we can assign our new variable the necessary object for querying a Fusion Table by adding the following code underneath the existing code that calls the map:

```
layer = new google.maps.FusionTablesLayer({
  query: {
      select: '\'Geocodable address\'',
      from: 'enter your Fusion Table key here'
  }
});
```

Next, we need to retrieve the actual Fusion Table key for the Chicago traffic fusion table. To do this, open Google Drive and search for the Fusion Table you created in Chapter 7. Once the table is open, select

(Continued)

Tools > Publish to pull up the sharing options for the table. If the table is private, an option for changing the privacy can be accessed by clicking "Change visibility." In the next window, click "Change" and then change the privacy option to "On – Public on the web." Save the changes and return to the table. Click on "File" and then "About this table" to see that the table is now available to anyone on the internet. This is also where we see the id for the table – a long string of numbers and letters. Copy this code and paste it into the HTML file. The code should now look something like:

```
layer = new google.maps.FusionTablesLayer({
  query: {
     select: '\'Geocodable address\'',
     from: '1pK-FSuDiB3Y3YfHVHA_Avy5w9SgUBGwGgddrlbvx'
  }
});
```

Now we include one additional line to add the Fusion Table layer to our map:

```
layer.setMap(map);
```

Before saving the HTML file, change the zoom level to 10 so that we zoom closer to Chicago than before. So our final JavaScript (the portion of the HTML file located between the `<script>` and `</script>`) elements is now as follows:

```
<script>
      var map, layer;
      function initMap() {
        map = new
google.maps.Map(document.getElementById('map'), {
          center: {lat: 41.83, lng: -87.68},
          zoom: 8
        });

layer = new google.maps.FusionTablesLayer({
  query: {
    select: '\'Geocodable address\'',
    from: '1pK-FSuDiB3Y3YfHVHA_Avy5w9SgUBGwGgddrlbvx'
  }
});

layer.setMap(map);

}

    </script>
```

Refresh the map in your browser and the Chicago traffic count points are added to the map (Figure 14.16). If the Fusion Table layer does not appear, make sure that the Fusion Table is public and that the table id is correct in the HTML file.

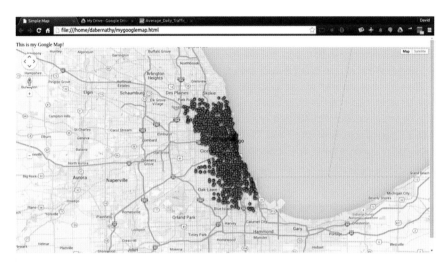

FIGURE 14.16   Chicago map showing traffic count points © Google

This exercise has only scratched the surface of how to create maps with the Google Maps API, but it has hopefully given you enough of a base to be able to work through the API, create your own Google Maps, and embed them in a web page. The Google developer page includes many more tutorials as well as a thorough reference guide to the entire API to help you further your skills in map development. If you plan on creating and publishing Google Maps on the web, it is also a good idea to read over the terms of service (which is true for any of the web mapping applications covered in this chapter). While the Google Maps API is freely available, there is a limit to both the ability to edit a map and the number of hits an online map can receive without incurring a cost. Partly because of this, some web developers have turned to an alternative online mapping application that remains completely free and provides more editing capabilities: OpenStreetMap.

 **Exercise 4: Using OpenStreetMap**

We can think of OpenStreetMap (OSM) as a sort of Wikipedia of mapping: unlike Google Maps, OSM is not owned by any one organization and is freely available to download and edit. We saw how OSM and its Nominatim can be used for geocoding in Chapter 8. In this exercise, we will dive deeper into OSM to learn how to create or edit features on the map as well as use the base layers on the site to create our own web map.

(Continued)

To begin, navigate to www.openstreetmap.org and click on "Sign Up" to create a new account. Once you have created your account you can begin editing the map. Since OSM is open source and also has an editing API, there are many different editing applications to choose from, including both online and stand-alone software products. Here we will use the default iD editor that can be used directly in the browser.

To begin using the iD editor, click "Edit" at the top of the OSM window. OSM gives you the option to begin editing immediately or to go through a brief tutorial to practice using the editor. If you have never edited on OSM before it is recommended that you first walk through the tutorial. The iD editor adds aerial imagery as the basemap so that you can identify features and add points, lines, and polygons to the map.

Zoom to a place with which you are familiar and pan around the area to find a place or feature on the map that is not yet included. Note that the tools on the right-hand side of the map let you change the basemap features; the default is imagery from Microsoft Bing, but you can select from several other base layers depending on the features you would like to edit or create. The tools also include the standard zoom tools, an option to zoom to your current location, a tool to show additional map data, and a help option. At the top of your map are the tools for creating points, lines, and areas to the map, along with a button for saving your edits (Figure 14.17).

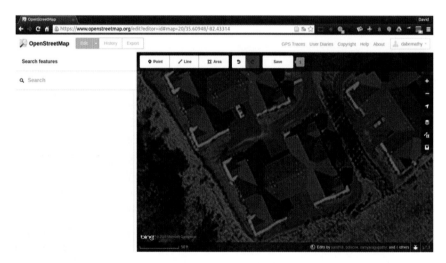

FIGURE 14.17 Microsoft Bing basemap in OpenStreetMap © OpenStreetMap contributors

Try creating a new polygon by clicking around a building footprint. Double-click back at the starting point to close the polygon. Once you complete the area it is highlighted as red, and a choice of feature types shows up on the left-hand side of the map (Figure 14.18). It is a good idea to first save your work before continuing so that you do not lose your edits.

Once the edits are saved, choose a feature type from the list to assign to the new polygon. Depending on which type of feature you select, you will then be prompted to add any additional information on the feature that you might have, such as a street address, name, elevation, etc. Continue editing and try adding a point feature to the map, edit the attribute data, and save the changes. Return to the main OSM window and view your edits on the map (this might take a few minutes, but your edits should eventually appear). You are now one of the more than 1.5 million people who have contributed geographic data to OpenStreetMap.

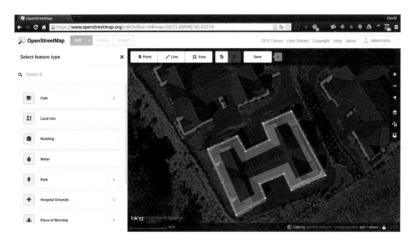

FIGURE 14.18 Creating a polygon on the OSM basemap © OpenStreetMap contributors

It is possible to share a link or embed an OSM map in an HTML file much the same way we did with a Google Map in Exercise 1 above. To embed the map, click on the "Share" button on the right-hand side of the map. From here you have the option to generate a URL, a shortened URL, or an `<iframe>` element in HTML (Figure 14.19). You also have the option to generate a static image and download it. Select the "HTML" option, copy the embed code, and paste it into a new text file. Add the necessary HTML elements and save the file with the ".html" extension.

FIGURE 14.19 Embedding an OSM map in an HTML file

As before, opening the file in a browser allows you to view and interact with OSM. Click on "View Larger Map" to return to the same area back on the OSM website.

Exercise 5: Using Mapbox

Another popular web mapping application is Mapbox. As with Google Maps, Mapbox has its own terms of service and is only free for the starter tier. Mapbox provides additional basemap designs that cannot be found in either Google Maps or OSM, provides access to Landsat imagery, and allows users to both draw and import their own vector data. Mapbox can be edited directly from the browser or from a downloadable software package called Mapbox Studio.

To create a web map with Mapbox, you will need to sign up for a new account. Navigate to www.mapbox. com and sign up for a free starter account, which gives you up to 100 MB in storage and up to 50,000 map views per month. Once signed in, click on "Maps" and select the online editor. This takes you to a map of the world and provides several basemaps from which to choose. The "Data" tab provides an option to draw or import data, and the "Project" tab lets you save your map as a project that can then be shared or embedded in an HTML page (Figure 14.20).

FIGURE 14.20   Choice of basemap styles in Mapbox © MapBox

Let us draw a feature on a map and save the embed code to HTML. Click on the "Data" tab, navigate to an area of interest on the map (the zoom controls are in the bottom left corner of the map window), and click on the "Marker" tab. Click on the map to place a marker. Options for a name, description, as well as the color and symbol of your marker and the precise latitude and longitude of its location, appear in the upper left area of the map (Figure 14.21).

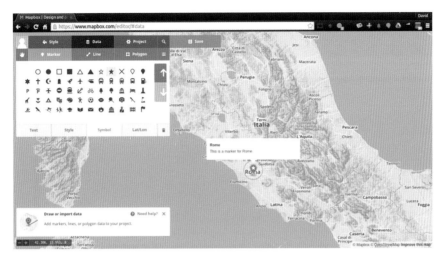

FIGURE 14.21 Placing a marker on a Mapbox basemap © MapBox

Click on the "Save" button to save the project, and a link and HTML `<iframe>` code appear in the window. As with Google Maps and OpenStreetMap, the embed code can be placed in an HTML file to be included on a separate web page.

Exercise 6: Using CartoDB

CartoDB is another web-based mapping platform built largely with open source tools and providing a free entry-level mapping tier. Like Mapbox, CartoDB provides access to several styled map layers to use as basemaps and the ability to import data, and like Google Fusion Tables it provides some basic GIS functionality for querying and symbolizing data. In this exercise, we will create a new project in CartoDB, import our Chicago traffic count data once again, query out a subset of traffic count locations, and plot those locations on our map.

To create a new CartoDB account, go to cartodb.com and click on "Sign Up." Once you have entered your user information and have an account, navigate to the CartoDB dashboard. From here you can view a gallery of existing maps, read documentation on the platform, and create a new map project. To begin our traffic count project, click on "New Map" and then select to create a map from scratch.

We can now connect our traffic data to our project. Click on "connect a dataset" and choose to upload a data file or connect to Google Drive to upload the file from there. Having navigated to where you have saved your traffic count spreadsheet, choose it to connect the dataset and add the data to your CartoDB datasets. CartoDB will then import the data and plot the points on a map. To change the default base layer, select "Change basemap" at the bottom left corner of the map window. Figure 14.22 displays our traffic data points on top of the "Nokia Day" basemap.

(Continued)

FIGURE 14.22   Traffic data points on top of the "Nokia Day" basemap © CartoDB, Inc.

Click on "Options" to toggle off and on map features such as title, legend, zoom controls, and more. Select "Add Element" to add a title box that can be customized and placed anywhere on the map. In Figure 14.23, all of the controls have been removed in the options and a title element has been added in the upper left-hand corner:

FIGURE 14.23   Traffic data map with added title box © CartoDB, Inc.

Now let us take a look at our imported data. At the top of the screen, toggle from "Map View" to "Data View." This view looks and acts much like a basic spreadsheet: we can sort the data by a particular attribute column, as well as add or delete rows and columns. We can also filter the data by using Structured Query Language.

Suppose we would like to limit our map to only a subset of locations with particularly high traffic counts. First, sort the data from highest traffic count to lowest by clicking the small black arrow next to the column named "total_passing_vehicle_volume" and selecting "Desc" as the order. The rows are sorted and we can see that the highest traffic count volume is 165,200 at 1550 South Lake Shore Dr. If we scroll down a bit we see that traffic volumes fairly quickly drop below 50,000, so let us make that our cutoff point. To query out all of the traffic locations with counts higher than 50,000, click on the "SQL" tab on the right-hand side of the screen. A custom SQL query screen appears, and we can see that the default query is:

```
SELECT * FROM average_daily_traffic_counts
```

The asterisk is the symbol used to represent "all," meaning that all rows meeting the criterion will be selected and plotted on the map. Since there are no restrictions other than that the rows selected must exist in the average_daily_traffic_counts dataset, every row is selected and plotted on the map. We can restrict our query to only those locations having high traffic counts by using the WHERE command:

```
SELECT * FROM average_daily_traffic_counts WHERE
total_passing_vehicle_volume > 50000
```

Click on "Apply query" and then click on the "SQL" tab again to reduce the query window. Now only the traffic locations with traffic volumes meeting our query are shown in the Data View (Figure 14.24).

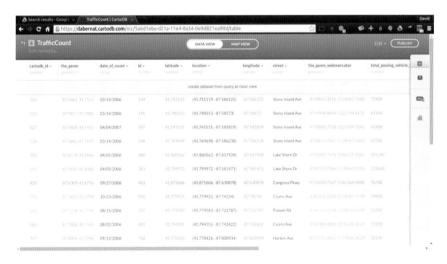

FIGURE 14.24 The average_daily_traffic_counts dataset limited to show only locations with high traffic counts © CartoDB, Inc.

We can now toggle back to our map view and see our queried locations on the map. Click on "create dataset from query" to save the queried rows as a new dataset and view the data on a map. Click on one of the high traffic count locations and select a field to be shown when locations are clicked – in this case we want

(Continued)

to use the `total_passing_vehicle_volume` column as our data to view when the points are clicked. Note that we can change the color of our pop-up windows, and we can also control what appears when the mouse hovers over a point but does not click on it. Change the color of the pop-up window when clicked to header blue and change the "hover" action to the `street` column. Now when we hover over the traffic locations we see the street address, and when we click on one of the points we see the traffic count (Figure 14.25).

FIGURE 14.25 Traffic count displayed for each location point on the map
© CartoDB, Inc.

Click the small arrow in the upper left corner of the screen, next to the name of the current dataset being viewed, to return to the CartoDB dashboard. Load the original traffic count dataset again to return to our full set of traffic data and select "Create map." A map of all traffic count locations on top of the default CartoDB "Positron" basemap appears. On the right-hand side of the map, click the "wizards" icon to see the available mapping options. The default view is the "Simple" map layer, which simply plots the latitude and longitude of each point and styles each with the same symbology. Below this option we can change the color and size of the points on the map, but not much else.

Change the map from "Simple" to "Choropleth." In the "Column" option, click on the dropdown menu to change the column mapped from `ID` to `total_passing_vehicle_volume`. Now our traffic locations are classified into seven different categories and symbolized from light to dark based on the values in that column (Figure 14.26).

Next, try changing the map layer to "Heatmap" and zoom in closer to downtown Chicago. A density map of traffic count locations appears, showing us areas where traffic counts are more prevalent (Figure 14.27).

Let us return to the "Choropleth" map layer, add some additional map items, and publish our map. Click on the "legends" icon on the toolbar on the right-hand side of the map, and change the legend template to "choropleth" in the dropdown menu. Uncheck "show" by the title so that only the labels appear in the legend. A legend appears in the bottom right corner of your map window.

FIGURE 14.26 Traffic locations classified into seven different color categories © CartoDB, Inc.

FIGURE 14.27 Density heatmap of traffic count locations © CartoDB, Inc.

Next, click on "Add Element" at the top of the map and add a title. Click the text inside the new item to make changes to the text and text formatting (Figure 14.28).

Once the map is complete, click on "Publish" in the upper right corner of the screen. As with the other web mapping applications covered in this chapter, we see a URL and an `<iframe>` element that we can copy and paste into our own HTML files. To see what the map will look like when embedded in another website, click on "Go to your map" under the "Embed it" option. A full-screen view of the map appears in a new browser window (Figure 14.29).

(Continued)

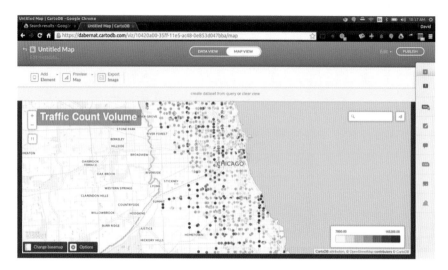

FIGURE 14.28 Choropleth map of traffic count location data with legend and title box © CartoDB, Inc.

FIGURE 14.29 Full-screen view of the map embedded in another website © CartoDB, Inc.

Exercise 7: Using OpenLayers

Yet another open source JavaScript library for web mapping is OpenLayers. OpenLayers supports several different types of tiled basemap layers, including those from OpenStreetMap and Mapbox, as well as multiple types of vector data formats. Significantly revamped in the latest version (OpenLayers 3), this mapping library can be accessed from a script from within an HTML page, similar to the Google Maps API, but the full distribution can also be downloaded and run on a local server since it is fully open source. In this example, we will walk through the quick start tutorial found at the OpenLayers website (openlayers.org) and then see how we can build on this basic map by adding additional components.

The sample code provided on the OpenLayers Quick Start page should look somewhat familiar, since it is similar to the code we wrote in Exercise 3. Essentially the code does three things: calls the OpenLayers JavaScript library, creates a placeholder for a map, and then runs the JavaScript needed to create that map. Let us take a look at these three components and then put the code together to create a map. First, we access the OpenLayers library with:

```
<script
src="http://openlayers.org/en/v3.15.0/build/ol.js"
type="text/javascript"></script>
```

Next, we create a placeholder for the map. This requires us to both create the placeholder in the <body> of our code:

```
<div id="map" class="map"></div>
```

and designate the size of the map in the <head> of our code:

```
<style>
      .map {
        height: 400px;
        width: 100%;
      }
   </style>
```

Next, we need to include the JavaScript code to pull a particular style of map tile, center it on a geographic coordinate pair, and designate a zoom level. We also need to transform the coordinates so that they match the projection of the MapQuest tile being mapped:

```
var map = new ol.Map({
      target: 'map',
      layers: [
        new ol.layer.Tile({
          source: new ol.source.MapQuest({layer: 'sat'})
        })
      ],
      view: new ol.View({
        center: ol.proj.transform([37.41, 8.82],
  zoom: 4
      })
    });
```

You can take a look at the entire code sample provided on the OpenLayers site http://openlayers.org/en/v3.15.0/doc/quickstart.html

(Continued)

Copy and paste the code into a text editor, then open it from a web browser. A map centered on the east coast of Africa appears in the browser window, along with basic zoom controls (Figure 14.30).

FIGURE 14.30   Map centred on the east coast of Africa with basic zoom controls
© Open Source Geospatial Foundation

Let us change the map center, base layer, and zoom level to create a map of London. First, change the coordinates to center on the coordinates for the city: 51.50853, −0.12574. OpenLayers puts longitude before latitude, however, so we need to change the code to:

```
ol.proj.transform([-0.12574, 51.50853]
```

Next, change the zoom level to 10. Let us also change from a satellite image to OpenStreetMap by changing the MapQuest layer from 'sat' to 'osm'. Save the changes and refresh the map in the browser to see the result (Figure 14.31).

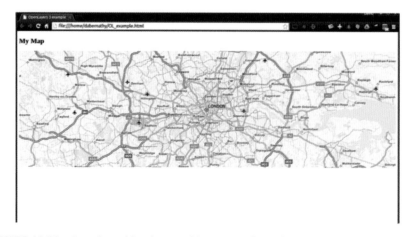

FIGURE 14.31   OpenStreetMap image of London © Open Source Geospatial Foundation

Now that we have a basic map, we can consult the OpenLayers API reference (openlayers.org/en/master/apidoc/index.html) to learn how to add controls, layers, and other components to build upon this basic code. For example, we can add a graticule to our map by calling `ol.Graticule` and designating the color, width, and symbol of the line we want to use. Add the following code to the HTML document just before the `</script>` line to add a red, dotted graticule to the map (Figure 14.32):

```
var graticule = new ol.Graticule({
  // the style to use for the lines, optional.
  strokeStyle: new ol.style.Stroke({
        color: 'rgba(255,120,0,0.9)',
        width: 2,
        lineDash: [0.5, 4]
  })
});
graticule.setMap(map);
```

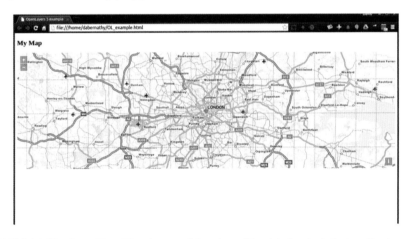

FIGURE 14.32 OpenStreetMap image of London with added red, dotted graticule
© Open Source Geospatial Foundation

The easiest way to learn more about using OpenLayers is to look at the dozens of examples provided on the openlayers.org website, where there is sample code for everything from adding vector layers to a map to creating interactive pop-up windows. The variety of basemap and vector formats that can be used in OpenLayers, and the fact that the entire library can be downloaded and installed locally, make it a good option for web mapping.

Exercise 8: Using Leaflet

The final web mapping JavaScript we will examine is a newer library called Leaflet. Like OpenLayers, Leaflet is open source and lets you bring in many different types of basemap tiles and vector data formats to create

(Continued)

interactive maps. Since it is a JavaScript library, the code looks similar to our previous JavaScript examples. In this exercise, we will use the Leaflet JavaScript library to create a map using OpenTopoMap (a map layer from OpenStreetMap designed to render terrain).

Start a new HTML document and include the following three lines in the `<head>` of your document:

```
<title>My Leaflet Map!</title>

<link rel="stylesheet"
href="http://cdnjs.cloudflare.com/ajax/libs/leaflet/0.7.3/
leaflet.css" />

<script
src="http://cdnjs.cloudflare.com/ajax/libs/leaflet/0.7.3/
leaflet.js"></script>
```

The map now has a title along with the necessary style sheet document and JavaScript library. Let us also style the map so that it fills the entire browser screen:

```
<style>

#map{ height: 100% }

</style>
```

Now move to the `<body>` of the HTML document. As before, we designate a placeholder for the map:

```
<div id="map"></div>
```

Next comes the Leaflet script. We first start the script and initialize a new map, including the latitude and longitude and zoom level. This code centers the map on Mount Rainier, Washington:

```
<script>
var map = L.map("map").setView([46.8529, -121.7604], 8);
```

Now we can load a tile layer. To load tiles from OpenTopoMap, we use `L.tileLayer` and point to the appropriate URL (the `z` represents zoom level, while the `x` and `y` refer to the geographic coordinates). We also include attribution information, add the layer to our map, and then end the script:

```
L.tileLayer('http://tile.opentopomap.org/{z}/{x}/{y}.png',
{
attribution: 'Tiles by <a
href="http://openstreetmap.org">OpenStreetMap</a>',
}).addTo(map);
</script>
```

Save the file and load it in a web browser to render the map (Figure 14.33).

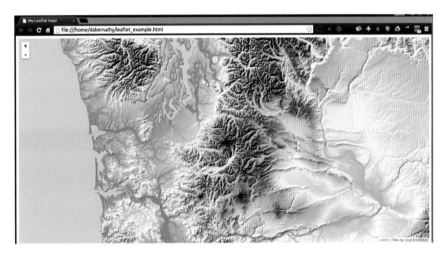

FIGURE 14.33   Map with tiles uploaded from OpenTopoMap © Vladimir Agafonkin

As with the other web mapping applications we have examined, gaining familiarity with the API is essential for creating more complex maps in Leaflet. To learn more about the Leaflet JavaScript Library, go to the API reference at leafletjs.com/reference.html.

Exercise 9: Using R with Leaflet

This final exercise of the chapter finds us returning to the R programming language, where we will examine the integration of R and Leaflet. The R package *leaflet* provides an easy way to access the Leaflet JavaScript library to create quick web maps. In this exercise, we will create a map of the Caribbean, add multiple base layers that the user can toggle between, and create a few point markers that include pop-up information. We can easily do all of this from the R command line.

Run R from a terminal to begin a new session (you can also use RStudio if you prefer). At the command prompt install the necessary R package:

```
> install.packages("leaflet")
```

You will be prompted to select a CRAN mirror and then the package is downloaded. Once complete, load the library:

```
> library(leaflet)
```

(Continued)

We can use the %>% pipe operator to string together functions. For example, we can use the following code to create a Leaflet map and bring in the default base layer of OpenStreetMap:

```
> leaflet() %>% addTiles()
```

This gives us the OpenStreetMap basemap at the default zoom level, along with some very basic zoom controls (Figure 14.34). Note: you may need to allow blocked content.

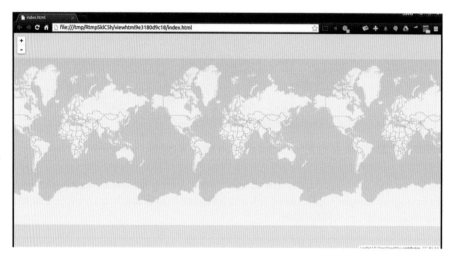

FIGURE 14.34 OpenStreetMap basemap with very basic zoom controls © Vladimir Agafonkin

To control the location and the zoom level of the map, we can add the geographic coordinates and the zoom with the setView() function:

```
leaflet() %>% addTiles() %>% setView(lng=-75.8,
lat=14.5, zoom=6)
```

This takes us to the Caribbean Sea region (Figure 14.35).

To change the basemap, we can use the addProviderTiles() function to pull in a different layer (to see available basemaps, go to leaflet-extras.github.io/leaflet-providers/preview/). Let us change the base-map layer to the Stamen watercolor layer.

```
> leaflet() %>% addProviderTiles("Stamen.Watercolor")
%>% setView(lng=-75.8, lat=14.5, zoom=6)
```

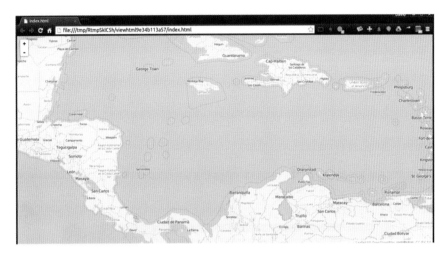

FIGURE 14.35 Location and zoom level adjusted to show the Caribbean Sea region
© Vladimir Agafonkin

We can add multiple base layers to maps as well. Since the watercolor layer has no labels, let us add the Stamen hybrid toner layer to give us those (Figure 14.36):

```
> leaflet() %>% addProviderTiles("Stamen.Watercolor") %>%
addProviderTiles("Stamen.TonerHybrid") %>% setView(lng=-
75.8, lat=14.5, zoom=6)
```

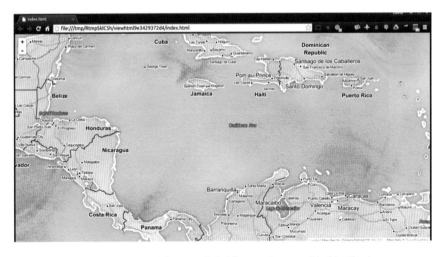

FIGURE 14.36 Watercolor and Stamen hybrid toner layers added to the basemap
© Vladimir Agafonkin

(Continued)

311

Next, let us create a map that lets a user toggle between two different maps – the default OpenStreetMap layer and a satellite image layer provided by MapQuest. To do that, we can use the `addLayersControl()` function to create a toggle control. Try the following code:

```
> leaflet() %>% addTiles(group = "OpenStreetMap") %>%
addProviderTiles("MapQuestOpen.Aerial", group =
"Satellite") %>% addLayersControl(baseGroups =
c("OpenStreetMap", "Satellite")) %>% setView(lng-75.8,
lat=14.5, zoom=6)
```

The resulting map now has a small icon in the top right corner of the map that lets the user choose between the two different map layers (Figure 14.37).

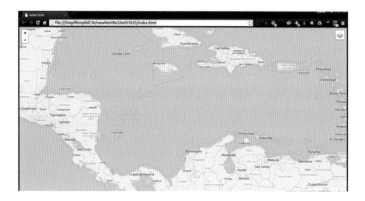

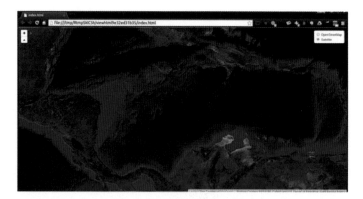

FIGURE 14.37 User toggle between OpenStreetMap layer and MapQuest satellite image layer © Vladimir Agafonkin

The final step of this exercise is to add a marker at a certain location on the map, add some text that will appear when the marker is clicked, and then include the option to show or not show the marker in our toggle control in the top right corner.

To add a marker and place it on the default OpenStreetMap layer, we can use the `addMarkers()` function:

```
> leaflet() %>% addTiles() %>% addMarkers(lng=-85.35, lat=11.61)
```

This defaults to a zoomed map focusing on the marker, so to zoom out we can use `setView()` again:

```
> leaflet() %>% addTiles() %>% addMarkers(lng=-85.35,
lat=11.61) %>% setView(lng=-85.35, lat=11.61, zoom=6)
```

To add some text to the marker that appears when the marker is clicked, we can simply add the text to the `addMarkers()` function like this:

```
> leaflet() %>% addTiles() %>% addMarkers(lng=-85.35,
lat=11.61, popup="Lake Nicaragua") %>% setView(lng=-
85.35, lat=11.61, zoom=6)
```

Now we can put everything together so that our new marker for Lake Nicaragua shows up as an option in our toggle menu (Figure 14.38). To do this, we create a group for our new marker and designate it as an overlay option (not another base layer option). The final code looks like this:

```
> leaflet() %>% addTiles(group = "OpenStreetMap") %>%
addProviderTiles("MapQuestOpen.Aerial", group =
"Satellite") %>% addMarkers(lng=-85.35, lat=11.61,
popup="Lake Nicaragua", group = "Lake Nicaragua") %>%
addLayersControl(baseGroups = c("OpenStreetMap",
"Satellite"), overlayGroups = c("Lake Nicaragua")) %>%
setView(lng=75.8, lat=14.5, zoom=6)
```

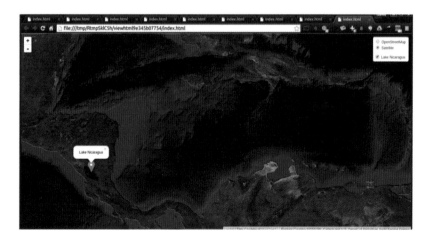

FIGURE 14.38 Lake Nicaragua set as a marker and toggle option © Vladimir Agafonkin

Chapter summary

This chapter has provided an overview of several web tools and libraries for creating interactive online maps. From Google Maps to Leaflet to new R packages, the world of internet mapping is a broad and rapidly changing field. While becoming proficient at creating complex web maps requires a deeper understanding of HTML and JavaScript, hopefully this chapter has demonstrated a couple of things. First, creating a fairly simple but useful interactive map is not terribly difficult, even without much knowledge of the underlying code. Second, there are many examples, code snippets, and online tutorials available to help you dive deeper, as well as a large and helpful user base for each of the above mapping tools. As web mapping tools continue to evolve and mature, it is important to be able to use these tools to work with your geodata.

Further reading

Peterson, M. (2014) *Mapping in the Cloud.* New York: Guilford Press.

COMPANION WEBSITE

Visit https://study.sagepub.co/abernathy for:

- Links to the websites and free software packages discussed in this chapter
- Downloadable versions of all datasets presented in this chapter

15

Epilogue

Weaving the Geoweb

In the third book of his trilogy on the intricate interconnections between technology and urban life, William Mitchell provocatively declares that "the trial separation between bits and atoms is now over" (Mitchell, 2003). Hyperbole perhaps, though Mitchell goes on to chart the many ways in which humans and their complex, nested technological networks – from the body to the home to the city and beyond – are so inextricably linked that we can hardly conceive of living without them. He calls himself a "spatially extended cyborg" whose many networks are both "essential to my physical survival" and "as crucial to cognition as my neurons." With a nod to Descartes that describes the human condition in this hyperconnected age, he writes: "I link, therefore I am." And this vivid depiction of how deeply networked we are was written before Facebook, Twitter, iOS and Android had even emerged to make these networks so much more pervasive.

Such is present-day life within the geoweb. The simple act of going out for a jog can trigger all sorts of data flows across multiple digital networks, assuming you take your smartphone with you. As you wind your way through the streets, your device can communicate with unseen satellites overhead to precisely map your route, the cell towers around you can transmit digital music from far-flung computer servers to the headphones in your ears, and software applications on your device can transmit your location and pace to your connections across multiple social networks. You, the seemingly solitary runner out for your daily exercise, become a node on the geoweb, pushing and pulling data across intertwining, interconnected data pathways.

Of course, as a node on the geoweb you are not only a sensor, but also something to be sensed. Your presence might be captured on a CCTV surveillance camera (or several of them), or perhaps a friend on a social network notices your proximity as you pass nearby. A retail store might also notice your presence, alerting you to current sale items or offering coupons when you are within a certain range. In the not too distant future, your movement might be anticipated and reacted to by a self-driving car. And when you return home, the lighting, climate control, and music might adjust to note your preferences based on your location and time of day.

We are all becoming spatially extended cyborgs, living in a world full of material objects that are themselves becoming spatially extended and interconnected. We apply the shorthand label of "smart" to anything that we can attach to the internet – smartphones, smart appliances, smart homes, smart cities – and being "smart" often relies on an ability to sense and interpret the meaning of time and space. A smart home must know our location; a smart city must understand the aggregate spatial patterns of thousands of networked individuals. And as more previously isolated "dumb" objects become connected nodes on the internet, location data will become even more synonymous with what it means to be "smart."

As defined in this book, the geoweb is a distributed digital network of geolocated nodes that capture, produce, and communicate data that include an explicitly spatial component. Exactly what this network consists of changes daily, and no doubt it will continue to evolve and transform itself in ways that we cannot fully anticipate. There are, however, some signs of where the geoweb is headed in the coming years, in terms of both the emerging technologies and the social implications of those technologies.

Most clearly apparent is the continued rise in the number of people, devices, and physical objects connected to the geoweb. The internet of things will continue to expand at a rapid pace, and many of those things will have the ability to produce and interact with geodata. A wide variety of new sensor networks will be deployed, consumer products and enterprise systems alike will be spatially enabled and connected to the internet, and the volume and variety of geodata produced will grow.

Related to this ongoing expansion of nodes on the geoweb is the increased interoperability between them. There is currently no single operating system or computer language for the geoweb, nor is there likely to be one soon, but continued advances in application programming interfaces and other efforts to improve data translation across multiple platforms will improve communication across multiple networks. Nodes in one part of the geoweb will increasingly be able to detect and react to the location, movement, and proximity of many other nodes in another part. Just as the number of nodes on the geoweb will grow, then, so will the number of pathways and connections between them.

Of particular importance to us as researchers wanting to harness the power of the geoweb are the ways in which we interact with it. As we have seen in this book, there are many software tools for creating and capturing geodata, from OpenDataKit to the R statistical programming language. As the geoweb continues to expand, we will undoubtedly create new tools and techniques for working with the vast quantities of geodata being generated. Already, we are seeing the deployment of GIS and other spatial analysis tools on cloud computing systems in order to take advantage of far more processing power than is typically found on the local computing systems at our schools and workplaces. Tools for distributing the computational workload of spatial analysis across clusters of computers, such as MapReduce or Spark, are making large-scale data query and analysis possible. Big data continue to be a hot topic across a wide variety of industries and research fields, and "big geodata" will certainly continue to grow in importance as the tools and techniques for working with them continue to improve.

At the same time, many of the software tools introduced in this book continue to expand in their capabilities for capturing, analyzing, and displaying geospatial information. The three open source GIS software toolkits covered are all extensible and expandable, with new plugins (QGIS), modules (GRASS) and packages (R) being created all the time. In addition, the large communities of programmers and enthusiasts supporting these projects continue to improve upon the core software code for each, providing us with reliable, open, and free software tools for working with geodata. There are many other free software tools out there that can be used for working with the geoweb, from Python to Geoserver, but the collection of tools covered in this book should give you a good idea of several approaches to the geoweb for the non-programmer. The primary goal of this book has been to get you up and running with geodata fairly quickly and easily so that you can pursue your own research interests and objectives.

SOCIAL IMPLICATIONS OF THE GEOWEB

Another goal of this book, as we saw in earlier chapters, is to ensure that we contemplate the social and ethical implications of geodata collection as we learn about some of the tools that can be used for gathering those data. The very strength of the emerging geoweb – our ability to capture accurate location data for a vast number of distributed nodes – also gives pause for thought. How do we take advantage of the geoweb without compromising privacy or sacrificing our civil liberties?

The tragic attacks in Paris in November 2015 provide a vivid example of the social implications of the geoweb. The earliest reports of the attacks first appeared on social network platforms such as Twitter, many including street addresses or other location data. These early posts were in turn used by others to construct preliminary maps of what was unfolding. Facebook's "safety check" tool allowed users to check in with each other to let them know they were safe, while the Twitter hashtag #PorteOuverte and a Google Map were used to share information on the location of homes being opened up to those seeking shelter in the city.

Of course, there was also a lot of misinformation shared during the attack and its aftermath, from erroneous reports of the Eiffel Tower going dark for the first time to doctored photos of individuals falsely purported to have been involved in the attacks. As in the case of the Boston Marathon bombing and other chaotic events that unfold in real time over social networks, weeding through the volume of data being generated about the attacks to find the most relevant and accurate information was certainly no easy task.

Within days of the attacks, both the French and the US governments were calling for bans on end-to-end data encryption such as that used on the mobile phones by those involved in carrying out the Paris attacks. Increased surveillance on mobile communication systems by giving governments a "back door" to encrypted data, combined with location data, could help prevent such terrorist activity, according to their argument. Privacy advocates disagreed, arguing that a surveillance back door would weaken the security of communication networks for everyone and would only spur the terrorist organizations to shift to other software applications and communications networks. In addition, any location information transmitted by a mobile device is likely to be found in that device's metadata, which typically resides outside any encryption software.

The geodata generated by mobile communication devices is but one component of the larger geoweb, but the debate over surveillance and privacy that has been fueled by attacks like the one in Paris as well as the information provided by Edward Snowden in 2013 demonstrate the emerging social issues we face as the volume and variety of geodata continue to increase. As we weave together networked geodata across multiple platforms, from environmental sensor networks to RFID monitoring systems to an ever-expanding collection of internet-connected things, a new geography is emerging that we are only just beginning to be able to make sense of. From the seemingly mundane social media check-in at a restaurant to the elaborate choreography of a smart mob engaged in social protest to the expanding "planetary nervous system" of networked sensors around the globe, we are building an exciting new era of spatial connectivity that we call the geoweb. And while the geoweb presents many potential obstacles – the social issues surrounding privacy and surveillance mentioned above, as well as the computational challenges in capturing geodata we have seen throughout this book – it also offers an increasingly important lens with which we can interrogate our contemporary world. We are in the midst of constructing an unprecedented mesh network of geolocated nodes that will produce untold amounts of information about our social and natural environments. Harnessing the power of the geoweb is one important way for us to try to understand it.

References

Adams, B., McKenzie, G. and Gahegan, M. (2015) Frankenplace: Interactive thematic mapping for ad hoc exploratory searching. *Proceedings of the 24th International World Wide Web Conference (WWW 2015)*. Geneva: International World Wide Web Conferences Steering Committee. http://dx.doi.org/10.1145/2736277.2741137.

Beaumont, P. (2011) 'Mohammed Bouazizi: The dutiful son whose death changed Tunisia's fate, *Guardian*, January 20.

Bryan, J. (2009) 'Where would we be without them? Knowledge, space and power in indigenous politics, *Futures*, 41(1), 24–32.

Castells, M. (2000) *The Rise of the Network Society: The Information Age: Economy, Society, and Culture, Volume 1*. Malden, MA: Blackwell. (1st edn, 1996.)

Cohen, N. (2011) It's tracking your every move and you may not even know, *New York Times*, March 26. www.nytimes.com. Accessed 15 July 2014.

Edwards, L. (2010) Study suggests reliance on GPS may reduce hippocampus function as we age, *Phys.Org*, November 18. phys.org/news/2010-11-reliance-gps-hippocampus-function-age.html. Accessed 5 January 2016.

Foster, P. (2015) Hacker "made plane climb" after taking control through in-flight entertainment system, *Telegraph*, May 17. www.telegraph.co.uk. Accessed 26 May 2015.

Foucault, M. (1979) *Discipline and Punish: The Birth of the Prison*. New York: Vintage Books.

Gartner (2013) Gartner says the internet of things installed base will grow to 26 billion units by 2020. Press release, December 12. www.gartner.com/newsroom/id/2636073. Accessed 29 May 2014.

Giles, J. (2005) Internet encyclopedias go head to head, *Nature*, 438(7070), 900–901.

Gladwell, M. (2010) Small change: Why the revolution will not be tweeted, *New Yorker*, October 4.

Golder, S. and Macy, M. (2011) Diurnal and seasonal mood vary with work, sleep, and daylength across diverse cultures, *Science*, 333(651), 1878–1881.

Goodchild, M. (2007) Citizens as sensors: the world of volunteered geography, *GeoJournal*, 69(4), 211–221.

Guardian (2013a) Verizon forced to hand over telephone data – full court ruling, *Guardian*, June 5. www.theguardian.com/world/interactive/2013/jun/06/verizon-telephone-data-court-order. Accessed 15 July 2014.

Guardian (2013b) NSA collecting phone records of millions of Verizon customers daily, *Guardian*, June 6. www.theguardian.com/world/2013/jun/06/nsa-phone-records-verizon-court-order. Accessed 15 July 2014.

Hamilton, M., et al. (2007) New approaches in embedded network sensing for terrestrial ecological observatories, *Environmental Engineering Science*, 24(2), 192–204.

Hewlett-Packard (2014) HP study reveals 70 percent of internet of things devices vulnerable to attack. www8.hp.com/uk/en/hp-news/press-release.html?id=1744676.

Khatib, F., Cooper, S., Tyka, M.D., Xu, K., Makedon, I., Popović, Z., Baker, D. and Foldit Players (2011) Algorithm discovery by protein folding game players, *Proceedings of the National Academy of Sciences of the United States of America*, 108(47), 18949–18953.

Laney, D. (2001) 3D Data Management: Controlling Data Volume, Variety and Velocity (META Group File 949). http://blogs.gartner.com/doug-laney/files/2012/01/ad949-3D-Data-Management-Controlling-Data-Volume-Velocity-and-Variety.pdf. Accessed June 2014.

Lanier, J. (2011) *You Are Not a Gadget: A Manifesto*. New York: Vintage Books.

Liptak, A. (2014) Major ruling shields privacy of cell phones, *New York Times*, June 25. www.nytimes.com. Accessed 16 July 2014.

Mitchell, W.J. (2003) *ME++: The Cyborg Self and the Networked City*. Cambridge, MA: MIT Press.

Pariser, E. (2011) *The Filter Bubble: What the Internet Is Hiding from You*. London: Viking/Penguin Press.

Peluso, N. (1995) Whose woods are these? Counter-mapping forest territories in Kalimantan, Indonesia, *Antipode*, 27(4), 383–406.

Pickles, J. (1995) *Ground Truth: The Social Implications of Geographic Information Systems*. New York: Guilford.

Rainie, L. and Wellman, B. (2012) *Networked: The New Social Operating System*. Cambridge, MA: MIT Press.

Reichelt, L. (2007) Ambient intimacy. www.disambiguity.com/ambient-intimacy. Accessed 24 May 2014.

Rheingold, H. (2003) *Smart Mobs: The Next Social Revolution*. Cambridge, MA: Perseus.

Rosen, R. (2012) Time and space has been completely annihilated, *The Atlantic*, February 14. www.theatlantic.com/technology/archive/2012/02/time-and-space-has-been-completely-annihilated/253103. Accessed 30 July 2014.

Shirky, C. (2008) *Web 2.0 Expo NY: It's not information overload, it's filter failure*. Video, September 19. Available at www.youtube.com.

Shirky, C. (2011) The political power of social media: Technology, the public sphere, and political change, *Foreign Affairs*, January/February.

Smolan, R. and Erwitt, J. (2012) *The Human Face of Big Data*. Sausalito, CA: Against All Odds Productions.

Standage, T. (1998) *The Victorian Internet: The Remarkable Story of the Telegraph and the Nineteenth Century's On-line Pioneers*. New York: Walker.

Surowiecki, J. (2004) *The Wisdom of Crowds: How the Many Are Smarter than the Few and How Collective Wisdom Shapes Business, Economies, Societies and Nations*. New York: Doubleday.

Thompson, C. (2014) *Smarter Than You Think: How Technology Is Changing Our Minds for the Better*. New York: Penguin.

United Nations (2014) The right to privacy in the digital age. www.ohchr.org/EN/Issues/DigitalAge/Pages/DigitalAgeIndex.aspx. Accessed 16 July 2014.

Wikipedia (2015) History of Wikipedia, in *Wikipedia*, December 25. https://en.wikipedia.org/wiki/History_of_Wikipedia. Accessed 5 January 2016.

Worth, R.F. (2011) How a single match can ignite a revolution, *New York Times*, January 21.

Index